INNERCIRCLE PUBLISHING

INNERCIRCLE PUBLISHING

The Twelve Sacred Principles of Karma

Library of Congress Catalog Number Pending Under the title:
"The Twelve Sacred Principles of Karma"

Edition 1

ISBN: 0-9720080-6-3

Edited by: Donald S. Moore
Page Design by: Chad Lilly
Cover Design by: Chad Lilly
Cover Photo by: Donald S. Moore

www.hairfield.com

Are You Aware?
www.innercirclepublishing.com

The Twelve Sacred Principles of Karma

Dr. Steven L. Hairfield ph.D
Donald S. Moore, editor

*"All truth passes through three stages:
First it is ridiculed. Second it is opposed.
Third, it is accepted as being self-evident."*

Arthur Schopenhauer (1788 – 1860)

Dedication

This book was written for all seekers. To this end, know that all experience on your path is your personal teacher of life. Know that all experience, whether external or internal, is the guiding light of you, for it may shepherd you to your true nature of Divine self, your home. Living the Divine being within you is your destiny, the underlying reason for life itself. Seek only the higher truths. All shall be made known and be laid before you from each moment to the next.

Truth is all there is to know!

– Steven L. Hairfeild '09

Table of Contents

"When all things are seen equal the timeless self-essence is reached."
Buddha

Introduction

I have written this book because it is deeply felt and believed that it contains the knowledge to change your life towards a much more positive direction, and to potentially lead us all toward global peace. Yes, this is a bold statement; however, at the very least, it will most assuredly guide us all toward *individual* peace. Why? Because we simply do not fully understand the long term impact each of us has upon our fellow humans, upon our world civilizations, and upon consciousness itself. You may ask me, "Well, how do you know?" May I share with you how this idea came to me, or more precisely, how I came to this idea? It was explained and shown to me first hand by several extraordinary teachers and Masters in the Far East.

Just how did I end up in the Far East, 9,000 miles from home, as a neophyte under the direct tutelage of the Masters? My journey began as an Army sergeant while serving in a Vietnamese village, Quang Ngai, in support of the Vietnamese 2nd Armored Division. During a walk in the village one morning, I turned a street corner and instantly locked eyes with a robed man walking on the opposite side. He scurried across to meet me and softly stated matter-of-factly, our eyes still locked, "Young man, if you do not learn to use your gift, it will destroy you." Without question, he got my attention. With the personal invitation by Master Hanh, what began as a benign curiosity quickly became my place of refuge and inner growth as I settled into a schedule of frequent visits to his Zen monastery, nestled amidst this war-torn country and close to the village. From this benevolent, humble teacher, I came to understand and value my inner tuition, or intuition, to follow my heart and the urges or impulses from within me. What can now be admitted through hindsight, intuition has further led me into very interesting experiences critical to my inner growth and understanding, just as it can for each and every one of us. It is the old adage, "follow your heart," or more precisely, follow what you feel on your path of life. Little did I realize how this experience was going to alter my life within a few years, and I sense most of you can admit the same regarding your current experience! We simply do things without realizing their long term effects.

The GI Bill provided me the opportunity to attain an undergraduate degree after my service enlistment; yet, six months prior to my graduation, I began to feel an urge to go to a place I had never been to, let alone thought of. The urge grew so strong as my graduation date approached, I absolutely had to make this journey, thinking there was much to learn. Having sold all my worldly belongings, except for a few personal effects, a sleeping bag and a backpack, I bought an open-ended ticket and flew directly to India, just three days prior to my commencement ceremony! As I found out later, I had bought the trip of a lifetime.

Although it appeared I was just following my nose after landing in Delhi, the truth is, my intuition, the urge, was guiding each step of my way, because I simply departed the plane, walked to baggage claim to pick up my gear, then headed out from the terminal not knowing what was ahead of me, whether an inch or a mile. Following only my inner guidance, I was not consciously thinking about my destination, for I simply traveled either by foot or hitchhiked. One day, I entered the state of Rajasthan, skirting the edge of the desert region known as the Punjab. "Whoa, how did I get here?" I asked myself when I became aware of my surroundings. I reflected upon days past and realized an inexplicable pattern had taken shape. As each night approached, I would find myself arriving at a village wherefrom a family would invite me to join them, offering me an evening meal and a place to sleep. To this day, I remain most grateful to all the families which were so wonderful and giving to me, a young American stranger. Each morning, just before I was about to leave

the village, an elderly man – a different man each day, mind you – would approach me, only to squat and silently draw a stick or finger map in the fine silt in front of my feet. Not knowing what else to do or where else to go, I took a leap of faith with the "road" map in my mind and followed its direction.

By accepting this so-called daily ritual, I ultimately reached the northern fringes of the Punjab. One day, I was thirsty for some tea and just so happened to approach a roadside shop which offered green tea, so I stopped and placed my order. With my cup of hot tea in hand – no Lipton's Iced Tea in this part of the world – I sauntered over to a shady, tree-side table next to the silt road and watched the scene before me. I became transfixed as I observed what seemed like thousands of travelers pass by on whichever mode of transportation they used, be it an elephant, camel, horse drawn cart, rickshaw, rickety bicycle, on foot, in a bus. As long as it worked and as long as they traveled, moving ever forward, I sensed their mode of choice was irrelevant. Having become so engrossed by the dust swirls and eddies created by this advancing human menagerie, I never noticed the two monks approaching, sitting down close behind me.

I was awakened from my reality show when I heard someone announce, "We have been waiting for you." Paying no mind to his statement since no one knew I was there, I figured the man was greeting a friend, so I continued watching the passersby. "Your name is Steven, is it not?" the same voice asked. The hairs on my neck sprang full upright as the hair on a cat's arched back as I slowly turned around, expecting Rod Serling to begin his narration for the next Twilight Zone episode! However, my eyes gazed into the softest, gentlest, deepest brown eyes I had ever seen. After the shock wave dissipated I answered warily, "Yes? How do you know my name?" The peaceful monk looked at me with an approving smile and simply repeated, "We have been waiting for you." I'm certain I looked totally dumbfounded at the gentle monks, as I had not realized anyone knew I even existed there. Yet, here they were sitting behind me, two monks claiming they have been waiting for an American named Steven who had never been to this part of the world! "We began focusing on you six months ago," the same monk informed me. I gasped, my

mind exclaiming, "What?—NO!...Wait-a-minute!" in total disbelief as I suddenly remembered my inner urge had also begun exactly six months ago. Yes, this all sounds incredulous and I totally understand your skepticism. I admit again, as each day progressed during that six month period, my inner urge literally overtook logic and reasoning to the point that I simply *had* to go to India. My Zen teachers taught me to follow what I felt, so here I was, facing two monks in complete shock.

At a roadside shop in "No Town" India, it came to be that Master Lobsang and Rinpoche Kiela came to greet me and introduce themselves, informing me, "You have come to learn the ancient knowledge and traditions, and about a human known as Issa." I stuck to their presence, "But how did you contact me? No one called!" They settled into a talk on consciousness, "We are all energetically connected in this higher realm." You see, consciousness was behind it all, from my six-month urge, to the village families each evening, even to the men giving me directions every morning. Consciousness is an extremely powerful tool in order to connect all these events, which at first would never seem to fit; yet, they *did* work together, perfectly merging to create my individual experience. Needless to say, my eyes widened as I became intensely riveted on this idea. How can anyone use this? Why was this not more commonly known?

I had many questions and they desired to answer every one; hence, they suggested I follow them. What I had initially thought to be a two to three-month trip turned into one lasting for many years, for I traveled and spent time in many different monasteries throughout India, Nepal and Tibet. While there, I learned hundreds of ideas and concepts, including the twelve principles of Karma and our interaction with them. Once internalized, these principles changed my life forever, giving me such a remarkable perspective on myself, people, and life, showing me why events actually take place and the precise manner in which they occur. Karma has allowed me, as it will for any individual, to see all others simply for who they are, not by how we judge them to be. In truth, it totally removes our judgment because we learn to see through the eyes of truth. It is my personal desire to share this information with you. If each individual took the

time to not only learn the principles, but to also live by them, they could attain self-mastery, learn what self-mastery truly means, and what it entails. Let us begin this journey as though we are learning to become a monk by what they are taught in the Eastern world; in other words, our class – Monk 101 – starts our journey through the twelve steps to self-recognition and self-mastery.

It is time to introduce you to the prime Principle of Life, the principle most of us seem to disregard; yet, we should not. It is as real as the human itself, and just as real as my initial experience in India. The Prime Principle is that of Consciousness, both individual consciousness and mass consciousness. Do you believe in this idea? If not, please realize that Quantum Theorists now use this very principle in many equations! In Monk 101, we all learn we are pure consciousness in the flesh and are purely and simply connected, not only to each other as human beings, but also to *all* things, including flora and fauna, the animal kingdom, our world, even stretching out into the entire cosmos. I understand how this may appear improbable; yet, it *is* the truth.

Whether you accept this concept is totally irrelevant. Truth remains, for all things are inseparably connected. One may not live without the other, for this is how we realize life and how we learn, through this inner-connectedness we each possess. If not so, then how do we know at times what another person is feeling, or know what another person is even thinking? Consider what happens when you think of someone you have not seen for quite awhile, perhaps asking yourself, "I wonder how he or she is doing?" Do you not run into them seemingly by coincidence, or hear from them in some way? Playfully put, you made a head call, whereby you connected your consciousness with theirs; essentially, you matched their vibration in that moment, and made a connection! The same happened to me when Master Lobsang and Master Kiela first connected by joining their consciousness to mine, how the initial contact was made and how it even strengthened over time.

So what is this consciousness thing? How and where are we all connected because of it? As an example, do you realize each grain of

sand must be connected to the other, that only from this connection can the grains of sand make up the beach? Do you believe the waves are separate from the beach? Actually, they are not. The waves must also be directly connected because they fashion the beach to exactly what it is, constantly shifting each grain of sand on and off the shoreline during the ebb and flow of the tide as we gaze upon it. The beach may not exist without the waves because each requires the other, one creating the other, to provide the beautiful scene before us. They are simply connected. Are there any other connections out there? Absolutely! The entire cosmos operates the exact same way. Would life exist without the sun? Would our planet keep its orbit without the magnificent gravitational pulls from the moon, the precise number of planets, and the sun? Though we are millions of miles apart physically, we remain connected. This holds true for all things, even though we honestly think everything is separate simply because it appears this way. This sense of separateness is, in fact, an illusion. And let us now go a step further. We, as the human observer, are also connected to the beach, including the waves and the entire cosmos. Why? We are one with them because *our* view has created the whole scene as our reality.

Now, how about the clarity of consciousness? Imagine if you will a crystal clear pool of water wherein we can easily see the bottom, no matter its depth. Now imagine each thought we have is either a crystal clear drop of water or a fine brown speck of silt, with the drop representing higher thought forms such as love, harmony and peace; whereas, the speck represents lower thought forms such as hate, anger, fear, plus "I am better than you." Both the higher and lower forms contribute to our personal pool; however, if we place more specks of silt into our pool than clear drops of water, their accumulation over the days, weeks, months, and even years of our lives, will eventually fill our once clear pool of consciousness. In this case we would feel trapped under the silt, would we not, as though buried under the quicksand of lower thought forms in our own individual consciousness? The truth is, for the vast majority, our individual pool contains nearly equal amounts of both clear drops and silt. Does this mean we are stuck with what we now have? Can it ever be filtered and cleansed to its original crystal clear state?

Although these answers will be explained in detail as we progress through Karma and its principles, I offer the short answer to the second question right now: yes it can!

I would like to give you the overall picture by taking this concept of connectedness yet a step further, moving from our individual pool of consciousness to the idea of mass consciousness, the accumulation and contribution of every human mind and all its thoughts, converging in one gargantuan global pool of pure, crystalline consciousness. Each living human, without exception, contributes to this original magnificent crystal clear pool of collective mind, adding to it each moment every day through our every thought. Aside from our spiritual self, we are each indelibly connected through mass consciousness and, considering what we individually have furnished this so-called super mind, one can easily understand the state of our world, for all our thoughts accumulating over the millennia have simply produced the Karmic return for its current condition!

Ask yourself, are you at peace or at odds with the world? Peace contributes crystal clear drops; whereas, the other contributes specks of silt, *both* kinds creating a return action as suggested by all Masters throughout time, in a variety of ways and in many languages. Put another way, this global pool is affected by what we contribute to it, and contains the power to create global peace through our clear drops, or global conflict through our brown silt, a purely conscious choice we each make perpetually. You see, if we exist, so does collective consciousness. If we have life, so does consciousness simply because we are inseparably connected. If we have consciousness, so does all life; therefore, global consciousness itself is alive. Truly, consciousness *gives* us life.

I sincerely hope every individual who welcomes what is offered within these pages may attain this higher level of self-realization and individual connection with all others and all life. The apparent difficulty we have in readily accepting this idea is that we look at other humans and all things with a pair of eyes through which we physically view separation. I repeat, separation is an illusion in truth. Yes, just as the pillars of the Parthenon are separate, so also are we –

physically speaking. But, in every other aspect, we are connected with each other for the purpose of creating collective strength and inner growth, contributing only clear drops of water by living in divine grace. This is the idea of living within the walls of a monastery and is the essence of Monk 101, to understand that we all, individually and collectively, contribute to consciousness, thereby creating our individual and global reality, respectively.

Being part of the whole, as each grain of sand is part of the shoreline, we have yet to fully realize our ability, the ability to think and choose with the unwavering understanding that each choice accumulates in the pool of consciousness, creating a ripple of consequence based on the ever-present twelve principles of Karma. All Masters are relentlessly aware of this. In truth, whether we place a heavy brown thought of silt or a light clear thought of a crystalline drop into the pool, it's like kind returns to us. Need any return consequence be filled with sinking silt or negativity? Absolutely not! In fact, only clear, lifting consequences may return if we simply have loving intentions behind all what we think, say, and do! Generally speaking, no one in Western culture thinks a return consequence will happen unless they make it happen. This is a great falsehood, for the ancients have told us there is no thing and no one above the Law, the Laws of Karma.

Under this Law there are twelve separate concepts or principles all working in union. The purpose of this book is to not only share them with you, but to also offer as much detail as possible, explaining fully how they work and relate to each other. May this book offer you knowledge of the ancient traditions by monastic teachings from the Far East, expanding you and your purpose in this reality. I offer one last question for you to consider before I continue: "What do you contribute to the overall consciousness of our world?" This dynamic alone can totally shift our world if every human simply realizes what they do contribute, and realizes they can change their contribution at any moment in time! This alone is such a simple and infallible concept in all its respects.

In the Far East they have a meaningful two-word phrase, Shanti Satyam, which simply means that truth brings you peace, freeing you

from the bonds of life. Become peace. Do not just think it. Don the cloak and clothing of a peaceful being and your life will transform into one filled with peace. As each individual adorns themselves in this fashion, the entire world will become enveloped in peace from its connection to mass consciousness, ending conflict for all time.

"And when we realize the essence of mind
even for one moment then truth is known to us."
Buddha

~ Chapter I ~
What is Karma?

Welcome to the experience of monastic teachings! As stated, we shall term it Monk 101. Most individuals in our part of the world seem to be seeking personal empowerment; yet, they are not certain what that is exactly. Allow me to assure you, it is not about having power over other people; instead, it is more in line with realizing our own power in our own life and in the situations we seem to encounter. If we understand its principles and what Karma actually is, we may realize outcomes which give us power over it, life and our self. In this book, the information being offered on Karma will assist you to not only attain the sense of being empowered, but will also most definitely guide you on the path of enlightenment or consciousness, along with having you realize how all things are connected, one to the other. I only ask that you "hear" and internalize what is shared with you in each chapter, and by living the teachings with purpose, you will gain all the desires of your heart.

You see, an empowered individual must first have power over them self, over their lower carnal nature. And by understanding Karma, this sense of being empowered is attained in a much easier fashion with the added bonus that they will go through life in a much more purposeful way. Having studied in the Far East for many years, I personally have come to understand and internalize these principles, observed how they operate irrespective of a personal belief system, and confirmed my own belief how people in this part of the world truly do not pay attention to the consequences of all what they do. Most people attach no meaning to the word "Karma" when overheard by another, or it is frequently mentioned through trite humor such as, "Oh, Karma will handle it," while internally believing Karma is a tool designed to punish. In truth, the above quote is accurate, and more times than not, Karma does not return in humor because it returns in like kind. Its sole purpose is to make sure the playing field remains level, to maintain equality in all things. This is true simply because all things were originally equal in their creation, and Karma ensures it stays this way.

I have often asked myself how an individual would explain a very ancient principle to the vast majority of people in the 21st century. My first answer would be that Karma is a genuine, natural, unrelenting Law of the Universe, the mechanism through which gives us experience as the Law of return action. Karma gave birth to life, in a sense, because the physical human and all things are the return action of the original energy of the Creator. We are the end result of the original Cause, and with us, Karma was given birth as one of the primary Principles of Life. We could go so far to say that Karma was and is the original creative power of the universal Divine mind, a purposefully empowered mind and thought. To think we are in Its image and likeness is simply staggering! No thought, no emotion, and no physical activity can be above or exempt from this Principle, which is why it is connected to the grand pool of Consciousness, to each and every thought, including their ripple effects on consciousness, personal and otherwise. Do you realize Karma, as a word and philosophy, reaches all the way into physics?

Newtonian physics states it as the Third Law of Motion, "For every action there is an equal and opposite re-action," with the prime idea that if this happens in one thing then it must happen in all things or it becomes invalid. Karma is also a principle underlying the way Doppler radar performs. How? As I understand it, when mathematician/physicist Christian Doppler was attempting to develop his idea, he became frustrated. After a rain, he went for a walk. He sat down on a bench and began throwing tiny pebbles into a small pool of water,

noticing the ripples traveling across it and wondered, "Once they disappear, where do they go?" From controlled experiments back in his lab, Doppler realized the ripples did not disappear at all; in fact, he discovered that every ripple, viewed as a concentric circle moving away from the point of impact, spread to all edges and depths of the pool, only to then return from whence it originated.

This is the purest evidence of Karma in action as all things return to their point of creation, including thought. Once thought is generated it goes forth to contact its like vibration only to return to its creator, the originator of the thought. Once the absolute power of Karma is fully realized, we could truly greet the circumstances of our experience, and to also comprehend the power of creation in the very act. So now I ask, "What pebbles do you cast into your pool of consciousness?" "What would you like to have as an experience?" "What would you like your life to become?" Karma has both the power to deliver it to you and the power to block it, thus taking it from you. Karma is a very powerful concept to learn and understand, let alone work with; yet, our very key is to actually work with it because we absolutely cannot avoid it! And to understand its operation, we must first understand the idea of consciousness, another concept we simply cannot avoid. Quantum Physics proved and accepted it mathematically and now uses this word frequently. So should we, for it is as real as the rising sun. Throughout Monk 101, we shall expand on the concept of consciousness because no stone shall be left unturned.

You may ask, "Does Karma have this kind of power?" One would think so if Newton and Doppler were correct in their discoveries. After all, Karma was a key factor in the creation of life! We should realize and appreciate the power we have and the power behind Karma. What goes on in our mind and what we think creates our life and experiences, both of which are 100% Karma and the action on its return; in other words, our circumstances or experiences are precisely what we each have produced. The question now is, "Do you believe it?" Honestly, a yes or no answer is totally irrelevant because Karma is truly real, constantly and continually, 24/7. I have a better question, "Do you accept it?" The proof is always present and right in front of you. If accepted, you then have chosen to watch this ever-present principle in constant action right before your very eyes. You will see it from everything you do through your thoughts and feelings, each and every moment, as you then gain the power to shift any and all things in your life and in the world. This is true empowerment! If declined, then your personal pool will remain cloudy at best with no chance of being cleared or filtered to its original pristine state.

Aside from referring to Karma so casually or in humor, I find it interesting that we do refer to it in the United States as, "What goes around comes around." This is Karma American-style, and it states the same idea; yet, we must accept it more literally and genuinely in order to ever have it work for us instead of against us. Correction here! Karma does neither because it simply works tenaciously in any direction we choose since it takes the human in a very literal context, even if we think otherwise. Being the producer of results in all we do or perpetuate, Karma returns to us exactly what we produced. In essence, whether we act responsibly or not is totally irrelevant, for every action carries its own consequence, as like attracts its like kind. Please remain ever-present and aware of this concept; otherwise, you may surely stumble on your path.

Karma is our ultimate teacher, the teacher of our true nature and the true ego-less self, as you will see while we journey together through the twelve principles. Its purpose is to have us realize the truth of life and our relationship to both it and each other. I have stated in previous works that the divine only creates in equality from divine substance into divine substance, and Karma ensures we live in that divine principle – exclusively. If we were to operate fully under the concept of Karma, a very natural divine Law in the full sense of the word, we would have no use for human-based Law. Now, what would we do with those Law-makers? Humor aside, the only reason we have human Laws is because we ignore the natural ones, ones which require no income, jails, or taxes, for they operate on their own accord without human intervention! How so? They are purely causes and effects as stated in Newton's third Law of Motion, with Karma being – to its very core – a universal condition and divinely-imposed on every individual. Interestingly enough, the Bhagavad Gita states: anything which is embodied cannot escape Karma or deny it as it

is ever-present. If I may add, Karma is the cause behind evolution, constantly changing, though we attempt to prevent it at times in our personal life.

If the evolution of life and all species are not able to avoid Karma, then how can any human? Ponder for a moment. As long as we think or believe we can prevent or even avoid Karma, which in truth we cannot, our true personal empowerment shall continue to avoid us. However, our life will work wondrously more smoothly in every activity once we consciously begin to work with it directly, learning to accept it and what it brings to us, which may very well be our special gift. Karma is the prod attempting to move us when we become seemingly stuck in our own quicksand due to the buildup of silt which we placed in our pool of consciousness. It is as eternal as the Creator, and the only Law to which we are bound to follow, knowingly or unknowingly matters not. Every advantage is given to us when we consciously follow Karma; otherwise, we are at the mercy of apparent circumstance.

To truly understand the principles, we must first realize it is not possible for any living being to exist without any level of activity, though we actually think we can be inactive at times. Even while sitting motionless on the sofa we can be mentally or emotionally active and still create Karmic effects. In truth, we are created as living activity – moving matter – and we learn the impact of Karma from all activities in which we find ourselves, whether they be physical, mental, emotional, or even a combination thereof, including the conditions to which Karma applies in these activities. By observing each activity, we then realize its cause, and from this process we begin to recognize the outline of Karma's path for us, indeed, the simplest and most fruitful of routes. As a small child, for example, we unconsciously utilize Karma while learning to walk. Do we not use the Law of cause and effect while making constant adjustments to our stance, swinging our arms, or even when reaching out to a piece of furniture for momentary balance? By paying attention only to the Karmic return of what we so created through each attempt, we ultimately learned how to walk. This applies to everything in life! Otherwise, by stubbornly remaining non-observant and resistant, the

very same path may become quite difficult, even nearly impossible, and we actually learn very little as we attempt to become so-called inactive. Please understand, from the mere act of resistance, Karmic pressure increases, following Newton's Third Law, because the act of resistance only creates more of itself, just as stubbornness creates more stubbornness. Each activity creates more of its like kind, each showing up as a unique circumstance. Truly, no other way exists since this is the primary focus behind Karmic Law.

As a student in Monk 101, the first area of focus for us neophytes would be self-observation with pure objectivity, learning to observe our self while in each activity without any self-judgment whatsoever. Judgment will quickly blind us from our true self; therefore, stay purely objective in our observation. Apply no condemnation. At first this may be difficult, but with practice it becomes much simpler to accomplish. Only from this viewpoint can we then distinguish the sequence of events to the same degree as a monk who knows precisely where they need to be in any given moment and is seldom caught off balance. As an aside, a monk is rarely caught off balance, if ever, because they understand balance as more of an internal event, not an external one as most of us think of it. If we do not like the results which create our imbalance, we merely change the preceding conditions; consequently, the results shift, returning us to a state of balance.

Continuing, we would learn to realize that we live in a world of natural Laws and to not only observe them, but to also master and utilize them for the benefit of our self and humankind. Imagine a planet with a truly balanced state of consciousness. The world would achieve a greater state of magnificence with all its people! Monks understand these Laws so well, they are able to teach them to others, just as I am attempting here. We are not in the grip of so-called circumstance; quite the contrary, we are in a world of natural principles and forces which may be used to bring about all we desire, as long as we understand and not violate them as we do constantly. It is this very violation which has brought about the world we have today. Does this make sense to you?

Karma is not a force that crushes; rather, it establishes a statement of conditions by which we are to live. From these conditions, results inevitably occur. Put another way, we see the results as an occurrence or experience which is entirely created by our own actions. Remember, they are not punishments per se, unless we live in self-punishment or dole it out by intentionally hurting, stealing, or taking from others. Also, I am not just talking about the physical things as you shall understand later. If we live in a fashion which is happy-go-lucky in a careless sense, ironically, this is exactly what will create our ongoing issues because we do not pay attention to natural circumstance. We will essentially become helpless and at the mercy of nature's forces while we remain ignorant of the natural process. While living in this fashion, we will most certainly experience misfortune and seeming failure, finding it a struggle to be truly happy and content with our lives. On the other hand, if we understand and are wise to these forces, we can master and allow these natural Laws to serve us as was originally intended. We must learn to realize that all natural Laws exist to enable us, not disable us, that our knowledge of them is necessary in order to utilize them, not to manipulate or violate them. Being a natural Law, Karma has a direct influence upon each of us due to its very inherent state, enabling us to virtually change our nature by altering how and why we do the things we do, only from the true knowledge of it. If we learn to observe the Laws in the stream of life, we will neither become caught in its eddies of confusion, nor will we bang into the rocks and logs of struggle which hide below, for we will safely and securely flow right by. I wish to first offer a few scenarios to help you understand how Karma works and interacts with us before we probe into each principle individually.

My first scenario looks at a homeowner who does everything possible in an attempt to burglar-proof their home. At first, this action seems innocent enough, perhaps even looked upon by others as a sensible precaution. I almost forgot to tell you, the only reason they are installing a security system is because they heard about other neighborhood break-ins. What is the potential return action through Karma? Even though the homeowner thinks they are taking care of house security during this whole time, they are actually sending out waves of fear into consciousness. Just as my Master teachers drew me to meet them at the roadside shack, so too does the homeowner attract the burglar to their residence by sending out the necessary energy. What energy? Why on Earth would this even occur when the purpose is for safety? Their underlying emotion is fear, and fear is a very powerful charge behind thought. It is one of the most powerful human emanations we have! In fact, the two greatest powers a human has through emotional energy are love and its exact opposite, fear.

Back to the scenario, the above could be termed as like mind or like vibration, one attracting the other. It could also be termed as the Doppler Effect, or the pull of electromagnetic fields, one attracting the other. Fear generated the event; prey attracted the predator. This particular homeowner truly focused on their fear of a break-in; whereas, the next door neighbor, all the while, may truly be focusing only on the absolute safety and security of *their* home, which by doing so, only safety and security would be attracted to the home by the very same Karmic principle. Please keep in mind, if the home of the fearful homeowner is eventually burglarized, this is most unfortunate, but it is neither Karma's "fault," nor is it a form of punishment. Karma was simply matching the originator of the vibration to its opposite in reality, as when a magnet or a magnetic force draws its opposite polarity. Think for a moment, if the monks could contact me from 9,000 miles away through the proper use of consciousness, imagine what we send out in our very own neighborhoods each and every day? Okay, what about the Karmic return for the thief?

From the perspective of a thief, the Karmic circumstance has a more far-reaching effect, aside from the potential jail time which is ultimately part of the Karmic return. Most thieves do end up in jail only because they do not know when to cease their activity. The Karmic return begins to set them up when they think it a lot easier to take from another person rather than to work in the traditional sense. By turning away from traditional work, they naturally must steal at a higher rate, honestly believing there is nothing erroneous in what they do! Of course, it can take time to catch them, but the more they steal, the more tightly Karmic principles take hold. When looked at in depth, what are the long term Karmic effects? From the very first effect, once they have stolen something, they are no longer

able to completely trust anything or anyone else, even to the degree of distrusting their own experience. Why is this so? In truth, we can only know others by how we know our self – another principle monks understand and utilize. You see, what we are, we see in others. I will expand on this principle in a future chapter. The bottom line is, if a thief is going to steal then how can they trust? This not only affects their material reality, but also their emotional reality. If they truly wanted another person to love and trust them, how could they return that person's love and trust? They simply could not because the wheels have already been set in motion by their own hand.

As the next effect comes into play, they run a very high risk of having things being stolen from *them*, following again the Karmic principle of equality; in other words, one may not have what does not belong to them. In truth, I could almost guarantee they will have things taken from them, for these are simply warnings given by Karma. To summarize, the thief has lost their traditional job, if any; they have lost the ability to trust; they have lost the ability to love and to be loved; they have lost the things they stole, and they will lose their freedom. All because of Karmic circumstance! Let us stir in two more effects on the thief: frustration and anger. Okay, why would these come into play? Once the Karmic returns occur, frustration will enter and compound itself in the thief's experience because, "nothing is going my way," while anger comes into play because of the jail time they will experience, about which they will always claim their innocence. Of course, who believes that? The thief got "hit" from every direction through Karmic return action, physically, mentally, and emotionally. Oh, one last thing. Thieves actually attract jail to themselves because of what they have now become: "trapped" in distrust. Even after all the Karmic effects have piled on top of the so-called thieves, they still have the ability to shift their experience into a totally new dynamic by understanding the principles of Karma and accepting the flow of a new direction. This change in mind creates new activities to which Karma may respond. Will the thief learn this lesson? Well, that is their choice – *if* they trust it.

It is time for a question if I may, "What is the experience of a Karmic return from our emotional body?" Love – true love – is vitally important to each of us and is the quintessential reason why we experience life; we want to attain it in physical form. As energy beings before we enter life, love is all what is known; however, as physical form, we get the full and intense impact of the idea. Do we not dream of love or seek it in some fashion in our world, just knowing there is someone who simply loves us for exactly who we are? This person loves us in every respect, no matter what we say or do. They love us completely from their heart, free of any conditions with absolutely no mental apprehensions or judgments whatsoever going on. My Master teachers informed me that we each have a twin flame or vibration, that we are too impatient in our search for them, hence the reason for such a high divorce rate in this part of the world. You see, if we would simply wait and search from our heart, we would find our twin flame very easily because the natural Law of Karma would lead us right to them.

I would like to share from personal experience because I finally have the twin flame of my life. My wife is an absolutely amazing person to be around, and I have absolutely no doubt or question as to how much she loves me. From our love, such strength, depth, and magnificence, abides constantly, 24/7. I truly feel it is the most extraordinary relationship any human could ever conceive. Can you have this, too? Absolutely! But, the truth is, you must be willing to walk this path *with* the other person, not *for* or *because* of them, but because of you. Additionally, from the perspective of Karma, you must become that person before they are even able to show up or even become attracted to you in your life. Love, in its truest sense, is like the purity and tranquility of the driven snow until shattered by our early experience of rejection, which will condition our subsequent experiences; hence, rejection in this area becomes fairly common for most.

At a young age, we can easily imagine rejection, whether perceived or real is totally irrelevant. Why so? As youngsters we simply do not have the wisdom to discern as we do when older or when we have more emotional experience in life. So, here we are, holding onto the pain of apparent rejection in our emotional body, wherefrom we actually create even more pain due to Karmic return action, as we

draw yet another experience of love and rejection to us! Does this make any sense? Such an experience therefore becomes one of the greatest errors we may have in the arena of love. In truth, it is all in how we perceive it! When we cut our finger we know where to place the antiseptic and band-aid; however, when it comes to our heart, how and where can we apply them? "So what do we do now?" you ask. By understanding Karma, we grow through it to negate any future Karmic influence; we simply learn to realize that the idea of rejection is nothing more than a teacher of self-acceptance. So forgive the experience and bless it as a lesson and move on to find the true love of your heart, your twin flame.

One day I asked Master Lobsang about the idea of love to which he replied simply and with deep wisdom, looking at me straight in the eye, "Young man, love does not know time or distance; it only knows love." Are you certain you even want true love in your life? Because, once you truly realize what this unconditional love thing is all about, you just may develop a fear of it. Yes, you may chuckle, but I am here to suggest to you that I most certainly did! The fear part, that is. You see, after my early experiences of emotional pain, I withheld my emotions from this idea of love, subsequently finding myself blaming my partners for my lack of feelings toward them. It actually became easier to show anger than to simply allow love to flow. How could I have love when I had no real experience of it with another human? I thought I had! Therein lies the answer to the issue. I *thought* I loved them; yet, I held myself from its experience. Love is not a thought; it is an emotion, a feeling. If one thinks they love another, it is not from their heart. It is from their mind. I came to realize Karmic return brought me a person who did not love me since I did not at first love myself. We must love our self first so the other may do the same. Remember, you and I are the originators of all our experiences. Once I realized the necessary ingredient was love of self, well, both you and I know the rest of the story.

Have you ever experienced a new relationship developing very rapidly? To instantly destroy it, you need only say to yourself, "This is going too fast!" which indicates that the relationship must be controlled. Ponder on this idea: if you are attempting to control love, how can it be love? Your control may very well be based on the idea of your fear from the very thing you would like to have the most. If this is the case, look at your need to control. Besides, this will only create a controlling relationship or a controlling partner through Karma. Master Lobsang also told me that if it takes longer than five seconds then it is not the twin flame. You may counter with, "Five seconds is absolutely not long enough to know a person!" Really? Here is the paradox. Love is instant, but learning who that love is may take a lifetime, and then being amazed by them. The key to the Karmic process is self-love first. If you do not, then you must ask yourself, "If I am not able to love me, then how may I love another? If it is not in me first, then how may the other love me?" Remember, what begins with us must end with us. This is the truth in all things, no matter how it may appear in the moment. Who creates it? You do for your experience. So, in reality, you must become open to the idea of like attraction, Karma on both ends of the scale. "Become what you seek and it shall find you," is the essence of Karmic Law, which will show more of itself as we journey together through the principles.

Because the idea of love is so powerful to the human, I want to take this in another direction for a moment, if I may. Love is the prime ingredient for creation of life, an extension of the Divine love by the Creator, and contains the power to make us successful in all we do. The love of a person, the love of a profession, the love of life are each the most significant thing we may hold dear to us; however, love may also bring the risk of betrayal. The first brings incredible rewards while the second may cost us all we have, with both aspects carrying Karmic circumstances unto themselves. Purely as an example, let us say you have found the person with whom you *think* you have fallen in love. Notice the word emphasis. Now, let us envision that many years have passed and you meet another person with whom you have an affair, which is very common in today's world. Most likely, you have absolutely no idea what you have set in motion and the full consequences of this event. Let me offer food for thought here. The Karmic return on this activity equals that of the thief because, in a sense, both you and the thief are stealing. The only difference is the affair steals an intangible object, the most powerful feeling a human can generate. This so-called robbery subsequently affects a minimum

of three people, up to two couples, along with all the children if we wish to compound the issue. All those affected by this activity will have difficulty in allowing another to love them, let alone having difficulty with loving them self. The adulterer or adulteress may truly think they are getting away with it, but – oh no – from the perspective of Karma, the wheels of return action are rolling. Although one Karmic return is divorce, I would like you to look into the deeper levels of this Karmic impact since there are so many levels which may surely take place, keeping in mind they are similar to those of the thief. No, there will not necessarily be jail time in the external sense of the word, but most certainly there will be jail time in the internal sense because many hearts have now been placed in confinement and stolen from the experience of true love.

Just how will this Karmic return play out? Although unique to each person and their situation, it can be illustrated using general examples since there are common threads to all potential Karmic outcomes. Do you wish to keep this affair a secret, or express the truth because you now know the ways to prevent brown silt from accumulating in your life from every circumstance? Here is a wonderful hint: the truth will allow more crystal drops to enter your clear pool of consciousness, thus diminishing the impact of the brown silt which you have already placed in your pool. And besides, it has been written throughout the ages: the truth will be made known. Do you believe there is any value in hiding it, knowing that it will come out in the end? The truth is, if you truly love the other person this would not have occurred in the first place, but because you think you love your partner, well, this is another story.

The affair really occurred for one reason only. There existed a level of unhappiness which we could have worked through with our partner; yet, most of us do not. Instead, we internalize the emotion until it festers into the affair. So what do you do? In everyone's best interest, you may consider entering a heart-to-heart discussion of the events. Address the truth with your partner in order to release your Karmic return, or to minimize it in a sense. Though it is after the fact, you must weather the initial storm, knowing there is going to at least be anger from your partner, and all the while remain calm during

this process. It is now hoped that you both will have the ability to communicate from the heart, not just the mind. Remember, through Karmic return, the truth now shows itself. What you thought was love, was in fact, not heartfelt; rather, it was simply mental. When the truth is offered, there is hope that it may be worked through with love possibly being discovered. Now, trusting each other will have to come into play, along with patience, two more levels of Karmic return.

On the other side of the coin, if your partner had the affair, how would *you* feel? Could you trust him or her? Ever? For most of us the answer would be an emphatic, "I doubt it!" The underlying question remains, will you ever have the ability to trust another person with your heart? Actually, yes! But only if you are able to truly forgive and release the event; otherwise, you may have the tendency to hold yourself back from a deeper, more meaningful experience of love, by constantly berating yourself on how dumb, gullible, or naïve you were to even trust that person in the first place. All because of one single event! This is generally the "normal" response from a knee-jerk reaction; hence, you embed the emotional trauma deep within you and push the emotional healing into the future.

Yes, even embedding and pushing the emotions will create a return action as does all things; therefore, be responsible for your part. After all, it did take at least two people initially to create that whole scene in the first place, did it not? And do not blame either yourself or any other since this will bind you to the very thing or person you do not like or care for. Ultimately, in order to achieve happiness through love, we must learn to trust no matter what we are faced with! From their perspective, monks do not hold any other person responsible for what they themselves have contributed in that particular experience. In truth, they would only trust and forgive in the very first place because they do not desire to carry forward any brown silt. Doing so would only "freeze" them in that particular arena. You see, when we trust, we must trust our self first before we may ever trust another human, just as we do in the arena of love. If we begin to blame our own being, we then become bound to it; yet, if we forgive and release it, we are actually bound to nothing and our personal pool continues to remain clear, further establishing our better future.

Next is patience. Patience creates high levels of tolerance with all others, most especially with your self. If you do not remain patient in all relationships and with all things, you run the risk of creating greater damage, damage not only to your partner, but also to your self by internally using all known expletives regarding how you were duped, all the while attempting to internally promise it will never occur again. Now you are internally – emotionally – in jail without having done anything – externally! Patience and trust go hand-in-hand, for without patience we may not trust anything as we literally rush in blindly. However, through patience, much in life may actually be attained and we would, in truth, have very little negative Karmic return since the idea of frustration would all but disappear, oddly enough. Through the eyes of a monk, patience builds trust while trust strengthens patience. A side point here, if we place our own heart in jail, we then create the return of finding another who also has their heart in jail, hence the reason why it is suggested above that you become your own partner. Ironically, you actually do in every circumstance; your own partner only appears physically separate from you!

Let us continue with the one who entered the affair, which probably would not have occurred if they had exercised patience and expressed the truth of what they were experiencing within their own relationship. But it is now after the fact. There are many Karmic ramifications or return actions, the vast majority of which will not necessarily be seen, but most certainly be felt. The so-called inappropriate doer most assuredly will not be able to trust any partner at any time until the situation is rectified through truth, most especially with them self since deception generally follows the affair. Deception brings more deception as a return action; hence, trust becomes deeply impacted. Even if the couple gets a divorce, trust glaringly remains an issue for the offender because they broke this covenant in the first place. Will the offender be able to love and be loved? Let us examine this.

Love, true love, is a cherished opportunity in our life, so once the affair occurs this opportunity becomes greatly diminished for all parties concerned, in most instances. Understand, a Karmic debt in this arena swiftly strikes at the heart of the matter, pun fully intended.

You see, fundamentally, the one who truly created the affair in the first place is the one who was betrayed; yet, they do not fully realize it at that moment. When opting for truth, however, this realization will come to them at some point in time. Self-betrayal then will be the largest of impacts from Karmic debt. "How does self-betrayal enter the picture?" you may ask. The offender ultimately betrayed their very own heart as well as all those involved, and unless they face themselves on this issue, it will continue to fester into every facet of their life. One facet is their ability to ever trust their partner, and in most cases, any future potential partner. Another facet is their anger at so many things, blaming so many external events for their present situation which, in truth, are an illusion in the first place. Karmically speaking, blame is denial of them self or their inability to assume personal responsibility, the very reason for swelling anger. Also, the idea of truth is entirely opposite of deception, the very reason for their experience of self-deception; they simply deny the truth of the matter. Once truth appears on the horizon though, deception disappears, thereby filtering their pool of consciousness back to clarity. It is very difficult to work through self-deception in order to locate the truth because the offender has become blind to the truth – another Karmic return – just as they had initially become blind to their commitment in the relationship.

What creates the idea of self-deception in the first place? By allowing, accumulating, and gripping onto internal mental and emotional pollution without releasing it. We actually block the activity of love by allowing and collecting this internal "smog," if you will. This deception accrues in, and truly contaminates, the heart because our ability to experience love has been diluted from its original state of purity at birth, the ultimate deception. Just in the arena of love, can you now picture the depth of Karmic return after having this affair? It violates one of the greatest principles we have to experience as a human being. The return is so deep and harsh because the heart is the powerhouse of our body wherefrom the power of any event is unleashed. If we are unable to trust our heart, we are then unable to trust in the power it may release, and as it diminishes, we begin to manifest a cold external demeanor toward people.

Once we take this stance we will then begin to progress toward the dominance of others and situations, simply because of what we did in our love relationship and to our partner. Ultimately, there is no value in this approach, nor is there value in anything which generates the path of a negative Karmic return. If we so choose, every negative return may be removed from our life if we consciously observe our actions and activities, both internal and external, each moment of every day, 24/7. Yes, I do realize this may first appear as a herculean task, one which you do not have time for, or so now you may think. However, I ask you to learn and work with it, for Karma will become automatic, actually requiring no additional time on your part. "What, no additional time for this huge task?" you may ask doubtfully. Yes! When automatic, you are constantly, objectively observing all aspects of your self while the external event unfolds right in front of you! This leads to a follow-up question, "From where do you see any additional time being utilized for this task?" By solely observing your self, you will undoubtedly see the areas needing change for your self-empowerment. A worthy practice indeed.

Let us return to Newton's third Law of Motion and let us take a more in-depth look upon its ideas. Do you believe this Law pertains only to the physical? May I suggest you read the Law again? Although it is based purely on a mathematical equation, you will find no mention or suggestion anywhere in this Law limiting it only to the mathematical or physical realities. Fascinating! Could it perhaps have greater applications, applying to all things physical, mental, and emotional? If so, it actually becomes a Universal Truth! Although I am not a credentialed physicist, I can offer you the following concept. Karma may be likened to the idea of a boat traveling through water. As the boat moves, its hull "slices" the water – action – leaving behind a completely visible wake – reaction – which then radiates outward to the shoreline. Now apply this same principle to an aircraft. Air provides lift under the wings – action – allowing the craft to fly, which then leaves its turbulence – reaction – behind. Don't we humans also move through the air, though much slower? If we are sitting or standing in place when a person walks by, do we not feel the slight breeze created as they just passed? We have the same effect with life; however, we do not see all the turbulence we create while

moving through our individual life, such as our mental and emotional aftermaths. They are indeed truly present, just as present and forceful as the boat passing through the water, or the aircraft flying through the air, or the human who had just walked by. Whether seen or felt, each wake has its original impact as well as its return consequence; therefore, the principles of Karma exist to help us understand the wake our personal vessel creates as it slices through each and every activity – our chosen action. This also includes all unseen activities which usually hold even greater power within. After all, the most powerful thing we have is our mind and thoughts.

To reiterate, this is not limited to just the physical, but includes all what we do, physically, mentally, and emotionally, for each creates in its own fashion some form of wake for its return activity. Don't stop here, for the return action will come, swinging now with both arms in either a positive or negative impact. Well, not physical arms per se. You see, while each experience unfolds, it further extends the Karmic return as our original wake crashes to the shores of our lives, attracting its like kind vibration or energy before commencing its return on the ripples. Karma's purpose is to actually enhance not only our personal experiences, but to also assist our creative power as the human. However, we are not able to use or shift the direction of this wonderful tool until we fully realize the extent to which Karma travels. We could operate in perfect symmetry by completely understanding our impact on life and events; yet, unlike the boat and airplane, the human does not create perfect symmetry in its wake. Do you see perfect symmetry from how the majority does things these days?

Yes, in some respects we do realize our impact, but I do not believe we have the full understanding of the long term impact we each carry. We impact not only ourselves constantly, but also the people immediately around us and the very natural environment in which we live. Do you believe otherwise? As mentioned earlier, there are many levels to Karmic return, for the impact of Karma encompasses not only the individual, but also every human. Consider this; we have a family Karma in which we create circumstance. This expands outward to the neighborhood in which we live, further expanding from the neighborhood to the city, expanding ever outward to the state, then

to the country, and ultimately to the entire world in which we reside. Now, how is this possible? It expands effortlessly and instantly due to our connected nature in consciousness.

Today we are faced with an ongoing debate on the cause(s) of global warming. Let us remember something about our physical sciences, from geophysics to astrophysics to even the medical sciences. Don't they each look at the physical only? Even the medical field looks at physical symptoms from a so-called physical illness. Karmically speaking, the physical is very seldom the cause; on the contrary, the physical is the end result of cause. If an asteroid impacts the earth, the resulting shock waves would most definitely be visible and felt. On the other hand, what would you say if the cause of an earthquake in this part of the world is actually due from the release of subterranean shock waves by bombs being dropped in other parts of the world, rather than two tectonic plates shifting as the media might swiftly inform us? Yes, this can be one of many reasons for the earth movements. If we, the human, require a release then would it not stand to reason that the land would also do the same? Land, just as water, will release shock waves which must be balanced at some point, so is there really a difference between the two when it comes to impacts?

Purely from a monk's perspective, I now offer you a supposition for which there is no physical proof; yet, there does indeed appear a connection. There truly may be another cause for global warming. I pose a question, "If you look at the world now and view the approaches of our masses, would you say there is peace?" Generally, you would have to say no since it is filled with the emotions of fear, anger, frustration, and impatience throughout the majority of continents. And, as each day passes, we hear of yet more and more deaths through acts of violence. Unfortunately, this is apparently the truth. Ok, what do these emotions have to do with global warming? Do you think they are unrelated, the same as between the bomb explosions and earthquake? Such would be the physical viewpoint, but this view has no true depth of perception. You see, if we are connected to each other through consciousness, it stands to reason that we are also connected to the environment in which we live. Please recall, if a principle or Law is universal, then it is true in every instance at every

level; otherwise, it would not be universal. If this is the case, when the majority of humans operate through any of the above emotions by asserting them outwardly to each other and their environment, we are then individually contributing a negative energy stream into the global pool of consciousness. And since each of the above emotions actually requires an increase in our energy, we essentially heat up. Once this occurs, do you now sense how global consciousness would now send the heat back to us as our Karmic return?

Based on the interconnectedness we each have through consciousness, the idea between global warming and our global pool of consciousness becomes directly related. Expressed another way, Karma acts as a request line for an experience, in a sense, and operates through the universal principle of Attraction, a Karmic principle to be discussed in a future chapter. In fact, our weather patterns are also operating as a direct reflection of what we are doing as humans. Does it really surprise you to witness today's weather in such turmoil? Why, it must be so, as it is the direct reflection, the Karmic return, of our own inner turmoil! You know, there exists one verifiable way to prove this supposition for certain. From this moment forward, let every human operate in peace, thereby negating all other influences. You see, we are the creators of our world. Which are we creating, peace or violence? Quite obviously, the answer is directly in front, staring right back at us!

Are you beginning to understand the idea of Karma? Let us travel in another direction for a moment to expand the scope of its action taking place in our world. How about the bird flu pandemic? Could we have created this, also? On the one hand, it appears completely probable according to the principles of Karma and our connectedness. Are you now asking, "How in the world did we do this?" Perhaps some light on this subject may help. No, I do not feel a hidden agency is creating this world event for a germ warfare exercise. From a more reasonable perspective, if we use antibiotics too often a virus becomes resistant, rendering the drugs ineffective and at the same time weakening our body's immune system. We now have a greater susceptibility to other viruses, do we not? What a vicious cycle we inadvertently created because we truly did not look long term! Fortunately, the medical

profession discovered this cause and effect. Unfortunately, not until the caregivers actually over-prescribed antibiotics for every little thing, did the governing bodies publicize the truth, stating such prevalent treatment is absolutely not necessary. Too late, though, for once the viruses began to mutate, they took a life of their own. We are exposed to an exponentially greater variety of viruses today than ever before!

Consider this, that within a few short years ago no mention or incident of bird flu even existed; yet, it is now schemed as the next pandemic. Are we really placing this idea in global consciousness? And the more people who fear it, the more its concept will spread and physically attract it, just as between the homeowner and the thief. In a sense, we have used a two-fold process to create this strain of flu. First, the viruses became resistant from the excessive use of antibiotics. Second, from the initial media frenzy over the first bird flu case, fear was brought into consciousness. Interestingly enough, this purported pandemic has not occurred as was originally projected. This makes sense because most of us have either not accepted it, or we have not given it enough energy – yet. I fervently hope we maintain this mindset; otherwise, it most certainly shall spread as extensively as the media has projected, if not more so. I fully realize how far-fetched these two ideas seem, how Karma may truly be the cause of global warming and the pandemic; however, it may not be so far-fetched after all simply because of our connected nature, our connection to all others and all life, through the common thread of consciousness. Yes, this includes viruses, too! If enough people input the idea and fear of the "bird flu pandemic" into consciousness, then it must come. If enough people continue to believe that global warming is fast approaching, then it surely shall. If you believe in war, you simply are not able to have peace. Karma applies in every direction, not just in those few instances we either accept or ignore out of personal convenience.

Let us now look at these impacts from the individual perspective because individuals make up the collective after all, our global pool of consciousness. Using one example, you – an individual – are driving down the street only to quickly cross a lane or two for your anticipated exit or turn. Not desiring to miss it, you had to cut in front of another

car which intentionally frustrated the other driver, no doubt. You did this knowingly! Now, two things will occur as the Karmic return. First, *you* are going to be cut off – or worse – at some point in the near future, and second, you will get to experience frustration yourself, maybe not when you are cut off in that instance, but most definitely in another circumstance and generally in a very short period of time.

Thank you for allowing me to use you again in this next example. Let us say you intentionally anger another. Then you shall also experience anger in one form or another, hence the idea: what you do to others you actually do to you. The majority does not see these incidents as being related; however, they absolutely are! They are as directly connected to us as the weather. One event created the other, which is why some people do not believe in coincidence. Would you like another, seemingly innocuous, example? Let us say you have finished shopping, and as you finish purchasing your items at the check-out the clerk gives you too much change. Realizing you received excess change, you still leave the store thinking, "The store won't miss it, and besides, it was their mistake, not mine." Karma disagrees because you knew the mistake, meaning you have now taken that which does not belong to you! On the other hand, I feel pretty certain you would have immediately requested the correct change if the clerk had first shorted you, is this not so? If you, therefore, know you have received the improper change, over or under, then do the proper thing. Correct it then and there, in that moment! Simply learn to follow your conscience, your inner voice, for conscience and consciousness are the connection. Okay then, what is the key to all this? The key is the intention behind what you do toward another. Karma holds us liable when we knowingly or intentionally realize any action; however, if it is truly inadvertent, the Karmic return is greatly diminished, possibly none at all.

Karma is like an ever-flowing liquid entirely generated by what each human does, an ever-flowing stream, either flowing in harmony or flooding its banks, in which case, it wreaks havoc on the community as it gushes every which way. This is the truth, no matter how or where you look at it, for it is all the same. If you choose to stay the course with me, you will realize that Universal Truth shows itself constantly

and consistently in all levels everywhere; in other words, if it is in one thing then it is in all things. If not, it is not Universal Truth. When enough individuals shift their direction then any city, state, or even country can shift its Karma into a new direction; however, it shall take many individual minds to accomplish this because, once a negative Karmic flow begins, it takes much effort to alter its course and resulting purpose. This flow may expand from one individual family member to the entire family, spreading forth to the local community, then to the state, and so on, until it permeates all people. Why does this occur? Once more, consciousness is the key. As already suggested, consciousness permeates all living things as it must, for consciousness is life, the very receptacle into which the ripples of every personal wake created by each human event is received.

I would now like to turn your attention to traditions, for each community and nation has them, each so diverse and unique in appearance. In the USA, the Southeast does things differently than the Northwest. Why is this so? The consciousness of the local residents creates the difference because each citizen who lives in that particular area generally has the same mindset. Although a community or region may vary from the whole of any country, there remain many similar nuances between the two. Additionally, when we view another nation, their traditions can easily differ from ours due to the pure and simple reason of consciousness; yet, there are levels or nuances of consciousness which remain constant between each. In truth, therefore, we *do* influence all others no matter the region or country! These principles are so simple as long as they are followed. They allow the stream of Karma to flow calmly and confined within its banks; otherwise, if we choose not to follow them, one country can potentially influence another as our stream over-flows its banks, overwhelming the other's realm of life. In turn, this creates uncontrolled acts and actions upon others as we attempt to control them in our own way. Now conflict is created. Being a universal Law, this can easily occur between two individuals, or between two families or communities, even between states. This begs the question, "Do you know of any conflicts going on in your area or the world at this time?" Now stay with me because control has yet another set of circumstances to go along with *it*.

What about this idea of control and controlling people? You understand this applies to the individual all the way to the full spectrum of humanity, nations included, do you not? Who is actually in control in the first place? From pure natural common sense, neither one single human nor one single nation should be in control, though some people believe differently. I suggest it is the Creator of life and each of us as individuals, and our grand pool of consciousness as Its messenger. Remember, our control is not outside of us, for we were never intended to control others, though we attempt to. Question: Who is a controlling individual? They are so domineering and very few of us enjoy this type of personality, isn't this so? Here's the defining truth of it: a person who is actually unable to control them self, and because of this, they in turn attempt to control everything around them, to make all things match them. This applies to the individual, a group, a major corporation, even to a state or a country!

For a controlling entity to feel secure it is compelled to have all things like it; else, it is intolerably insecure which is masked by anger. So now it must dominate all things around it. Can you imagine for a moment just how extremely frustrating this experience may be, that the only seeming gratification to come is when the entity knows it is controlling others? Unfortunately, as frustration increases so does the need for greater control. And on and on the cycle goes, and when will it cease? When they relinquish control! The Karmic returns for control are frustration and anger which happen to be two very great and efficient contributors of brown sludgy silt to our present-day global pool of consciousness. Could this be why we witness so much global violence? One can only wonder why people are now beginning to rebel against the idea of being so controlled! This indeed would be the Karmic return. But keep in mind, though, violence is never the answer, whether on a personal or global level, because violence can only create more violence. Karmic return strikes again!

Let us look into our field of medicine again, and yes, it is one of the most advanced in the world; yet, it simply does not or will not understand many things when it comes to Karma and illness. As mentioned earlier, the field relies on physical symptoms to reveal an apparent physical illness. Symptoms are messengers, in a sense,

only communicating which illness the individual potentially has; however, it is not the cause of the illness. What is now shared with you may seem very bold; nonetheless, I have seen it with my own two eyes during my sojourn with my Master teachers. Monks are taught how to *completely* heal other people; in fact, a monk can cure some illnesses and diseases that our high-tech modalities cannot. The reason is quite practical. Since there are so many remote areas, a monk is the only available healer, and from centuries of practice and through observation, the monk actually brings about true healing for the patient simply because the cause of the illness/disease is treated, not its symptoms.

If only our sciences would take into consideration a holistic approach, they would be better able to assist many more people toward health rather than illness, generally speaking. Holistic in this context may not be what you are thinking. A monk not only looks at the particular part in trouble, but also senses the manner in which all the parts make up the whole body of the patient; in other words, they view the patient in a whole sense. They incorporate lifestyle to dietary habits to work and family environment to the patient's mind. Many years ago, I overhead a cynical motto aimed at our medical field: We are about illness, not health. I immediately shook my head in total disagreement; however, after years of simple observation, this phrase may offer some truth, unfortunately. Figures do not deceive; health care costs are rising nearly exponentially; therefore, if the medical professionals genuinely promote health in all they do, why the deluge of diseases and recurring illnesses? Shouldn't the incidents be decreasing? Health stems from true nutrition which is not necessarily from only what we physically eat, to offer a clue. Nutrition in this part of the world is something entirely different from other parts of the world.

While studying in the Far East, my teachers thoroughly explained to me that our body and each of its organs have a very meaningful metaphysical representation. From this reference, every organ acts as a sponge, easily, quickly, and deeply absorbing the energy of Karmic return. A few examples are in order. First would be the lungs, which represent our ability to receive life, while second, the cardio system represents our ability to allow life to flow just as it is. How about the kidneys and liver? They represent our ability to filter the issues we encounter through our daily lives. And what do you suppose is the meaning behind the digestive system? Of course, it represents our ability to digest and release those same issues. The sexual organs represent the idea of being guilt-free or free from feelings of guilt. Our wondrous body is one very large chain of chemical reactions directly influenced by our mind. So let us now look at the mind, body and experience with relationships, each connected to the other through the power of electromagnetic fields, as one attracts the other. Do not stop here! We offer more food for thought.

Additional information ought to be revealed for you about the controlling person discussed earlier. You see, this person runs the risk of many health challenges, two of them almost certain. Karmically speaking, this individual will have lung and heart issues which are greatly increased due to their innate ability to interrupt their flow of life. This flow becomes interrupted because they need to control the people and issues around them, and when they are not able to, the control literally eats at them. One, they cannot accept – breathe in – "no" for an answer, thus developing a higher risk of respiratory issues. Two, they cannot allow life to simply flow; hence, they develop a higher risk of heart and/or cardiovascular issues. I have had the opportunity to chat on many occasions with respiratory therapists, personally asking during our conversations, "What kind of mindset do your patients have?" The therapists with whom I have spoken suggested, in summary, "I have run into stubbornness, short tempers, and even receive quite an earful from my patient, who attempts to tell me, in no uncertain terms, how I am to do my job." Now what does this sound like to you? I also asked, "Have you ever had a person with respiratory issues who was very peaceful with an easy-going demeanor?" And the answer is? "If I do, chances are extremely rare." Do you notice a connection here? It would appear, indeed, that the possibility is present, especially if our connectedness is a Universal Truth. Does it make sense that our organs are also directly connected to Karmic return, just like everything else? Simply stated, mind is cause and the effect is the physical illness or disease.

Let us peer into heart disease for a moment to reveal another potential Karmic result, remembering it represents our ability to allow life to be just what it is, to let it flow. The United States may very well be the "Heart Issue" capital for the entire world. Can you now understand why? Could it be that so many people have the need to control, that they simply do not allow their life to flow freely? When we look at the clogging of arteries is it really because of *only* what we eat? Is it because of our heredity or genetic DNA? Perhaps; yet, there could be more here than what meets the eye on this one, too. We fail to realize, our body is a miraculous chemical interaction giving us life. Ponder for a moment, what if this chemical interaction slowly closes up our arteries due to our closed mindedness, that it is not simply the food alone we ingest? When we look at the ramifications offered us by Karmic return, we may now hold a slightly different viewpoint, do we not? Again, our body is one very large chemical reaction, the chemicals of which are controlled by our mind, directly influencing the chemical exchange taking place within each cell. If our mind is polluted by the need to control, it would appear Karma would direct its return in the appropriate arenas, namely the lungs and heart. This is why in monastic studies the Master teachers would suggest the necessity to relinquish control in order to maintain a level of optimum health. A monk does not attempt to control anything outside of them self since everything outside is simply what it is. Wisely, they allow it to remain without any interference whatsoever. Are you beginning to realize the body, mind, and experience connection behind an illness or disease?

In truth, most health issues are genuinely created by this lack of internal connection to external events, a time when the body is literally not at ease, or in *dis*-ease. Tremendous healing could truly take place, totally and completely reversing these effects, if we but simply change our mind and viewpoint towards our interactions with life, our experience, and all humankind! Some may still feel this connection cannot be correct or at the very least misguided; yet, we do hear about hundreds of people going through amazing physiological shifts and healing a so-called incurable illness by making major lifestyle changes. When the ailing individual commits to such a drastic and thorough change, it is most fascinating to witness the degree to which their

personal accumulation of Karma shifts. Is this telling us there is also a connection between lifestyle and Karmic return? No one that I am aware of has ever looked at this from the perspective of Karmic Law! It is interesting when these people do make the change. It is as though their illness no longer "fits" their new way of living, and so it disappears. Perhaps it is wise to keep in mind that when we change our lives, our Karma follows.

Kindly allow me to touch on just one more important area relating Karma to the physiology of the liver and kidneys. Physically speaking, these two organs are important filters, paramount for the maintenance of blood and bodily purification. If we have any issues or harbor any level of ill-will, these necessary attributes shall have a greater degree of difficulty because they will most certainly become clogged or blocked over a period of time. If we are going to heal our body from any disease, use the primary healing tool, our very own mind. By first clearing mind of the issues with which we are unsettled, we stand a much better chance to become whole in the process. Once the organs are cleared, the medicines and procedures would be more effective, if at all necessary. Unfortunately in most cases, relying solely on medical assistance may only help temporarily at best, for the blockages will more than likely return. Remember, all things are represented through our organs and how they function. All we must allow for in this arena is the flow of life. Clearly, holding onto or having an issue with absolutely nothing is the best and most peaceful path, for this truly promotes optimal bodily function.

Inner peace is truly the optimum ideal for perfect health. In all my years working with monks, I never found one who was not at peace or at rest in each moment, and I never saw one become ill. I include myself while living amongst them. Do you believe it is much simpler to live in a monastery? Possibly so, but only to a small degree. I saw firsthand the operation at work, twenty-four hours a day, seven days a week, all accomplished without effort. You see, in their view it is the real world because they simply do not live in a hectic fashion. Even in our world, what some term as the outside world, who or what is requiring us to live in a hectic fashion? Although I live in this so-called outside world, I easily maintain my lifestyle of a monk, simply

because I enjoy it and choose it. Fundamentally speaking, unless we choose to live in a peaceful mental state, we shall remain hectic because our minds are hectic. Reflect on this viewpoint: it is not as much about where we live as it is about how we live.

You see, one could live peacefully in any environment. The only requirement to maintain true health is to accept the environment without struggle. A monk would certainly advise us that holding onto anything will have its long-term impact upon our body. Cease what you are doing internally to your self, and your health will begin to change for the better. Take this moment to just stand back and view your life as an observer. How do you interact with it? This exercise may help you to understand the Karmic interactions taking place within your body; in fact, take another moment to listen to your body. What is it attempting to tell you about your health? By spending these few moments more often, we would realize what we accumulate within our chemical interactions through our experiences, and in so doing, we may then shift it to create health in place of *dis*-ease. My message to you is, without the body we have no ability to physically live. To have health is living life in the optimum sense of the idea, so eat well and slowly. Be at peace with all there is, especially with your experiences, then life will give to you what you seek.

Within the last few words of this chapter, I offer one more analogy in my attempt to deepen your understanding of our reality and Karma. Come visualize with me for a moment. In your mind's eye, imagine consciousness as a lake in the pre-dawn hours, its surface reflecting as though a highly-machined telescope mirror without a single ripple on it, the trees clearly appearing to be hanging upside down along its shoreline. The water surface is truly magnificent to behold and to be a part of. A water skier's dream, don't you think? Oh look, there they are, getting into the water from the opposite shore! They are really enjoying the smooth water surface with their friends! I do not sense they are even aware of the other arrivals. Late morning, we now see many boats and skiers enjoying the placid waters, now including the jet skiers, and families with children spread along the shoreline, laughing, splashing and enjoying their outing.

Wow, it is afternoon already? Look at the lake now! The water surface is no longer smooth; instead, it is now filled with deep ripples as though boulders had been dropped in it. Choppy crisscross waves splash the shore, even the silt has been raised from the bottom due to all the surface activity and resulting wave turbulence. Now, what you saw in your mind's eye is much like consciousness as we first arise each morning. Initially, nothing is on our minds, for we are in a placid mental state, crystal clear. As we become active we begin placing more into consciousness by planning or dreading the day. As our day becomes filled with experience, we have become choppy in our minds and interactions with events, hence raising the silt from the bottom of our pool to its surface, appearing much as the lake in the late afternoon, only in our mind.

You see, the choppy waters are the myriad of thoughts we send forth without our realizing it, and like the Doppler Effect, they will return to us once they have garnered the experience through Karma for the return action. Upon their return, they begin to churn us inside, pushing our personal silt of memories to the surface, thereby clouding our mind. We now must filter through these previous events; otherwise, we have just allowed them to go within to block our body and its organs from our optimum state of health. This is our life, day in and day out; yet, it need not remain this way! In truth, we can have everlasting tranquility within our bodies, no matter what the outer world is offering us as experience.

We may be peaceful with all people and circumstances by understanding and operating through the principles of Karma. This is entirely within our sphere of control and ever-present as long as we do not create waves on our own pool's surface. Through the twelve principles of Karma, I hope you soon realize that you have more influence than you may have ever dreamed of. A divine human truly empowered! Through the realization of your direct influence, you attain optimum control and self-mastery in all you strive to do and accomplish. May your journey be in peace and in wholeness!

"The light of any lamp dispels in a moment
the darkness of long eons;
The strong light of the mind in but a flash will
burn the veil of ignorance."
Buddha

~ Chapter II ~
The Great Principle

Now that you have an idea of how Karma works, and its true nature and purpose, the twelve sacred Laws will now be presented to you, individually and in the same order they were offered to me. The words "principle" and "Law" are actually synonymous terms, and are wholly interchangeable throughout each chapter. Our journey begins by introducing you to the first of the twelve principles, termed as the Great Law or Great Principle. It was shared with me in this manner and with these words offered from my Master teachers, "*What you sow so shall you reap.*" There is almost more causality in this one principle than in all the others, so it may be considered the greatest of the Laws, hence its name and place in the sequence. When you fully understand this first principle, not only will the scope in which you operate narrow, but it will also add greater overall flexibility to you and your life.

Understanding the Great Principle will also help you understand the other principles, for they in themselves shall become much simpler and have less impact in your life than they do now. No, they do not go away, but you will soon know what they are and how they operate. Living by their ageless wisdom, your life does become easier, at least in the sense of knowing your outcomes long before they ever arrive.

In truth, this is the key to all life experience which we bring to us. Oh, I can hear you, "What does he mean, '*we* bring to *us*'?" Yes, you read that correctly, for it is as though circumstances come to *us* by our request. What goes into life and consciousness first occurs through each of us as our individual experience, and then expands outward to the collective experience. Depending entirely upon how we each view our experiences, Karma simply reflects their like kind back to us.

This first Law determines how life shall progress or evolve, individually and collectively, whether it creates turmoil, stress, even war, or their opposites, such as love, compassion and peace. It totally depends on what we individually first decide to plant. They teach in the East: if there is an effect, there is always a cause which created that effect. One simply may not exist without the other, which is the exact premise behind Newton's Third Law. If you want peace and joy in your life, in your home, the neighborhood, all countries, even the whole world, simply start where you are, by doing something about *you*. I suggest, quite literally, that we place our focus on our self first, not on others as we do most times. When we focus on our self, we are much more aware of what we do than what others do; in fact, this is the one main key to Karma. It is all about you, not them. Allow all others to take care of themselves and their own responsibility in what they do; besides, when you are focusing on others it distracts from the most important part of your life – you. Here are three questions you might ask yourself: 1) "If I am helpless and fearful, do I really cause them?" 2) "Subsequently, do these really draw more of the same experience to me?" 3) "Am I, in fact, creating negatives in my own life simply by focusing on the fears and helplessness of others?" Truly consider these questions as they have a large impact on each of us both individually and collectively.

While studying with the monks in the Far East, I vividly recall the day when Master Lobsang approached me, stating in his simple manner, "It is time for you to learn the ideas of cause and effect in us humans, known as Karma," and further impressed upon me that these were going to be some of the most important principles I would come to learn during my sojourn with the Master teachers. Further, he wanted me to internalize them in a very specific order;

therefore, they were introduced to me and discussed, one at a time, allowing me many a moon to learn and internalize each one so that working with them would be simpler for me, just as I will do for you through this book. He said, "Once learned, you will know how your life will unfold before the effects or events even appear in your experience. You will also learn to realize how you are directly able to influence your life with greater ease by internalizing and living them, not simply thinking them." Following his request, "Come walk with me," I began my exposure to the ideas of Karmic Law and to circumstances created by cause.

During our walk one spring, just as we approached the crops beside the monastery where monks were busy planting and harvesting, Master Lobsang turned to ask me, his index finger pointing toward the fields, "Young man, what do you see?" I confidently replied, "Why, Master, I see my brothers tending the fields. Some are tilling the soil; some are planting seeds, and others are harvesting some early crops." He stated that we should sit under the shade of a tree so we could begin the principles. He talked about Karma, much of which I related to you in the last chapter, and indeed, he fully understood I observed Karma in the physical sense; however, it does not end here. Karma runs much deeper as it intertwines itself in all things, like the roots of a plant which we do not see under the soil. We merely see the results of the seed, but not until after it has sprouted, much the same way Karma itself works.

We plant the seed and it naturally knows to shoot and spread its roots to take hold in the soil, only to spring into life. "Do you know what your mind, emotions, and physical self do?" my teacher posed for me to ponder. "Yes I do, Master!" I immediately answered. He offered, "You may know what your body does, as we all do, for that is clearly seen. Most of us, however, do not realize the impact our mind and emotions have on the body. They are, in fact, our most important part because they determine our life, both in the short and long run. I venture to say, if we truly know their degree of impact, would we not be more judicious in how we operate with them? Would we not become more aware of what we are thinking or feeling? Would we not know what our thoughts are doing? Would we not be more focused on the types of thoughts we emanate? If we truly are, then perhaps we would not allow them to wander as we currently do. These are all things more powerful than we may have ever imagined."

My teacher continued, "These two tools – thought and emotion – actually do determine our outcomes in material life and we never know what those will be until they sprout and grow, at least in the way we now plant and nurture them. As they grow, we have what we term as the experience or effect of what we planted, and at times, whether it be a day, a month, or even years later, we see the mature growth of what we planted. The return action from our creation is actually known as our created cause and it is what we term our experience." Master Lobsang further stated that these two personal aspects not only affect us directly, but they also affect those closest to us, which then affects our community, only to continue their ripple effect ever outward to the entire world as they move straight into the idea of consciousness, wherefrom they are shared with every human and *their* experience in life. The mind and emotional arenas of the human impact consciousness and collective mind directly, while the physical body simply executes what these guide it toward. Master Lobsang simply offered, "This is the Great Law which all people should learn to understand: *What you sow so shall you reap*. It is the prime basis of cause and effect." Most likely you have had at least one experience which you did not particularly care for, am I correct? The truth is, you created the experience through the return actions of Karma, and whether or not you believe this is totally irrelevant, for the fact remains, the Great Law is the Universal Truth behind all experiences.

What is this so-called Great Law? What is this prime principle of life really all about? How does it work? Allow me to share this as my teachers taught it to me because it is very important, especially to realize we can work with it, but only through knowing how it works. Repeating, the Great Law of Karma states: *What you sow so shall you reap.* You may shrug your shoulders while thinking, "Oh sure, I have heard this before. Didn't Jesus say this in the Bible?" Although the Christ is the one who is most quoted for saying it, he in fact did not originate it. Records show, He was taught this principle along

with the other eleven Laws of Karma during His sojourn in the Far East. Yes, most certainly, all twelve principles are quoted by Him throughout the Bible, but in different phrasing.

The Great Law was actually recorded in the Vedas, the oldest known philosophic text in the world, a text predating Jesus by at least two millennia, a text even older than Buddhism, a teaching which holds the greatest number of practitioners who abide by this very principle. It is written about in the Bhagavad-Gita and stated by Krishna, in approximately 150 BCE. If I were to choose only one principle to follow, the Great Law is by far the only one we would ever need practice through all of life because of the simplicity in its purity. Look at its simplicity as the manner in which you would plant each seed in the ground while its purity shines though the manner in which the seed innately spreads its roots to accept the nutrients provided by both water and soil, thirsting for growth. We tend to think sowing a seed as simply planting a crop or garden like the monks that spring day; however, where the human is concerned in life, sowing is not limited to only physical action and activity.

In every action perpetrated by us, we plant seeds which, by their very nature, must come to fruition and bear their own fruits. For a moment, imagine this prime principle as strictly literal – it is more than we may want to realize. Now ask yourself, "Which seeds am I planting in all I say and do?" When answering, please be very truthful with yourself, and when answered, take an honest and open introspective look at every circumstance in your life, openly viewing it as an impartial observer. Doing so you are more easily able to see the fruits your seeds have yielded. Perhaps now you can understand why your life is precisely the way it is. Now don't blame me. And it is certainly no one else's fault! Be careful, placing blame on anyone or anything outside of you negates personal responsibility. The subject of blame shall be expanded on in a later chapter. Also, removing every idea or feeling of blame is vitally imperative during this process as you transform your weed-filled garden to a luscious fruit-filled grove.

If not seen in the physical, then what exactly are the seeds we sow and how do we plant them? Do you realize we plant them in

everything we do, constantly and continually? Ironically, this was part of creation and is our divine gift in reality. We have the divine gift of planting weeds or fruitful lives; it is our choice, but not until we realize what and how we plant, thus the idea of these twelve sacred principles. These are planted in every act, action, thought or emotion in which we emit, and to think they are all under our control should we so choose! There is no way around this. In truth, our own lives are our very own creation through this very principle according to Master Lobsang. The simple concepts and ideas of Karma are to get each one of us to become aware of what we plant, not how the planting may be avoided or even circumvented, which is actually not possible. There are actually three varieties of seeds for which we are responsible to plant, the physical seeds which are contained in and seen from our every physical action or activity, and the more subtle seeds contained in our mind, the very powerful mental and emotional ones with the emotional seeds being pre-eminent since they contain unrivaled power. In a general sense, it is the latter two, interestingly enough, that actually create all the physical activity because they generate each physical response or action to what we think or feel toward something.

Let us first begin with the mental seeds, followed by the emotional ones, only to end this chapter with the physical seeds since their return consequences are the easiest to realize. The physical seeds are the simplest to weed through and they also seem to grow or materialize the fastest without requiring nearly as much nurturing as do the mental and emotional ones. The mental and emotional seeds are a bit more complex by their very inherent nature because they are invisible at first, while at some future point they will manifest in either a positive or negative return. Interestingly, it is precisely these two realms – the mental and emotional – which are both within our sphere of control as physical action follows these two. Human seeds are similar to plant seeds in that, once they are buried beneath the soil of our mind, they elude our eye until they sprout. Once they break the surface, are they a weed or are they what we intended or desired to plant? Can we easily tell the difference? In this scenario we must wait until they sprout so as not to inadvertently remove what we actually desired to plant and have grow in our life. Our journey begins with the mind and its inherent nature of: *What you sow so shall you reap.*

Do you believe mind and thought are synonymous? If you do, are you certain? You see, a monk would not believe so because mind is the store house whereas thought is the resultant activity of the mind. Mind and its activity create individual thoughts through the chemical activity of our body in relationship to experience, and its key factor to operate with Karma is to remain present with it, right-now-this-moment. By remaining present we will know what our thoughts are doing as they echo through the mind, thereby knowing precisely what we are planting in that moment. One of the first things taught in a monastery is to always be present since this is the most powerful place in which to reside. Where does the creation of events actually occur in life? In the present! Initially, remaining mentally present is difficult because the unfocused mind has the tendency to drift like a butterfly, fluttering from one flower to the next without any rhyme or rhythm. Therefore, to know what we are planting we must hone the mind to always be present in all we do.

How do we do this? Let us offer an analogy by using the wild mustang, a horse found in the western U.S. If you were to catch one and immediately place it in a very confined space, you would quickly realize your level of difficulty in keeping that horse contained. Here is a wild animal, roaming wherever and whenever it pleased during its entire life, much like the mind. The next moment – slam, click; the mustang is locked in the smallest of pens. You kind of think the horse would rebel a bit? Yes it would, as would also your mind which has been roaming freely all through its life as well! But if you gradually, slowly over time, rope and fence the horse in until it was confined, you would find this process much less difficult and the animal would most likely stay calm. The same holds true with our mental attribute.

For our entire lives we are taught to control only our body and our emotions, but very seldom our mind. Generally, this organ flails almost perpetually, wandering hither and yon as the butterfly, continuously creating and bringing about return effects from all the things it plants from mindless meandering. This reminds me of the story of Hansel and Gretel who left a trail of bread crumbs to mark their way home, only to have the crumbs gobbled up by the birds and forest animals. This simply implies that we forget or ignore our seeds

and our thoughts, believing each as inconsequential, while in truth, each and every one carries a weight or return impact. Yes, each and every one of them!

Remember this Universal Truth, for it is not that some seeds will sprout and grow, but rather all seeds must come to fruition, each one carrying equal weight. I remember Master Lobsang thoughtfully asking me, "What if the one you call your God heard everything you thought and considered it as your request for It to do something for you? Would you change the way you think?" "Why yes, Master!" I replied in shock. "Good!" he emphatically stated, "For that is precisely what occurs as it is generated by our mind! Every single thought has the power of creation behind it. Even the most seemingly flippant thought carries the exact same weight and impact as the most loving thought. They each have the power to attract its like kind, and to subsequently bring it to us for the experience." This is truly powerful in its full scope! The mind is the most powerful aspect of the human as a steering mechanism for our life. And to think we have the choice to either operate it in the divine sense by planting divine seeds or to operate it purely in the fashion of a simple physical human, completely alone and separate from the entire cosmos. Which is your choice? Choose wisely in this matter as it is literally life-altering in breadth.

Just how do we go about training our flailing mind? From the perspective of the monastic teaching, it becomes simple after diligent practice: always keep our mind and thoughts where our body is. Another way of looking at it would be what Master Lobsang taught me: keep your thoughts right where your eyes are looking. Have the mind always follow the eyes. Now you are present. And that's it. This is being fully present, and by maintaining this, we subsequently create presence and empowerment. Do you realize the basic principle behind meditation is keeping your mind exactly where you are? I fully understand many people do not believe they have any time to actually meditate. The truth is, we all do!

Let us peek into the typical American mindset, one which goes about its daily activity as a fluttering butterfly. When at work, it thinks and plans for what it is going to do for the upcoming weekend.

What's this? Wonderful! – a call just in from a friend and now both minds get excited about an evening event. Oh no, another call, and in the very next moment it begins a shopping list for that evening's supper. I ask you, where is "work" in these three activities? When "mind" arrives home, it can only seem to think and worry about the work not completed, which must now be added to tomorrow's list of work tasks. These scenarios imply that our mind is not truly present in either situation, though our body was. It is no surprise then to think we do not have the time to meditate. Generally speaking from a mental sense, because our minds are adrift in the ocean of life, we are perpetually undoing ourselves at every turn as we plant the seeds of our lives. We simply are not consciously aware of the seeds or events around us until after the fact, and unfortunately, we may very easily overreact to most situations because our mind is allowed to operate as in the above scenario.

We generally think of where we are not instead of focusing on where we are; therefore, we are surprised or startled by events because we are not focused on where we are in reality. Understandably, could our reaction be the very seat of anger, simply because we are caught by surprise? Herein rests the issue. A test question before continuing: Are you with me? Right-here-right-now? Is your mind present with your body? Good! Being in the present, we would have the ability to act on events, not react to them, while adding the ability to focus our mind on any given thing in each moment. The Zen tradition calls this mindfulness, which is one of its primary teachings, to always and perpetually be present with our body. Certainly this takes practice. And mind you, never force your mind for it will quickly behave as the wild mustang; instead, gently nudge it back to the present each time it drifts. If you find this difficult, then simply focus on your breath and breathing. This practice will free your mind from drifting and return it to the present wherein you will realize which seeds you are planting in your life. Rest assured; life becomes easier.

So how do we remove this mental flailing in order to train our mustang mind? First, just realize how simply being present may be. While driving, you are usually focused on your destination more times than not, right? This means you are actually living in the future;

therefore, your mind is not where your body is. Because you already know your destination, I suggest you simply stop thinking about it, thereby eliminating this mindset. Focus only on the driving wherein you remain present, totally away from the future since it is purely a moment which will not arrive until the proper distance has been achieved, not one second sooner.

A few good reasons to keep your mind with your body while driving: 1) it diminishes your chance of getting in a hurry. This will only create more pressure as its Karmic return; 2) it diminishes any level of stress. Because you are operating in the present, you are planting seeds of peace; otherwise, operating in a future moment can only plant weeds of stress. Put bluntly, stress damages the body in the long run; 3) it diminishes any probability of an accident because you know what is going on around you – *at all times*; 4) it diminishes the possibility of road rage because, again, there is no stress. Road rage may occur when a driver feels that others are slowing them down, or are interfering or blocking them in some manner. Why? All because they are focusing on where they are going and not as much on what they are doing!

There is another perk for focusing only on your driving. It keeps you out of the past since those moments have already occurred. Not convinced? Then keep this in mind. The future is a place wherein you are not physically able to live because your physical body may only be in the present, which is where you really are. Besides, living in the future keeps everything in a future moment, not the present! When it arrives, the future automatically transforms into the present, the time when all events take place and is where you can realize what you had planted. Remember, the idea and real value of being present is our knowing which seeds we are planting in any given moment by our mind. This is termed, "presence" or "being mindful." Karmically speaking, living in the future will only bring stress, worry, even frustration; on the other hand, living in the past simply replants the seeds of old experiences, and when seeds are replanted, we seem to encounter cycles in our experience. The added advantage of driving in this manner is actually the purpose of meditation. What, you have never heard of driving meditation? In truth, by genuinely staying present in any activity, we are actually meditating. If time was our

excuse to not meditate, it appears no longer valid, for here is one way of doing what we thought we don't have time for.

We pose two questions, "What causes us to worry? Why do some people do this more than others?" The true cause of this mental ailment is not being in the present, not remaining right behind your eyes. Consider this for a moment; just sit back and ask yourself, "Right in this very moment, is there anything or anyone to worry about?" Okay, how about in *this* moment! Now in *this* one! I believe you get the idea. We worry of future moments or things from our past because in the present there is no time to get caught in worry. Try it out; you may be surprised. First, let us offer a point to ponder. Worry is just as powerful, if not more so, than focused, purposeful thought. You still plant the seeds and are scattering them everywhere, thereby creating evermore worries.

You know, most of us certainly have the propensity to worry. Interestingly enough, living in the future is the primary cause of worry. Okay, here is an example. What do you call it when a person looks at their current checkbook balance today, then anxiously thinks of the bills that are due at month's end? Here they are, only on the second day of the month! You cannot tell me that they are not worried about how they are going to pay the month-end debts, which are weeks away. You see, they are mentally living at the end of the month, in the future, worrying over something which will not occur for another twenty-eight days or so from now. From this one worry and without even realizing it, they are actually planting the weeds of lack in their personal life for future growth, permitting Karmic return to plant even more weeds through other avenues of stress into their life. Would you rather train to always live in the present, each moment free from worry and stress?

I agree we have things to work with in the present; however, there exists no time to worry or even stress over anything or anyone else since we are presently working with precisely what we need to say and do in this particular moment. Maintaining our focus on the task at hand, such as reading each word in this sentence, we are simply in a state of meditation and no longer concerned about any harvest

coming our way through the Laws of attraction. Living in the future has never resolved anything ever in our lives; instead, it leads us into wishful – future – thinking which carries no true value in our present. Worrying over lack may only bring more lack into our reality. Why would we want that as our experience? Of course we do not! So stay focused on abundant living in the present, then it shall surely come to pass by the principles of Karma.

Can we practice our presence and mindfulness when walking? Absolutely, for when you focus only on walking, you even add another dimension to the activity by also focusing on your breathing; in other words, not only do you focus on walking, but you also focus on the power of your breathing and its rate. I love to ask an audience if any one knows *how* they walk. By far the majority of people say yes; however, once they are questioned on the specifics of their walking, they quickly realize they really do not. This reveals that even while walking they live in a future moment, only thinking of where they are walking to or drifting with their thoughts, which is not nearly as important as simply walking, aside from the exercise. When focused during a walk, we would know things like our natural stride, whether we step flat-footed or heal-to-toe, how our whole body sways, how our arms swing, how we are breathing, whether labored or easy. We would allow the body to tell us how it is performing, aside from not stumbling over the root in our path if we are not present. Being present allows us to observe and know what we are planting physiologically, mentally, emotionally, and experientially, and is the very key to understanding this one single principle of Karma. This is why it is called the Great Law, for it teaches presence by disciplining our mind to not drift as the butterfly. Even if we do what is known as power-walking, it is far more beneficial to keep focused on the walking aspect itself, rather than on the idea of power-walking. Yes, we do it for our health, but being in the present is by far the healthiest thing anyone can do for themselves, for consciousness, and for all of humankind. Why for humankind? Because this also creates presence in consciousness! The truth is, one could easily state this now becomes God or Christ consciousness simply because we now command presence.

Why is it best not to think about power-walking? The results of power-walking are future events; hence, in the current moment, they are not so important. All pressures of life are of the future or future goals; being present removes them from our mind, and we will notice there are very seldom any pressures whirling around in the present. Do you truly believe that Olympic athletes train without stress or injury? Do they think only of their present training? You mean there is no pressure for achieving the Gold medal, a future goal? There most certainly is, if they look only at the future event of the Gold; otherwise, by remaining present, winning the Gold medal right now in this moment, their Karmic return shall automatically "train" them toward that level of achievement. So which style of training can be considered the most powerful and most beneficial for the athlete? Practicing presence in what they are achieving. The truth is, any time our mind begins to drift, past or future, bring it back to the present by simply focusing on our breathing during any activity. Now, no thing exists for us to worry about. Breathing brings presence. A wonderful gift indeed!

This very same principle of being present applies to every one of our events and activities, whether while we work, drive, walk, run, speak, or even cook. No matter what we may be doing at any given moment, do not allow the mind to drift. Be only present with what we do, for this helps train our mind in this ancient and powerful art of mindfulness. By implementing this one technique, do you realize you are actually meditating the whole time? We would also be aware of precisely what we are sowing along with the full knowledge of what we are going to reap according to my teacher. You see, once we harness this method of being present, we enter the realm of being in perpetual consciousness because we are consciously aware of our life and events as they unfold. Living in this fashion, by purely being present in each thing we do, brings a high degree of clarity to us each moment. Please stop and read the above sentences again to your self. A monk would never be out of the present, nor need any other human being since this is all a state of mind, as is life; after all, our mind creates our life.

Being present is realizing what we are now placing – right this moment – not only in our life, but also in consciousness, and we realize it shall come to fruition at some point. Life is our garden and it is up to each of us to know what we plant, for if we do not, then we are planting carelessly without any idea which seeds have been buried in the mind. No one would plant a vegetable garden in this manner because there would be no organization to it. Not only would there be no organization, but the plants themselves would also tangle all over and through each other, much like our mind does. The same would apply to life. Do you ever wonder why the events of your life have occurred the way they have? Do you now have a better understanding? Either way, you have an opportunity to now replant your garden with the proper seeds. Learn to stay present. I fully understand it takes practice, and the older we are, the more difficult it may seem to be. Age and experience of mental drifting creates the apparent difficulty only because we have allowed our minds to drift aimlessly on the sea of life for the whole time we have been alive. No matter the difficulty it is well worth the journey. The good news is, we have the ability at any time to take hold of the rudder, to reinstate our authority as the true captain of our ship, thereby becoming fully empowered by the use of this one single idea!

Just how is this idea taught in a monastery? This answer will be demonstrated throughout the entirety of this book because different stories are shared in each lesson as they unfold with each principle. Although the Masters first teach by the same method I am now offering you, they do use many teaching techniques to assist the student onto the path of being present automatically. Allow me to share one of their extremely effective methods. Shortly after my arrival at the monastery, I recognized a pattern. Each time I walked with one of my teachers, the greatest of lessons would take place. One day Master Lobsang approached me saying, "Young man, walk with me." I exclaimed to myself, "Cool, another great lesson for me!" Not yet knowing just how intuitive Masters are, I was unaware that my teacher had immediately sensed my rise in excitement; therefore, he knew I was anticipating the lesson more than being present. So we began to walk and walk – and walk – in complete silence. As both the walking and silence continued I sensed my impatience growing because the longing for my lesson was intensifying as we continued our walk. Can you guess the topic of my first lesson? Clearly it was to learn patience

and to remain present until the teaching began. Never knowing exactly when it was going to occur, I had to wait, understanding the lesson would come in the appropriate moment. Yes, we could walk for hours and miles before the lesson would begin; yet, many events may unfold during such a walk. In monastic teachings they use very non-traditional methods to instill the traditional lesson.

The best and most humorous of all teaching techniques they use in monasteries is the "waking" stick. I fondly recall my first encounter with a "waking" stick, of which I was a recipient many times, I admit. What is a "waking" stick? Many hikers use it in this part of the world to assist in walking. Yes, most people refer to it as a walking stick; however, in the East it has a dual purpose, the first to assist in one's walking, the second to whack the neophyte if they are not in the present moment. Wait-a-minute, I can just sense your body stiffening and eyes widening! It is not at all as threatening or hurt-felt as you may perceive, for when a Master senses the student's mind wandering off, he would gently hit the student, making a flat strike from which a loud "WHACK" would resound. If this didn't jog the student back to the present, then nothing would, and the student would probably be asked to leave the monastery.

Alright, back to my own first encounter with this tool. We were walking for what seemed forever as stated above. While I was experiencing my impatience for the lesson, Master Lobsang sensed my wandering mind. In a very swift fluidic movement, I heard this loud crack. I was stunned at the speed and dexterity of his movement, and as I looked at him with an expression of, "OK, what was *that* for?" he simply stated, "Stay present, for you shall miss nothing in all moments. Never allow your mind to drift even for a second, for you do not know what you plant in that moment in time." Then we both began to laugh as I finally realized, just in that moment, that the crack from the stick actually did not hurt. You see, it was the sound which so-called shocked me back to the present. Thereafter, I welcomed the "waking" stick. Or should I say it welcomed me? This instrument seems most unorthodox, but it is most effective in serving its purpose.

Being patient and present are our first two major lessons! Both

are important tools to use on our path to wisdom and consciousness, empowering us to truly know our self; otherwise, all we will ever know is simply how we judge ourselves to be – purely illusion. It is never the Master's intention to hurt anyone, but I must admit, the "waking" stick is an effective tool to insure the student's attention for the lesson. I ask you, "If we are not present, then how can we learn?" It follows, "If we are not present, how can we understand the written words in this book while reading it?" If not present, then not possible. We may not learn anything while caught up in our own thoughts, let alone hear anything, as long as we are busy thinking of something unrelated to the lesson or words in this book. Unfortunately, the purpose behind the "waking" stick method has been entirely misconstrued in current times and is considered abusive, most especially in this part of the world. In a common sense reality, a "waking" stick should neither hurt nor condemn. Personally, I found it humorous after awhile, yet constantly effective. So, in order to return to the present, let us utilize our personal invisible "waking" stick by consciously and mindfully focusing on what we are doing each "waking" moment. Are you still with me?

Presence is the greatest single thing we may accomplish in our life because it can tremendously assist us in all things, even increase our productivity in what we do within each moment. With the extra time, perhaps we can then meditate at the beach or the mountains! Looking now into the power of the mind, many of us claim we believe and know the power of this human attribute. But do we really? I sincerely ask because it is the single most powerful thing we have in our present day reality. I was once told that a single human brain, if totally converted to electrical energy, could power the entire city of New York without even a single flicker from a light bulb. For ten years! Or be transformed into an explosive device, it would be *more* powerful than an atomic bomb. This is real genuine power if the theories stand correct. So imagine what we each could do if we harness and focus this type of power, individually and collectively! This may only be accomplished by being present with it, knowing that everything we do is done with complete present intention. However, look at the human today, aimlessly using this wonderful, nearly limitless energy source in such an unfocused mode of operation to the degree they

are mentally wasteful with this energy dynamic, exhibiting so much flailing motion in their thinking process. Athletes are told to be efficient in movement, to waste no motion; great for the body, but who is training their mind? This all inclusive principle reveals and explains the greatest aspect of life: be efficient with our mind since it generates our thoughts.

I would like you to focus with me for a few moments, to visualize something. See yourself yielding onto the interstate highway from your local onramp as you intend to travel from coast to coast. Set the car on cruise control as you settle down to drive for the next hundred miles nonstop. Now, drive with your eyes closed. What?! Alright, open your eyes and tell me how far you went! I would say not very far at all, correct? In a sense, this is what we do with our minds; we close our eyes to its operation more times than not. This is why learning to focus the mind becomes paramount in our daily lives. This single mechanism has the ability to both create and destroy our lives! Through Karma's return activity from our requests, the mind and thoughts may do either, however slowly or rapidly by what we allow the mind to do in any given moment. This is yet another reason why it is vitally important we know what the mind is doing.

I do not imply we enter a constant analysis of it, wondering why it does what it does, for this will not assist us and would be wasted energy, though it is currently what most of us do anyway. From analyzing, more times than not, we allow our minds to overpower or overrun us, an effect which could be eliminated when we remain always present. Our language is most fascinating! When we look at two simple words, "analysis" and "analyze," all we need do is look at the first four letters of both words to know why this action can be a waste of mental energy. Humor aside, it is far simpler and in our best interest to keep our mind present. Do not even think of wishing for it to do something under your control because you are wishing for a future event; hence, it will never be harnessed. Simply keep present with it, or keep it present with you is the best viewpoint. When viewing this first principle of Karma, you may now clearly see your mind as the garden wherein most seeds of experience are going to be planted.

I submit, every single thought you have has the potential of creating your next experience. Do you accept this? If not, kindly indulge me and keep reading. Along with my fellow neophytes, we were taught this idea: the Creator hears *all* things our mind sends forth and actually considers it a request to take action on it. All monks totally accept this idea, including me, for it has repeatedly shown itself to me through all the events of my life. If this idea challenges you, here is some food for thought. Purely from a scientific perspective, from the foundations of both chemistry and physics, anything showing evidence of vibration is alive because it has movement. If so, then each thought has life because it generates a vibrating, living, electro-magnetic field. Displaying an electro-magnetic field now implies magnetism travels through it or with it. Once you create and emanate the thought, it has life and magnetism, radiating outward solely to seek its ideal twin, attracting its like kind energy field, only to then return to you, its creator. *You* planted the seed, and it now returns with the fruits of the vine which may be either bitter or sweet. Do you recall the homeowner and the thief in the first chapter? By securing the home, the owner's vine of fear bore the fruit of the thief, actually bringing the thief to the front door by their unconscious request which, by the way, is how most of us operate. We appear to operate unconsciously or with our eyes closed! A few questions are in order here, "Have you ever thought about a person whom you have not seen in quite a while? Well, what happened? Did you hear from them or, seemingly by accident, bump into them?" Understand, you thought about it and it brought you the answer – Karma in action! So-called success or failure occurs just the same, for we either draw the event to us or push the event away simply by how we think about it.

Events are brought to us not only by how we think, but also by how we actually feel about what we think. If the last sentence just confused you, please do not despair or enter into analysis paralysis, for I am with you through this. Just stay with me, for I am going to go out on a limb a ways. You see, the combination of these two energy bodies – thought and feeling – creates what has already been referred to as the electro-magnetic field. This field stays in perpetual motion because we constantly think and feel towards all ideas and events. The stronger the level of emotional involvement, the greater

the reality of the thought, much like the thief who was empowered by the owner's fear of being robbed. Know that negative thoughts and emotions are just as powerful and creative as the positive ones because, from the viewpoint of Karma and consciousness, there is absolutely no difference between positive and negative. Only to the human is the difference perceived; in fact, we can easily say that both Karma and consciousness implicitly trust us to know what we create since they certainly do not. "They don't?" you ask. No! The human does the creating; whereas, Karma and consciousness are the energies, solely the impersonal mechanisms which deliver our creation. In truth, the human is the singular power source generating its own purpose and existence. The Laws endure for our usage, a concept never considered in this part of the world. We are the force behind our present reality in two ways: 1) through our mental interface with mind consciousness and 2) the Karmic return brought on by this infinite connection. Thought is our most powerful contribution to our personal life. It then radiates to global consciousness, either further intensifying the choppy surface on the lake or contributing to its early morning calm, smooth as glass.

Do you now realize that a single thought is one of the most dynamic and powerful seeds we may plant? It is written in the Dead Sea Scrolls: a single thought is more powerful than the greatest earthquake, mightier than the lightening which cleaves the ancient oak tree. It even has the power to overcome death. These scenarios certainly offer an image, don't they? How incredible to know that thought is the most potent attribute we have, that thought is how we navigate through life, that thought contributes to life through the use of our own mind. No wonder being present is extremely important at all times! One flippant moment of mind has the potential to create severe personal destruction in so many areas of our life, even to the degree of potentially including the life of others. With just the single idea that all thoughts are seeds, can you even comprehend the sheer volume of seeds you have scattered all along your life's path during each and every moment? Perhaps you can now more easily conceive that we all have unconsciously created one of the most impenetrable wild jungles of thought ever witnessed in any part of the physical world. To even realize that Karma and consciousness take us literally on every thought is staggering!

There is still more! We will now probe into the deeper side of our prolific seed generator by looking at the return activity which is certain to occur at some point. Remember the homeowner and the thief? Do you realize the owner and thief are of like magnetism, each at the opposite end of the magnetic spectrum? Another scenario: two people are in a hurry while driving their vehicles, motivated by their speedy mindsets, of course, which may very well be generated by their sense of being late or not having enough time. Being two impatient people, they have just increased their odds of creating a collision, perhaps even running into each other! How unfortunate this is. Instead of focusing solely on their driving in what I term a "mind-IN-body" experience, they each preferred to focus either on their destination or other activities in their day. They simply got ahead of themselves. Oops, that is not accurately put. Their minds got ahead of their bodies, which is why being present is such a valuable tool. From common sense, we know like attracts like. Well, this principle also works through the Laws of Karma. "I want to know how this really works, Steven." Alright, we know thought generates a vibration, producing a magnetic field or charge. Now operating as a magnet, the thought actually attracts its like energy stream to the person who created it. Put another way, once created, the thought stays in life until the moment it locates it's like thought or experience. It then returns in full force, so to speak, even if the individual has totally forgotten all about it. Every moment is created in this fashion, a simple and elegant process, yet generally completely ignored in reality. Have you ever heard the phrase, there are no coincidences? Do you believe it? If so, we then know why the events happen as they do and it is a simple concept by which to live. In truth, every monk is aware of this, the simplest of all principles.

Thought is the basis of all creation, for it is how our Creator created life through Its own realization of the very principles It created. Ponder on this: if the Creator operates by these principles, then wouldn't it make sense that we are also bound to these very same principles of creation, all through the energetic dynamics of mind and thought? You see, thought connects us to each other and to life, creating the dynamics of our individual and collective experiences.

Rather than traveling peacefully in perfect symmetry and alignment with each other, we seemingly prefer to dodge and sideswipe each other while speeding down the highway of life, thus creating conflicts as we careen off each other. Do we not witness this in our everyday life? As our conflicts increase daily, the surface chop of the lake rapidly intensifies. It would appear today that life is all about who is in control, and of course the Karmic return we are seeing is the rebellion against that control from all directions, individually and collectively. Consider the rising conflict between people and nations. It would seem we are becoming living demonstrations of nattering nabobs of negativity!

As our mind goes we go, too, without fully realizing we just planted in so many bifurcating directions. For each emanating thought, its like return is created. Thought is the prime reason for the Great Law: *What you sow so shall you reap*, as infinite as life itself. Science says the human mind operates at about 2,500 thoughts per minute. Realizing each as a seed, coming first to fruition then to its balance, can we really deny all what we have in our world today? It's all from our thought! Personally speaking, are you even aware of how many extraneous thoughts you emit each and every minute? What if each of these attached a return to it? Knowing this, would you not quickly change the way you think? It is my sincere belief you most certainly would. For example, when you think of someone as being a bonehead, then rest assured, you can look forward to your own bonehead experience. Have you ever thought another as being foolish? How much time passed before you had an experience in which *you* felt foolish? Remember, all things return to the creator, even a single flippant thought! Karma is relentless in this arena, expanding into all forms of thought, into every emotion and physical action, especially where another human is concerned. I do not know of any way around this, for *no* thing and *no* human are above the Law. I fully understand the potential confusion going on inside the Western mindset and the difficulty it may have in conceiving this paradigm shift. The bottom line is, be totally responsible for what you say and do without concerning yourself about what others say and do. You may recognize this viewpoint as we explore each principle, for they are all related.

Let us now move into the next aspect of sowing and reaping with Karma, switching from the mental arena to the not so obvious emotional one. "Another area we must take into consideration?" you may ask. Absolutely, because we not only experience Karmic returns based on what we think toward life, but also on how we feel toward life! In fact, our emotions truly determine the actual extent of the Karmic return once it is generated through the power of hatred, fear, and love. Keep in mind, the basis of life is only about love and how much of it we are able to offer in every circumstance; thus, if the emotion is anything other than love, the return experience in this arena shall simply have a heavier effect upon us, revealing itself based on how we feel about our self and toward others. Your expression may be asking me, "What do you mean, heavier?" Like thought, love is a very powerful emanation to send forth, the second attribute of the electro-magnetic fields we generate. Our thoughts are considered the magnetic generator and our emotions are the electrical charge necessary to generate the full field. When we combine our mental and emotional energy streams into Karmic actions, in other words, adding our emotion to the thought, the original and simpler magnetic force now transforms literally into a "heavier impact." It is literally a more powerful electro-magnetic field, creating an even greater impulse and tremendous pull to the Laws of attraction because of the electrical charge our heart gives to experience.

Through which field, our mental, physical, or emotional, does our memory have its most profound impact and elicit our response? Certainly our emotional field since this field alone can energize the memory. The deeper our feeling about the memory, the stronger and more powerful the memory grows. Generally, we all seek unconditional love or unconditional acceptance, correct? And to truly have this experience, we are going to experience rejection along our path. "Are you saying our rejection is guaranteed?" you might ask. Well, yes, in a fashion. Since we have a propensity to withhold from the overall experience of unconditional love, we literally cut the experience short. Why? Because when we withhold, our Karmic return does likewise, merely allowing the experience of unconditional love to reject us. In truth, this rejection actually represents a teacher of sorts to strengthen our ability to love and to accept all experience

unconditionally. And if we are going to love free of conditions, then rejection has absolutely no power because we simply love. The Christ once stated, we should love our enemies. Rejection is our enemy, isn't it? Please understand when it is said, "If you actually withhold yourself while in any experience it will withhold from you by not giving you the depth of the experience you seek." You may never realize this if it were not for the positive influence given you by Karmic principles. You see, our emotional body is by far the most challenging aspect to learn until we go through the process and ultimately realize that withholding is of very little assistance except as a wonderful teacher. By withholding, we will not move forward as efficiently as we are capable of; in fact, withholding will swiftly chain us to the heaviest anchor we may ever create. So how does this anchor work? Are we able to disconnect or cut the chain?

In essence, the anchor is actually the memory we carry along with us, empowered by the emotional feeling(s) we give or attach to it. Purely as an example, let us say you are going through emotional trauma concerning the idea of love from the spousal affair offered in chapter one. To deepen the image, let us say you had experienced your spouse's denial for months, if not years. Suddenly, you discover the truth. You not only realize the affair is going on, but you also find out that it is with your closest life-long friend! For this scenario, let us also keep in mind one more thing. You were totally and deeply in love with your spouse during this affair. I truly understand. This level of emotional shock can easily bind you for a very long period of time, if not for life, as you become anchored in the memory of this heartbreak. As a result, the power of your emotion continually feeds this unfortunate memory and it now prevents you from experiencing the idea of true love again. How? You will withhold your heart from every future potential partner with whom you come into contact. Must you be stuck carrying your "anchor and chain?" If you know the anchor will stay with you until the original event is forgiven – *completely* – are you willing to cut the links or release the bind? Certainly the affair is a very difficult experience to forgive, but not impossible. Being free of conditions means precisely this, being able to forgive and release. By so doing, there remains no bind or anchor.

Interestingly enough, Karma will assist you in accomplishing this task if you view your present experience with love only through your present emotions, not with the past ones. In this manner, the present frees you from the past memory because you are no longer there. You are here. At first, this is not so easy to do; however, it can indeed be accomplished through practice. By so doing, you will accomplish emotional freedom from the past by being purely in the present, and you would inevitably discover that this new experience – a new relationship perhaps? – is positively the best ever for you at this time in your life! I am not saying the memory will disappear; I say you are no longer emotionally bound to it, for it is merely a thing of the past now. This allows for the new to enter your life because the anchor chain has been cut. Have you ever felt the relief when an emotional burden has been released? Truly an uplifting moment! You see, when you operate out of the present, there is never a past or future. It is truly your gift, which is why it is called the present. I do not imply that we don't plan for the future or ignore the past. I do imply, however, that we live only where we are, right wherever our body is, so stay present with it! In this example, therefore, we are not bound to the past because we no longer have any emotional attachments to it. It merely becomes past experience. It is better to experience emotional freedom than to be emotionally bound to a past memory, most especially if it carries any emotional trauma. To once again realize the power, be present!

Moving on, our emotional memories harbor the greatest trap by laying the heaviest anchor for the human. According to my monastic teachings, as long as we hold to the past we are casting the very same seeds in our present, thereby *unknowingly* seeking an actual repeat of the very same events, events that we *knowingly* prefer not to have! I realize this is shocking and hard to conceive but it is the truth. Have you had experiences repeat in your life? If so, this is the reason behind them! It is my personal hope that you understand this concept because you are simply replanting the very same seeds. Put another way, when the same pitfall arrives once more, we seemingly go into shock, not at all realizing we actually re-created it. Do you honestly believe you will truly avoid another pitfall by vividly remembering the first one with such a deep emotional attachment? Does this make any sense?

Through the power of the emotional body and its attachment to the thoughts of old events, we instantly restore our past Karmic debts.

There is no need to repeat a cycle once we have had the experience of it, unless we did not get the teachings on the first go-around. If we have not gleaned the message of the original Karmic circumstance, it must repeat until we gain the true knowledge or lesson of the experience, intact with the emotion completely released before we are able to move forward once again. These lessons all come into play when we do not give our all to what we desire. Remember the idea of partially loving someone and its resulting experience? If a universal truism, does this same idea apply to other areas in our life? How may one desire to succeed, yet only go after it half-heartedly? Will their success truly occur? What if a young person desires a career as a professional athlete but only half-attempts during their training? Can you hear the coach yelling, "Next student!" when he or she realizes their apparent lack of desire? Whatever and wherever it is we seek, if we do not give it our best, the odds of accomplishment are greatly diminished primarily because of Karma. Are you surprised? If we produce only half of what is necessary then only half will return. There is no way around this, not even half way! This is indeed a Universal Truth because it applies across the board to all things. If we are allowed one "must" in life then this "must" be it. By all means, we "must" be present and focused mentally. Release all past binds and anchors in our emotional arena. Presence and focus allow us to physically live and move, free of fear. In truth, they nearly guarantee fulfillment in any endeavor we so decide to pursue.

Now I would like to examine the Great Principle through our physical activities, the last arena. To start, we must realize our physical activity has its basis in not only what and how we think, but also in how we feel about what we are doing. Sometimes we may do something which feels good to us but seems to hurt the other; whereas, at other times we may do something which does not feel so good to us but feels great to the other. Heads up, a pivotal message exists here! We must become more aware of how *we* feel, rather than how the other feels. How the other feels is truly *their* responsibility, not ours. This is

not to say we can go around and intentionally do or say things to hurt or negatively affect others. If we do, the like kind return impact from Karma shall be most significant! Karmically speaking, of course it would be in our best interest to act with consideration and sensitivity, but if we are going to become empowered then we must only own how we feel, otherwise, we are giving our self away as we live according to how others feel. This will be explained further in my discussion on the Principle of the Mirrors in chapter six.

I can just hear some of you saying, "This is not how I was brought up! I would be called inconsiderate and selfish by not thinking of the other person's feelings first!" Allow me to explain further. First, a question, "Do you *really* have any control over how any other person feels, let alone knowing what they are truly feeling?" I answer by way of placing you in another example, in which case you live in an unhappy relationship with another person. You stay in it, however, because you desire to not "hurt" your partner which, without realizing, solely fills your own life with emotional torture. Are you following me in this? Well, this certainly makes sense because your Karmic action can only return torture to you since you continually live in that mode of emotion. Another pivotal message here, no human has the right to actually assume they have so much power over another human as to control their feelings. Allow them to choose how they are going to experience their own emotions. "You make me feel" is totally impossible since, in truth, "you" are not able to hurt "me" because it is up to "me" to choose which of my own emotions I so wish to feel at this moment. How you handle your own emotions is purely a matter of *your* personal choice, not the choice of any other person, certainly not mine. Of course, for the most part, we do not want to intentionally hurt another; yet, there are times such hurt takes place. If we do not intend to hurt the other and it occurs nonetheless, very little negative Karmic action will return to us, though it may happen with the other person if *they* choose hurt feelings. Now the "anchor and chain" is in their court and they must choose to deal with it – or not. If, on the other hand, we choose to intentionally hurt the other, this becomes a different matter, for the Karmic return will most certainly barrel down on us.

Certainly, up until you began reading this book, there have been times when you had unknowingly set up your own return action, but you can never catch a monk unawares, for they always know what the return will be by the very seed(s) they had sown, and they always plant with the intention of a good harvest. To "hurt" is not a positive planting, hence a harvest chock-full of heavy weeds. Here is another pivotal message: the power behind physical actions lies behind the intention of the mind and emotions, our two personal motivators in every activity. Peaceful living only requires an individual to feel good in all they do, and quite naturally, only good feelings return to create an even more peaceful nature. If we so choose, we all could view life as monks, solely being fully aware of the process behind each seed we create and plant. We, too, can know the precise Karmic return by the outcome of our harvest. It shows itself as experience. Because of this understanding, we now have the opportunity to shift the process into a much lighter direction, into the higher vibrations of love, compassion, and peace. Before this chapter ends, let us offer a few physical actions along with their potential return. Keep the following points in mind though: 1) the physical is obviously the easiest to see, 2) the power behind all physical action is more difficult to see, 3) the internal experience unfolds the external physical activity. Cause creates the effect and to see the reverse is extremely difficult. We may not see cause because of the effect; therefore, it helps to understand that what we do is the cause, and what we experience is the effect. Look at things objectively, perhaps as an impartial observer standing next to you. Cause may then be seen more easily since you no longer get ensnared in every effect generated by you through cause. Experiential understanding now comes to you automatically.

All physical activities are obvious by their very nature as has been stated. From physical activity, the subsequent return is generated faster because it is not from our subtle bodies, our mental and emotional activities, because the latter two must first locate their equal before the return. Physical actions will, therefore, typically experience a faster Karmic return. For example, if we strike another, chances are we will be struck back. As the thief, if we steal from another we will have things stolen from us. So what is the main ingredient? The fact they are both done with selfish intention through one's physical

activity. By living perpetually in the present, no physical activity would go without our notice, unless our mind and emotions are totally impervious to our actions. To my way of understanding, such level of detachment is virtually impossible, unless the person thinks so arrogantly that all what they do is completely acceptable. Yes, these humans are in our world.

Let us consider a simple day-to-day action. As you open the door into a building or room, you see another person following just behind you, and yet, you choose not to hold the door open for them. Happens every now and then, doesn't it? The action is now deemed rude simply because your intention was to not do the proper thing. What will the return now be? Your own experience in being treated rudely! What if that person gets hurt as the door closes on them? Yes, your experience will be of like kind. A simple rule of thumb exists here which you may certainly count on. Your return is always in like kind with the possibility of even a greater return depending completely on your individual circumstance. Okay, let's say the person became injured, and we now add that you offer no real remorse towards them, only to callously comment, "You ought to be more careful!" Later in the day you trip down the stairs, completely baffled as to why it happened. Yes, even these two seemingly disconnected events are related! Depending upon the circumstances of the initial event, physical experience can become even more extreme, with some carrying into another lifetime! Some teachings say we are in this life solely to rectify Karmic events done in another. Okay, certainly this may be the case, but be assured of something. Most of us, if any, will not remember our old Karmic debt, for we simply have difficulty recalling them in this lifetime!

Just for the sake of discussion, I would like to show how far-reaching Karma may extend itself. Whether reincarnation is true I leave entirely up to you. What follows is a picture I would like you to see. Let us say you inherited a great deal of wealth in a previous lifetime, and since you did not earn any of it, you had great difficulty in handling it wisely. Indeed, you squandered it all away, down to the very last penny. Compounding this example, you never assisted others in any way with this wealth; instead, you chose to spend your entire fortune solely on you and all your pleasures. Do keep in mind,

this level of pleasure is solidly rooted in selfishness and is totally self-serving. Karma, therefore, ensures that in a future lifetime, you find yourself totally destitute or find money as a great personal struggle. No surprise here since this Karmic event was created when you had frivolously spent away all your wealth in the previous lifetime. You now receive your lesson in the present experience. And the lesson is? You shall forever remember to not be selfish. Once the soul knows this, the individual would never again be selfish in anything they do. What does this mean for you in today's world? You would always hold the door open for others and would very probably be in service to others as a Karmically-accomplished soul operating in your particular body.

Allow me to go out on another limb here and discuss what is occurring much too frequently in our modern-day world. Do you suppose a murderer has a Karmic return? Would it be serious? Although perfectly correct in concept and however unbelievable this may seem, the murderer would be murdered in their future lifetime(s) by the same number of people whose lives they took. If all people took this into consideration then murder probably would not exist; however, because Karma is not actively taught in Western culture, many believe they can get away with whatever they do. Not really. This leads me to ask, "Once you "leave" this world, do you believe all the deeds you created will remain here?" Regardless of your belief, the truth is, you take them with you from life to life to life, etc.

This is termed as dross or heaviness to the soul. The soul, for the most part, is blameless in these acts; however, it does accumulate what we do, hence the idea of dross or heaviness. Unfortunately, those who receive capital punishment think this is it, the end of it all, without ever realizing this is just the beginning of a very long cycle. Remember, Karma keeps all of life on a level or equal playing field, and in reality, Karma is our true form of protection against injustices. Master teachers have been offering the following three phrases since time immemorial, each intended for us to fully understand, no matter the language or country of origin: 1) "All things shall be balanced," 2) "No thing [no one] is above the Law," 3) "What you do here you lay up for yourself in heaven." Each human should take these literally, for the Law is inescapable.

All seeds must come to fruition in all things. The Great Principle of Karma was created quite possibly as the greatest Law by which any human could ever live, a Law to end all world wars and crime if our specie would simply choose to abide by it. What one does is what they receive, and all we can do is come to this one realization, for no one is above the Law. Let us check our history for a moment. Did not a "war to end all wars" already occur in our early twentieth century? Obviously, war creates more wars and resolves absolutely no issue. Any country attempting to dominate the world only did so for a very short period of time before it would lose in a war. No crime has ever gone unpunished, although some time may pass. No individual has ever gotten away with anything which did not support humanity as a whole; they never shall because of the twelve principles of Karma.

These principles are more far-reaching and relentless in their purpose than any legislated or material Law created by the human. No judge or jury can set you free from these principles because you, yourself, are your own judge and jury. It is your responsibility to pay your Karmic debt in full, including any interest from resistance. Most importantly, no one is to blame since Karma is a natural blameless Law which began with Creation and is how it all occurred in the first place.

If this is what God knew and used then so can we as individuals. These principles are as absolute as life and are immutable. Ironically, it matters not at all whether we know of these principles or even believe in them, but when we do, the principles shall put more direct influence within our very own hands, giving us a greater level of control over our personal dynamics by empowering us to the fullest extent possible. From this Great Principle we would realize all what we do, that our action is purely the result of the seeds we had sown in our lives, which now begs the only question: "Is this what I desire to harvest?" If yes, then plant and nurture your seeds in the fertile ground of your mind. If no, then plant nothing by taking no action. By doing so, your life would unfold as Karmic return brings abundant flow from one peaceful moment into the next. I encourage you to remain constantly aware each moment of the seeds you prepare to plant in your own pool of consciousness, thus allowing the Great Law to become very powerful and ever-abundant in all what you do.

"If you cannot find the truth right where you are,
Where else do you expect to find it?"
Buddha

~ Chapter III ~
The Principle of Creation

To begin this chapter I would like to ask you a very real and truthful question. Did you receive an operator's manual when you were born, you know, a manual instructing you how to work precisely with life, to live fully and effortlessly in life? Do not feel embarrassed because neither did I, at least not until I began studying under my Master teachers in the Far East. In the form of the twelve Principles of Karma, I offer the manual to each of you in this book. Do you remember the Great Principle, the first principle of Karma and the creative power behind all seeds we plant along our highway of life? This Law guides us to become aware of not only the present in which we are always involved, but also the number and types of seeds we set in motion, intentionally and otherwise. With the first principle now behind us, let us journey onward to the second by developing our ability to further enhance our knowledge in the true nature of life's creative forces.

Karmic Law is indeed purposefully designed, helping us understand both ourselves and life on a much deeper level. It also assists us in developing a natural harmony or flow in all what we say and do, thus the idea of an operating manual. In a sense, Karmic principles actually do provide our operating instructions, but only if we read, comprehend, and follow them. Otherwise, they will just as easily create disharmony due to their natural precision and our unconscious

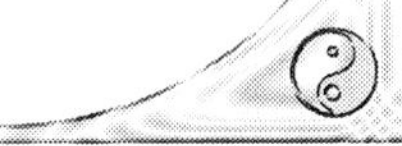

interaction with them. Stop and take a moment to envision a life filled only with harmony, purpose, and complete abundance in all aspects. In truth, life is exactly this until we interrupt it, only because these principles remain unknown to us. Life is more real than we may have ever imagined, decisively purpose-filled, but not necessarily for the reasons we may think. Life is genuine and it is about growth, spiritual growth or awakening, realized or not. Life teaches us to be spiritually living creatures, to reach into the infinite divine with Karma meeting this purpose in all respects. These are the main reasons why there is no way around the Law of Karma, for there are absolutely no loop holes in the principles contained therein. The Law is the manual from which we can elevate to this higher view of life. The principles themselves are our teachers, willing and able assistants guiding us to live in and honor all of life, urging us to reach this supreme state of being, a loving, divine, empowered creator, which now is a perfect segue for the introduction of the Law of Creation.

In the eastern world, the Law of Creation is cited in this context to which I learned while walking with my teachers. Rinpoche Kiela looked at me and asked, "Young man, what if all events in your life are simply because of you? What if you draw the people to you that you do? Do you realize that you are responsible for all of the events that take place in your life?" I had to consider these for a few moments. Then he flatly stated, "*You attract to you what you are, not what you want.*" Allow me to share this once again, italics mine: You attract to you what you *are*, *not* what you *want*. "This principle is the very key to the reality of why your life is the way it is," he continued. "Your life can be no different than you yourself are, because life is your exact mirror image by Karmic principle. This is one of the primary keys since life is about magnetic fields of energy, the reason why it even exists in the very real sense. Humans are the only living beings able to shift the dynamics of life in any given moment. No other living creature may do this, for they are simply what they came in this world to be. A rose may not be a petunia and a cat cannot become a dog. We, on the other hand, may be anything we choose through the use of Karma's dynamics, the very principles which also let us know we are the very first cause in our individual and collective lives."

My mind was now reeling from all of this information, and I think Master Kiela knew this by the smile on his face. This Law of Creation supports and strengthens my assertion made in the last chapter on how we are a walking, breathing, thinking, electro-magnetic field generator, and how we attract every experience to us through what we plant each moment. Master Kiela went on, "This is all completely controllable. We are able to directly influence it for any purpose we may see fit, keeping in mind that the intention is never about power over another, nor about power itself. Such intention would ultimately be a purpose of great error which can only create and perpetuate negative Karmic responses. On the other hand, Karma can make your life almost magical in your daily process when used wisely."

No human can actually gain power over another unless it is first given to them. Wait, I'm shaking my head on this concept because, the truth is, to believe we can have power over another is to simply believe an illusion, one that we created in this reality. I suggested in my previous work, "*A Metaphysical Interpretation of the Bible*," that all things were created equal. If not, then our Creator would be flawed. If this is the case then the principles of Karma would be an illusion. However, Karma ultimately ensures equality with all things, human and otherwise. This concept remains uppermost and imbedded in all creation along with the second principle. It simply confirms that we individually live with what we create in each and every moment, and to own the responsibility for it. After all, we brought it into our experience!

Let me go out on another limb with you for a moment. Suppose inequality is the truth in our reality, known as the Law of Inequality. When living under this Law by the concept of "better than," one experiences difficulty in a variety of ways, especially if they attempt to cover it over in some fashion. And by covering it over, do they not actually create their own isolation from an emotional perspective? I ask, "Have you ever met an emotionally cold person?" The truth is they actually believe they have power over others, or so they think. This is truly Karma in action, not the Law of Inequality! Have you also met people whose actions remain oblivious to them, yet are intensely clear to you? And they are extremely quick to support their denial of the action! These individuals have developed the "better than" approach, and in most instances are completely unaware of the walls they have built around them, a Karmic return. You see, Karma guarantees equality in all respects since acting from "better than" can only return to the individual what they first created for themselves. By their own actions, their pure isolation remains confined behind immense walls while being surrounded by people who think they are "better than." The Law of Inequality, therefore, is a bona fide ego-created illusion by its very nature, working contrary to love and connectedness, two very true divine attributes of the human.

When you read the Law of Creation, the second principle of Karma: *You attract to you what you are, not what you want*, how do you respond in thought? Perhaps something akin to, "No, I did not ask for this! These things and events did not come into my life because of me." Forgive me, for I must affirm, "Yes you did create them." At first, I admit, the truth of this matter was very difficult for me to realize and internalize. You see, our energy base as the human attracts every event and circumstance to us, and it is a combination of many things. This so-called base is not comprised of just our thoughts, for it is also made up of all our fears, all our moments of hesitation and exaltation, all our heart-felt emotions, and all what we hold on and let go. These are our individual dynamics, and their sum equals our beliefs. Test this out. If you believe you are going to fail, you simply cannot succeed. If you believe you are un-loveable then love will elude you, or you will get a façade of it. This is also why the first Law is so very important because we reap what we ourselves plant. We are the seed itself. We are the magnet which draws our experience to us.

These dynamics or beliefs develop through our upbringing and subsequent experiences, an unending cycle of events which only validates our beliefs again, and again, and again. From the monk's perspective, this is why beliefs must broaden through flexibility, to ever-expand as we grow and change from each learning experience into the next. In a later chapter we shall discuss for you the Law of Change and this one may surprise you in its range. In truth, beliefs should never be static; however, countless humans think otherwise according to their indoctrination, or so they believe. Forgive me, for

this is simply a falsehood. If you are in doubt of this simply look at the world as it is and you will see the simple truth in the power of beliefs. As previously discussed, Karma is our guide, not our so-called enemy or punisher. Consider this, when one does not allow belief to shift and change, there shall occur specific Karmic returns for it and they continually repeat with the intent to wake the person up, to shake the shoulders a bit to get their belief to change. You shall realize this when we journey further to the appropriate principle. We grasp onto old beliefs entirely too firmly, when in truth, we could be more flexible with them, which is what the Christ intended for us to understand when He suggested that we cannot put new wine in old skins. And this is simply another version of how Karma works as we interact with life and experience.

Although your beliefs are direct influences from what your dynamics have become, remember, every one is changeable because only you have the full responsibility of changing yourself. According to the manual instructions given by my Master teachers, if we shift our beliefs then our dynamics will follow suit. This is ultimately in your hands. Without ever blaming circumstances, can you accept the idea that you have attracted all the events in your life, just as I and everyone else have through how we actually see our self – our belief? This does not have to be a complex process; in fact, it is simple by its very nature. You know what you like about you and what you do not. These are changeable at your choosing. The Principle of Creation actually suggests that living a healthy, abundant, and successful life requires absolute full participation by you, the individual. Remember in the last chapter when we discussed doing things half-way or holding back? If I may *should* upon us, in reality we should never hold back from anything or anyone in life since life has very little to do with which race, creed, country or belief we have. Yes, these are external circumstances; yet, they need not define your internal energy dynamics, for your personal definition is entirely up to you. It is all about what we have become as opposed to who we are in all moments. We truly can control this, should we choose to, by taking full and active participation in all of life, pouring our full nature into it, holding nothing back! At first, like the mind, this takes great effort, but it does become easier as we work with it, and we begin to really

learn our own nature rather than others'; otherwise, we actually ask to be short-changed in our experiences which I am certain you have felt at some point. You now may understand the "why" of this.

It was shared earlier in the first chapter how we are all connected in the idea of oneness through consciousness; yet, this is much more far-reaching than just the external ideas of connection. The second principle indicates we are also one with our self. While studying in Nepal, one of my teachers asked me, "Why do you see everything as separate from you?" I answered, "That is how I was raised and is how all Americans are raised, Master," and pointing my index finger, "I see you next to me and that monk over there. I see a tree about 12 feet away from us and a shrub next to my foot. They are all separate, aren't they?" He offered, "That is simply an illusion. All things are one and the same." I became deeply puzzled and he could see the perplexed look on my face. He continued, "As humans, we are all the same physically. Other than how we look – the only true difference – we all think the same, feel the same, and act the same." He even went so far as to say if I was thinking of something then he probably would be thinking of it, too, at the same moment. What he said next was interesting and formed the basis of the statement above, "There truly is no separation between the internal and the external."

One of the prime causes of disease – *dis*-ease being more accurate – is our belief in seeing and living in separation between the internal and external. This merely implies we are ill at ease with the external environment we created. This unsettledness or seeming separation is the cause of our illness. Put another way, if we are not connected internally then we have inner division because we are now disconnected. And if we are divided internally, does it not stand to reason we would be the same with the external, our environment? This is why we find so much disagreement with ourselves and what we do, with each other and what others do, even with the world, my Master teacher offered. He suggested that I practice this inner union and then observe my outer world. Once mastered, it gives a whole new meaning to life and individuality. As one who took his suggestion to heart, this practice is deeply humbling. When you not only experience the connectedness of life, but also live in this manner, it is much more fulfilling because you live "wholistically."

The difficulty we each may have in comprehending this shift in perspective is very understandable; yet, the whole basis of Karma rests on our union between the internal and external environments. You see, we are directly connected from the inside to the outside each and every moment. There is no such thing as separation. Separation is pure illusion, for it is all one. Yes, every thing does manifest uniquely from the other; however, everything has its basis in the exact same energy streams. Only its physical manifestation gives the impression of separation, which is how the mind operates with it. Look at this concept in the following way. For us to even "see" there must first be the appearance of separation or void so we are able to walk, for example, between the trees instead of walking into them. Let me go even further by asking, "Why do you see the table or any other object?" Because there is nothing around it, correct? This nothingness allows us to see the table, and every other object for that matter, and basically allows us to navigate and handle all objects more easily; yet, this void gives us the illusion of separation. "Nothing" is actually one of the prime keys to how we learn and gain intelligence – BUT – it can also offer us a minor hindrance as we seek the idea of consciousness. Why? Because "nothing" can truly and easily enter your perception of seeing individual separation. You may desire to read that sentence again. In truth, we are not even separated from earth since it is simply a different manifestation of matter supporting life. As the earth goes so does life. As the human goes so does life. The Law of Creation guides us to understand this very concept, and by unifying our internal with the external, we can "see" more clearly and easily what we individually manifest or create.

Allow me to throw a curve ball at you to reveal the depth and breadth of this principle. Even if we do not care for our experiences, even if we deny our relationship or physical connection to them, we still remain directly responsible for them purely because of our mental and emotional connection to those experiences. Talking about our internal connection, I mean there exists no separation between our mental and emotional arenas. Certainly they appear separate whenever discussed; yet, they are not, for both the mental and emotional aspects directly influence each other, just as we directly influence each other. And because this is a universal principle of life, this concept applies not only to each of us individually, but also to all of us collectively. The Law of Creation is simply attempting to alert us about this fact of life, the connection between every thing and every experience. It is suggested we learn to not see any separation from our inner being to our outer world. As the Principle states, our outer world is precisely the way it is purely because of how we are in our inner world.

If you feel your life is in chaos, forgive me, perhaps you are the same on the inside. If you think your life is not organized, perhaps you are not organized on the inside, for your mind is simply disorganized. If you have a peaceful life then you are peaceful internally. Choices create these ideas in how we feel; therefore, if we choose differently, we then change our internal self which subsequently takes us in a new and different direction. And just because a certain choice worked once does not necessarily mean it will work yet again. In truth, we are surrounded by and directly connected with clues to our inner nature, constantly and continually; yet, we may not even realize it. Our outer world is not separate from us, never was never is. It *is* us! It is what we choose to see and accept internally before we may ever shift it externally. We spend entirely too much time working with and on the external by giving it power; yet, we are the very ones who actually hold the power. In current times, so many humans seem powerless. You really can take control of your life by working on the interior of your self. Just don't give your power away.

We fully realize the challenge you may have in understanding this concept; nonetheless, it is the truth and it does apply to every single living thing. The outer world is our Karmic circumstance being shown to us in all respects. Interestingly enough, for the most part, we are not willing to accept this idea that our true nature is signified by what we have all around us. We can now realize the truth if we so choose. There is no sidestepping or escaping from this concept, Karma being what it is and magnetism being what *it* is. Expressed another way, our outer environment is a direct reflection of how we are inside. If you know a person whose life is in disarray, they are in disarray on the inside. If you would like your outer world to become organized then become organized internally and the outer will naturally follow this path. Certainly it may take a few moments to catch up to you, but be

patient and wait for it; it will come and your life magically becomes organized. To shift anything externally, the internal shift must come first, not the other way around as this part of the world has been taught. Simply focus and control the inner and the outer follows you wherever you go. It's your lead!

One beautiful fall afternoon Master Lobsang asked me to walk with him. We left the monastery and headed toward the forest. Now realizing that my teachers may walk for hours before speaking, I simply followed along in silence and patience. Approaching the trees, I walked on a pathway while Master Lobsang wandered along beside it, moving gracefully and effortlessly around tress and bushes. We continued to walk in silence until he looked over at me and asked, "Why do you walk on the path?" I replied, "I can easily see it, Master. It's well worn." He nodded, smiled, and fell back into silence while continuing to meander around and through the foliage. A few moments later he looked at me again, stating, "If you continue to follow the path you are walking on, young man, it could become so deep you would not be able to get out of it." He fell silent. I looked over at him, "Master, you are not talking about me walking, are you?" He looked at me thoughtfully, "I am talking about your mind and how it operates."

He went on to explain how mental routine could easily turn into a rut from which it would be extremely difficult to free myself. You see, if we are repetitive in our choices, this stems from our mental routines, clearly the most predominant type of thought process from which we seem to operate. I am not entirely sure why we do this. Perhaps we actually believe a routine will make our life simpler or more comfortable; however, in the eyes of Karma this is not so. Why? Mental routines are quite possibly the most dangerous form of habit we can fall into, whether we remain stuck in the rut for a complete lifetime or for only a brief portion of it. How may we climb out of mental routines? During my teachings, Master Lobsang suggested I learn to do everything free of routine, to start small such as pulling my pants up my left leg first instead of the right one, or cleaning myself in a different order, or walking off the well-worn path. "If you break the small routines then the most significant one – how

you think – will also become easier to break," he instructed. Being a typical young American I took his instructions to heart and went full tilt by exaggerating them, taking them to the extreme. My level of awareness ballooned to watching every minor routine and minute body movement. You know, after a short time had passed, not only did I perceive how my choices changed in a myriad of ways, but I also realized a choice was very seldom made twice. Additionally, my mind and thoughts had naturally shifted! I still practice "non-routine" each day.

May we offer a rule of thumb here? Just a simple one which may assist you on your journey in this world, something to help you on your Karmic path of creation. Well, we all know and like the idea of people liking people who like what they themselves like, right? Silliness aside, in essence we like people who are just like us since they match us in personality, dress, music, diet, travel, or whatever it may be. The rule of thumb is, if you want loving people around you then simply love. Being loving becomes your magnet to subsequently and automatically draw only those kinds of people to you. Trust it. They *will* find you. It is who you are, so how can an unloving person be drawn to you? They cannot. In fact, it will never enter their so-called unloving mind to do so. Chances are they would be repelled by you. If this occurs, do not be disturbed, for it is their choice. Allow them that choice.

If you are routine-oriented, those around you will be identically the same as you yourself already are. Remember the rule here: *You attract to you what you are, not what you want.* Simply become the magnet to draw into your experience whoever and whatever it is you choose. If you desire to surround yourself with smart people then become smart in virtually anything. They will be in your life because it is who you are, or more precisely because it is who you have now become. If you want the perfect mate, simply develop the traits which you envision in your mate, then life itself will automatically deliver those traits to you as your mate.

Never build a façade because that is what you will get in your pursuit of the perfect mate, another perfect façade, who will ultimately be

exposed at some point in time. They *have* to, for the truth always becomes known. This principle is about living the truth of our inner nature; otherwise, we are living a lie, an experience which will ultimately surround us through Karmic return. Hint: in your best interest, you best admit to this sooner rather than later because Karma is relentless in its purpose and will fulfill your every desire, whether you choose truth or a lie. This inner truth is ever-changeable by its very characteristic because it is you who has direct influence upon it; however, by not realizing or choosing to take control of it now implies that you accept other people and circumstances to have control over you. Self-empowerment does not exist under these terms. It is a free agent.

Who you *were* is never as important as who you are – *right now*. But it is up to you to do the shifting; otherwise, it most assuredly will stay with you right where you are, and your same cycles will continue as they have been. The message conveyed by this principle is the knowledge that we create our reality from within us, not from without. In other words, what shows up outside of us is purely what we had originally created within us. Nothing may come into our lives without our direct influence on it. Whether a thief, abundance, poverty, or health shows up, it matters not to natural Law. As mentioned earlier, Karma is solely the mechanism; therefore, our belief, including our choices based on that belief, will determine what we draw to us. You will find this true one hundred percent of the time. If you desire a different life, no matter what it may be, change you to match it. Then it will come because you will draw that change right directly to you through experiences.

You attract to you what you are, not what you want is a very viable idea, which is why it is listed as the second of the twelve Karmic principles. Our seeds become us, for they are what we have planted, nurtured, and grown, first internally then externally, so it would stand to reason the Principle of Creation would indeed follow the Great Principle. Let us re-examine the homeowner's situation, the one fearing a potential home burglary. Through fear, the owner attracts the very thing they fear the most: having their possessions stolen. Fear is actually a dual edged sword. From one side of the sword,

the emotionally fearful owner attracts the very reason for their fear, directly to them self into their home. From the other side of the sword, the owner's personal possessions clearly have the power and control because they are looked upon as more important, hence the owner's need for home security. Fear is the key in this instance, and through their sense and need of protection from the fear, the owner had to secure the home and its belongings!

When thinking of monastic living, do you believe monks don't desire anything? This belief holds true only to a point. In truth, the underlying idea is the power of desire and what it may do to a person. Trust me, from personal experience I know and believe the monks are fine and happy simply being with themselves since they know this can never be taken from them. On the other hand, a desire can be taken. You see, when we give a desire the title of ownership, what we think we own now actually owns us, so much so that it totally affects how we truly feel about our self, which now means we have completely transferred our power to one or more external things. This way of living is absolutely contrary to the original idea of life.

You are the one with the true ability and power until you give it away to external things, to others, or even both. Unfortunately, this has become prevalent in current times. Do you ever wonder why you do not feel empowered? Perhaps now you may realize why. We all give it up! We may give it up to things, family, religion, even to a government. By giving our self away, we are no longer the human we were born to be. Because the outer has been granted unconditional power to now control us, we have "contractually" agreed to live our life separate from our innate divine connection between our inner and outer environment. If left unchecked, desire can completely consume and overpower the individual, involving and allowing the ego to misdirect them entirely. Of course, once this occurs, frustration and anger swells within the individual as these two emotions, along with their Karmic return, perpetuate this creative motion. To a monk, this is the biggest reason why desire is controlled and why they are filled with content in all they have – them self. In fact, they are willing to give away any personal possession at any given moment since it is not as important as life itself. Life is the greatest of possessions one may

have, and it is the one thing we truly require. Only when we own our self are we then fully empowered over all things.

It has been revealed to you that Karma may swipe both ways. Either while swinging in the negative direction or in the abundantly positive one for you, the principle remains relentless. These first two principles show us this because, if we plant self-serving seeds then their like kind shall return to us; whereas, if we plant with wisdom then wisdom abounds all around us. The Law of Creation, though, is more pronounced and profound in its effect because its purpose is to reveal our true nature rather than our illusions of self. Through our experiences, the second principle guides us to realize what we, in fact, have created. If we do not desire our creation, we may change its direction.

Keep first and foremost in mind, we may not be able to change the set of circumstances so created; however, our creation may be redirected, thereby changing the set of circumstances and consequently the experience. Like the Creator, we must also realize at this point that we may never *un*-create. All we can do is take what has been created and shift the direction of the creation until it becomes what we originally sought. The words make it quite clear; we were made as co-creators, not as co-"*un*-creators." This is very specific even in Karmic Law. Once we have a thing or the experience, do not struggle with it. Just allow it to play out as it is; otherwise, it may easily become compounded, leading us only into complete confusion and disarray. Also, denial of any personal responsibility for the environment will not assist you or anyone else in any way. Denial will only slow the progress of what you are attempting to create. It is far better, therefore, to simply create again through another set of choices until the choice is perfected. The truth is, if we do not claim responsibility, then we sink into the depths of self-denial. As you know by now, Karma will take care of this also, by continuing in its uncompromising fashion until we can no longer deny our self and the events surrounding us. By stubbornly staying on the abysmal path of denial, Karmic action will actually increase the possibility of greater pressure from the events we experience; thus, I suggest self-admission as the shortest and least dramatic path.

When we deny our self, we actually acknowledge, in a sense, that our life is nothing and that our life is an accident. But it is not! Living in this mindset now implies there is no purpose in our life. In truth, we do have purpose; else we would not even be here. If we do live by this mindset, then in a way, we live haphazardly or are heading toward disaster; either way, our path becomes neither easy nor simple for anyone because life would be erratic. And it makes total sense, doesn't it, that such life could lead us into thinking we no longer have control? So what is the answer? Our emotional mindset is the creator of this lifestyle. Let us peer into typical moments through which this mindset lives.

As an example, a few pages ago you may have been excited or joyful; yet, in this moment you may now be perplexed, and within several minutes from now you may find yourself frustrated or angry. The reason behind these shifts is totally irrelevant. Except for one. Each emotional swing simply told you the outer world now has direct influence over your otherwise perfect moment, or that you did not necessarily like the results of the experience. Both are judgment calls. Do you realize these unwarranted emotional switches actually pulled you out of the perfect present? They poured more fuel on the fired-up emotion, which in turn rang all the bells and blew all the sirens just for your attention. It worked! You totally immersed yourself in your frustration or anger instead of staying in that perfect peace-filled moment.

Seeds are garnered from either type of moment; yet, because of the emotion now rattling you – consuming you – only more of the exact same emotional experience will come to you. Once frustration sets in, have you ever noticed that it always seems to increase? Simply put, Karma responds to that emotional instant as your request for yet more of those like kind emotional incidents! Remember the quicksand idea described in an earlier chapter? Put in this context, the more we allow ourselves to feel frustrated, the more fuel we pour on its fire and the thicker our consciousness becomes. We become engulfed by the brown silt of frustration as it pulls us into its downward spiral. Please understand, during each of these fleeting moments of emotional expression, we will draw to us its like kind energy source.

But remember. Do not believe for one iota that we must remain stuck in the spiral. We can shift it at any time by merely changing our perspective. As always, it's our choice.

So how do we shift the moment? If I may suggest, just don't give it any power. This is not to say simply ignore it; just do not give it your energy. It will dissipate all on its own. Simply view the negative emotion objectively without analyzing your outer experience or pointing to the person who you believe caused your feeling; otherwise, the feeling will only intensify and exacerbate your experiences with it. You see, we are actually feeding the feeling when we work with it in this fashion. By allowing the feeling to be what it is, the "why" or purpose of the feeling will show itself when ready. Analyzing, on the other hand, can truly block this internal discovery. "If I do not analyze, then should I blame?" you may ask. Certainly not! The blame or cause for what we are feeling is not at all outside us; it is internal. We must learn to own the feeling; after all, it is ours, nobody else's. Blame eliminates our own responsibility for the feeling, thus allowing an external influence – another human (?) – to control it. It is best to use objective observation because the answer will then become obvious, sooner rather than much later. Keep in mind, though, never get down on or berate ourselves, for doing so will surely strengthen the feeling and the Karmic return shall magnify our personal experience.

Adding a new variable or dimension to the episode, suppose we vilify another person during our moment of frustration because they either asked whether we are okay or if they can help. As an emotionally-charged human in that moment, we do have the tendency for lashing out, especially with the person closest to us, unfortunately. Such an emotional outburst has now transformed our frustration into a moment of anger levied at most likely a genuinely innocent person or our partner. Now we have two Karmic returns heading right at us, one is increasing frustration and the other is return anger, coming either from the other person or from another direction! No one else has brought these upon us. We do well enough on our own to attract these two scenarios. Yet, if we were to use these principles with wisdom and focused being, neither of them would ever occur because we are aware of them and nothing more.

From a monk's perspective, the most efficient way to shift the moment is by allowing the emotion to exist simply for what it is. Let us say you are experiencing frustration. Okay, just acknowledge its presence without feeding it and it will dissipate out of its own accord. The same is true with any emotion: simply allow it. It is there for a reason, and rarely will it have anything to do with an external event. While working with the monks one day, I recall a moment of sadness. A Master gently asked, "Why are you sad?" I answered with what I felt was the reason for it. The teacher looked at me and simply stated, "Then enjoy the experience of your sadness, young man." Perhaps you believe his answer was callous; however, his intent was genuine as I internalized its true meaning.

On our path of enlightenment we encounter many teachers, some traditional, others non-traditional, still others appearing as an enemy – an emotion too! You see, when we encounter a so-called enemy, we are to view it as a teacher, and as such, it should be honored as our teacher. Through honor, the enemy goes away and the teacher remains. The idea is to sense the emotion and allow it to instruct us, and yes, they most definitely do! When we think of an enemy we generally think of another human or animal; yet, do not limit the scope of this since any negative thought, emotion, or experience may also be considered an enemy. These are actually internal enemies. Does this surprise you? It should not. You see, we have the feeling of being attacked, truly an internal enemy; therefore, we are the one doing the attacking within our being, and we use negative emotions created by our own frustration or anger, to name a few. See them as your teacher with, "What am I being shown about me in this moment?" in mind.

Take the emotions of frustration and sadness simply as examples. I feel fairly certain no one desires to cozy up to either emotion; instead, we may indeed consider each as an enemy, both of which we are better off without. An emotion like frustration or sadness is indeed an enemy when we fight it because the emotion shall only grow; however, when we look upon it as our teacher, by allowing this inner experience in order to learn from the emotion, we actually eliminate it, never to return, for it has now become our friend, even our closest ally rather than a looming enemy. This subject is discussed further

in the next chapter. In reality, we still create within those moments when we allow a myriad of emotions to come and go, and most likely, the very same is recreated, over and over, time and again, without ever realizing we are the one doing it. But taking the opportunity to understand the emotions, we then are able to create even greater things in our life since we now understand their origin.

The emotions, as the mind, are the wild mustang, and at times, we genuinely believe we are a victim of circumstance. This is purely a mental trap. We are not victims, truth be told. Climb into your driver's seat and allow whatever you feel to dissipate on it's own without feeding it any further. From common sense, we all know our feelings dissipate as well as all thoughts. Simply let them. And do not hold onto them. Realize a return action shall come, by what you do or not do in that moment, but through the dissipation of the emotion this now diminishes the potential of the return activity. On the other hand, if you grapple with the emotion, it will become your strongest enemy, intensifying and growing evermore so through Karmic return action.

I would like to explain why most of us experience emotional peaks and valleys – up and downs – at one time or another throughout life. Do you know the one-word answer? Karma. The somewhat longer version is simply because we are neither present with our mind, nor with our body. In all my years as a monk, I have yet to witness any fellow monk express an emotion other than peaceful joy. Anger and frustration do not appear to exist in their very nature, no matter which monastery I visited at the time. Additionally, monks are joined by a common thread; they are perpetually present in their life with whatever they do at the moment, never losing focus. I am fascinated to hear most people share with me their sincere belief that monks only sit in meditation all day long, doing nothing else. Granted, they certainly do this for part of the day; however, they also perform their daily tasks and meditate while doing those tasks, such as cleaning the grounds, tending the fields, exercising, even cooking and walking. I must tell you, a monk accepts a 24/7 job. Where is the "easy" in that? This alone was a major learning experience for me, just being present all the time no matter the goings on. This experience changed

my outlook forever, for being present does not allow for worry since neither past nor future can exist in this moment. When we master this, we can only see perfection in all things; hence, any possibility of extraneous influences, both mentally and emotionally, is greatly diminished. Perfection resides only in the present moment.

In truth, the one thing influencing our emotions the most today, more times than not, is our memory of bygone events. Although it is now nothing more than a fleeting memory, what we are experiencing this moment can immediately trigger that particular memory or one from a similar experience due to a person, place, thing, or to any one of our senses. A current situation can inexplicitly refresh a memory from which we will instantaneously recall every emotion that had welled up within us during that past experience. Doesn't it make sense that the past is now directly influencing our present experience? Could this be a Karmic return? The answers are yes, but not necessarily for the reasons you may think. Perhaps the surge of emotion(s) occurred to bring about the healing of an old wound instead of exacerbating it. Mind you, Karma works in many ways. You see, when we look at this principle: *You attract to you what you are*… there certainly may be a part of us needing repair. And for whatever reason, whether we are unable to do it ourselves or refuse to face it, Karma will make sure we ultimately do, in one fashion or another, in one lifetime or another. In this particular instance, the memory reappeared to clear and heal our old wound in order to eliminate our sense of heaviness regarding it. Deal with the heal and allow it to do its work for you.

How may we use this knowledge and very principle in our everyday life? May I begin with your greatest dream, the one you are wishing for right now? We each have one, I know. First, it is suggested that you stop wishing for it. "What? You do not want me to have it? Am I not worthy of it or something?" you might be asking. Besides a no answer to all of the above, allow me to offer the truth of the matter. "Wishing for" something or someone actually blocks you from ever reaching that dream since the wish is solely embroiled in wishful thinking, meaning it has no reality or substance behind it. To achieve your dream you must simply become your dream so you match the reality of it. The moment you reach this state of being, the dream will

truly find you; thus, you will not have to look for it. Do you know you have just utilized the Law of Creation, the second principle of Karma, to fulfill your dream? Forgive me for repeating it yet again: *You attract to you what you are, not what you want.* Comprehending this principle, as with any new understanding, may initially be challenging; yet, I ask you to just learn to properly place your focus, to remain in the present with that focus because, once achieved, your dream will indeed seek you out.

And when it is stated to "focus," this means there are no other visions besides the one of your dream. Entertain absolutely no doubt or fear at any moment in time, nor any wavering for even one second regarding the dream. It is always present with you. Notice the mention of "always present." You must see it in your present constantly and continually. If you honestly love your dream, then you can easily love and maintain your focus on it. The trap to watch out for is the potential sense of frustration arising from the seat of impatience, which may show up because the dream has not physically appeared just yet. Impatience is nothing more than your own mind playing a mind game with you, no pun intended. I ask you to not go there because, once you do, your dream becomes delayed or even blocked from you due to this negative sense. Simply keep the dream present with your loving focus. Eliminate the idea of frustration. If impatience ultimately does come into play, then honor it as your teacher by practicing its lesson – patience. The impatience transforms into your ally and no longer interferes with your dream. When we dream, also learn to observe any and all emotions associated with it. They may very well be the same teacher who actually shows you how to achieve the dream.

I vividly recall my inner nature upon my arrival at the first monastery in India. The place and surroundings were so peaceful. So, too, were all the monks. On the other hand, my own being was not at all peaceful. You see, within a few short years prior to my sojourn to India, I had returned stateside from Vietnam, still very much wound up from my experiences in the Army. Being very angry and frustrated with my life, I desperately wished to be as peaceful as the gentle monks all around me. I just had to have this for myself! That was all there was to it. Later, there was a time when I even felt envious of them because they were all so very graceful in everything they did each and every moment. Master Lobsang noticed my emotion and gently asked, "Young man, why are you so envious of the other monks?" I replied in agitation, "I want for myself what they have, but I do not seem to be able to get there!" According to non-traditional teachings, his answer was simply another question, "Why don't you just see it and allow it to come to you?" "Oh sure, easy for you to say!" could very well have been my thoughts in that moment, only because I did not yet realize the message. Master Lobsang explained further, "It is not to seek what you want, but to allow it to find you." This made absolutely no sense to me at the time; yet, because he saw my deepening frustration, he continued, "If you seek something, it means you do not have it," as his face softened in thoughtful humor, "And you will probably never have it as long as you believe you must look for it. But if you focus on it as though you do have it, then you would soon realize you do, indeed, already have it, for it has shown up in your life."

So I stopped looking for it and my frustration began to slowly dissipate until I "woke up," realizing on one particular day that I was just like the other monks, peaceful in nature. On that day, it simply "showed up" because only the presence of peace now existed within me. The world became peace-filled. Did I do anything magical or mystical? No, I simply stopped looking for peace; instead, I allowed it to exist in me as I became it in that present moment. And it remains there to this very day. My life, therefore, is peaceful along with the people around me. I have applied the very message I now offer to each of you, to become the dream within you first, to fully realize that your inner world drives your outer to what you experience in every given moment. I have applied this same idea in so many areas of life, always with consistent results as long as I patiently wait for it to find me. And it always does.

By sharing my personal experience with you, it is my intent to have you understand that life, both individually and collectively, is nowhere near as complex as we make it out to be, and that we seem to always look for something. Because we are all equal under the eyes of

Karmic Law, what was just shared in the above paragraph will work for not only a single individual, but also for all humankind. Imagine if all people in all nations simply focus on being peace in the present, right-here-right-now, what that would do by itself. Can you really see a world without any turmoil? Yes it is that simple! The key to it all: see what you dream, be patient, and allow it to work its way into your reality.

In this part of the world, patience has almost become a non sequitur; however, only from patience can the other Karmic returns which we had previously put forth be truly worked through, after which there will no longer be anything to slow down our dream from reaching us. There exists a wonderful side-effect to this Law of attraction. The more we use it, the stronger it becomes. In fact, come to think of it, I suggest we begin with small things, then work slowly toward our larger dream of life. This would help us develop understanding in three areas: 1) attain a greater degree of patience, 2) significantly lower the chance to encounter frustration, 3) realize just how the process works. Although smaller inconsequential things may appear to have less weight to them, attracting them, nonetheless, shall truly show us this is not only possible, but actually very real. Once you master this, then all things will come to you. Just one crucial caveat here: you must be able to handle it!

What do I mean? Purely as an example, suppose you do not understand the idea of money, when all of a sudden, you have millions of dollars, perhaps as a lottery winner. Well, the odds are very high that the windfall will be gone in no time. How can you "lose" so much so fast? The reason is because you truly have no idea, or training, on how to handle such a large sum of money. You may simply squander it, through no fault of your own, by miscomprehending the full responsibility in having it. Now it may be lifetimes before you have that same chance again. The point is you must be fully prepared for the dream's realization because it now creates a whole different set of circumstances with which you must work. Do you realize nearly every aspect of your life must transform to match the dream? Are you physically, emotionally, and mentally ready? I believe the wording is: you cannot put new wine in old skins. In other words, you cannot have your new life while the old one still exists. This simply will not work. In the long run, do not yearn for the old after the new has arrived, as this now begs the question, "Do you truly desire what you seek?"

Allow me to now sum up this principle for you because, just as the first one, this principle leads us right into the next one. *You attract to you what you are, not what you want* incites great depth to one's learning, an idea by which to operate and live in handling all of one's circumstances through life. Let us begin right now, right from where we are, to realize we have full creative power each and every moment of our life, creating with and through these very principles constantly and continually. In fact they tell us precisely how to accomplish this through all of our individual and global activities. Again, there is no way around the Principle of Creation and never should we attempt to *un*-create, for it only wastes our time and energy – absolutely fruitless. You see, even if we think we have *un*-created or destroyed something, we merely created something new and different; therefore, once it is present just accept it, both mentally and emotionally.

In a sense, the act of creating is much like rolling a ball, which is very much how we operate our life. Once the ball rolls, we need only nudge it every now and then to keep it rolling; however, be always careful and aware, for if we nudge or push too hard then we need to frantically chase the ball, in which case we can most certainly feel lost or sense we are attempting to catch up, all because our life has slipped ahead. And do you know what? We will miss our very own life in this process, all the while we are endeavoring to catch up to it! So what does this all mean? Do not let what you create get too far out in front of you; instead, always keep it close to you by being present, thereby making it a whole lot easier to maintain the rate at which you create. It will certainly get out of hand otherwise, and if you struggle with it, even to the point it stops, you are still creating. Remember Karmic return? Struggle creates only more struggles. The truth of the matter is, we are never behind. This is not possible. So if you feel you are attempting to catch up, you are living in the future and nothing more; on the other hand, if you remain present, you then miss nothing at all since the ball rolls with you at your own pace of life.

Continuing, what if your ball moves too far ahead? Simply realize you are being taught to not push so hard, to realize you are attempting to create at a faster rate than you are able to handle. When this occurs your emotions and mind begin to race, at which point it is suggested you cease all activity by implementing a Zen tradition wherein it is stated, "Sometimes the best thing to do is nothing at all." Doing nothing slows the ball. So too will your life. Our life is always in our hands; yet, it is completely out of our hands while we live in the next week or future month instead of right where we are. Neither are we able to live in our yesterdays. Even though we allow our mind and emotions to drift into either of these energies, do you realize we are still creating? If we create out of yesterday then we have those same experiences, and there is no one who is able to create out of the future. Yes, we do create the future, but only from our present. Einstein once stated that the past, present, and future are all going on at the same time. Considering the way we operate in the mental sense, his statement runs true. The reality is, this moment is the only one which exists wherein the past, present, and future all actually meet, as one creates the other in oneness.

Remember, the seed of creation is carried in all things as it is ever-present. The human should also be ever-present. Therefore, keep your presence and know which seeds you plant. May they be the fertile seeds of creative power from each moment you have available to you. As your emotions or thoughts shift and change, know they all carry this creative power within them. Only you determine the field into which your creation will return, either positive or negative. Karmic Law is the mechanism; you determine the direction. The energies of the cosmos are all pure by their inherent nature, and the human decides how to handle its purity.

While present in mind, we can shift and change our present moment into any thing we so desire, into any idea we so choose. These energies give us life and the power of thought, along with the true energy source of our body, the emotions. All the emotions we emit can simply be considered a request because they are responsible for creating our personal electro-magnetic field, the energy from which seeks its own like kind. Most importantly, it is the like kind return

which actually seeks us! From all we generate, we originally created it through this very principle of Karma, the Principle of Creation. Always remember these words: *You attract to you what you, are not what you want.* Change what you are, then your life changes with you. It has been your choice since the day you were born, for it came into life with you because of the Universal Truths of life, and it will leave with you when you transition. In truth, it will bring you back for yet another festive lifetime and another opportunity to learn the Laws of divine creation so you will ultimately live as the divine principle which you are, the principle extolling your true nature, a deeply humbling experience indeed. Is it coincidental that the third Law is known as the Principle of Humility? I don't think so. Only perfect flow!

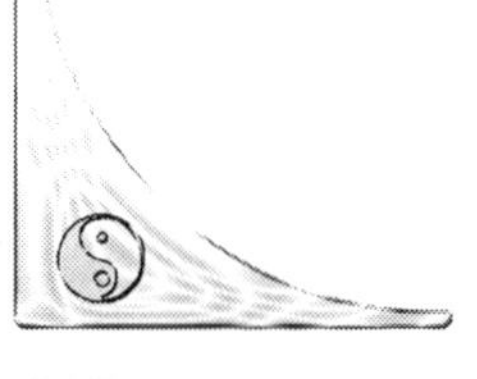

"When you have thrown off your ideas as to mind and body, the original truth will fully appear."
Zen Master Dogen

~ Chapter IV ~
The Principle of Humility

We now enter the third principle of Karma, the Law of Humility, a truly magnificent principle in its precept. It is the one principle which has assisted monks to simply be who they are each and every moment of their life – reverently humble. Do you easily envision monks as a very gentle and easy-going people? This was consistently observed at every monastery I visited. No matter the circumstance in which they may find them self, their demeanor and nature remains totally unfettered. They never were at odds with any thing or any human because they will simply stand aside in their humility. Monks are appreciative of life, honoring it in each moment, continually enjoying just being alive and aware of that life. Interestingly enough, the monks did indeed give up their own country in the name of this Law because they believe so much in these principles, and are deeply committed to firmly live by them rather than merely think of them as a matter of convenience.

Monks know they will live on, no matter the location. Where they live is not a concern, for there will always be a roof over their head and food to nourish their bodies. They remind me of a young supple tree, its limbs and trunk gracefully bending in the wind without any concern about the wind's strength or direction. The Principle of Humility is about learning to be humble rather than being so gregarious about our self and life, to honor all aspects of life for what

they are, instead of what they are not. Contrary to the monks, we in this part of the world have become very rigid and brittle. Watch out if the wind blows, for the inflexible limbs of the tree may snap or break apart in direct proportion to both wind speed and direction. But do you realize we can be just like the monks in the way we choose to live each day and without really giving up anything? By understanding the ideas of this principle, then to live it, our humble nature would be a breath of fresh air because, in current times, the Western culture is entirely consumed at being the best at whichever wherever with whatever for whomever. I am willing to bet you may think humility portrays weakness. Not at all! In truth, it is from this very attribute that we shall become aware of our divine nature. Do you realize humility is the source of our sovereign strength? We call it flexibility. It was also once stated very clearly, the meek shall inherit the earth. Did the Master Christ intend for us to understand this very Law?

As you continue reading this book, you will soon realize the most significant goal of Karma, but I will tell you now. It is to guide the human towards that level of awareness when they simply transform to the best divine human they may possibly be. It is our individual birthright to live in this nature. The bottom line truth is, these principles shall make certain of this outcome, assuring us of reaching this goal, whether it occurs in this lifetime or another – our choice. The sole reason for life is for each of us to overcome the pull of the body and its lower physical natures. In fact, the faster we master these principles, the easier our life becomes. Humility is an integral part of our divine nature, and to achieve this ideal, we must journey under the principle offered by its Law, a Law wherein many of our most significant lessons of life reside. I say the following with my full encouragement and support. When traveling under the Principle of Humility, its path can become the most arduous one you may ever undertake in any one lifetime, purely because this Law is the greatest teacher as it reveals who you truly are. Is this really possible within one lifetime? Yes! From your perseverance and acceptance, this one principle is about facing your self for what you have become, which is exactly what most people do not wish to do! With this realization you can more easily shift into your proper direction. I now ask you a question, "Why is it best to use a map when undertaking a cross-

country trip? Well, would it not be significantly more efficient and easier to arrive at one's destination rather than to follow one's nose, turning any which way at any which time?"

Similarly, the principles of Karma are the road map to our full realization of life and who we are, but only if we choose to follow them. The third principle guides us to understand that we are not about *what* we are; rather, it is about *who* we are through realizing we are not our things. We are not our hair, our partners, our children, nor are we our house, our car, our career. These are the "what's" in our life. And they have created the "what" we have become in our life. If properly utilized, these things may possibly contain the ability to power our divine creativity; however, they have most certainly diminished our ability to accept divine humility. This is because the "what's" have done nothing more than feed our physical ego. When utilized as a learning tool, the "what's" are quite wonderful because we gain experience through their proper use and they assist us towards our self-realization of who we are, not what we are. On the other hand, when used solely to accumulate more "what's," this direction travels entirely opposite from the original intention because the "what's" appear to have totally diminished our Creator-given ability. Just as important, we have allowed the "what's" to create our illusions and judgments of life and people. One could easily say our "what's" now have become our stumbling blocks to higher attainment. Do you notice the desire for more in our world today? The "what's" have simply overpowered us, appearing to thoroughly enjoy feeding our ego-based mind. In truth, they bolster our insatiable ego in all respects while humility nearly recedes into a faint and foggy memory.

What is the Law of Humility? How does it work and how do we apply it? In answer to the first question, the Law simply states: *What you resist persists for you.* Interestingly enough, as a start to the second question, the idea behind this Law is that we not only choose our enemies, but we also give them their apparent strength. Oh yes, we do indeed choose our very own enemies, and we then boost them into what appears as an infinitely strong and insurmountable position. This may sound very ludicrous; yet, it is an accurate assertion based on personal experience and understanding of Karma. Before you

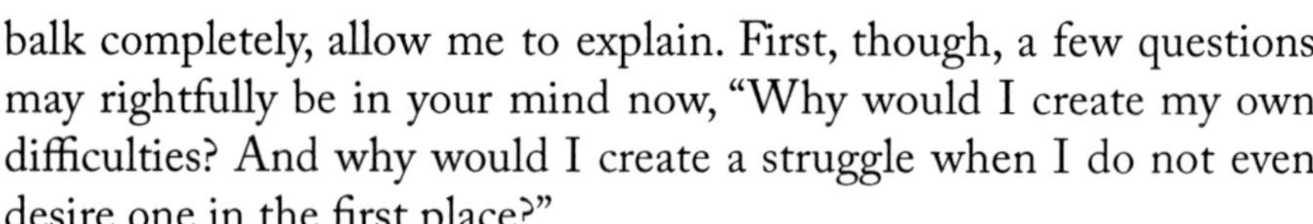

balk completely, allow me to explain. First, though, a few questions may rightfully be in your mind now, "Why would I create my own difficulties? And why would I create a struggle when I do not even desire one in the first place?"

Keep in mind, an enemy is not necessarily limited to an adversarial human, a person who may physically attack or thwart us in some fashion. It can be our career, our partner, our child, a family member, or even an item we own. Metaphysically speaking, an enemy is anything, animate or inanimate, which takes away from our peaceful nature. It is any thing which pulls us from our divine source. It may even be our own self, which reminds me of the old saying, "You are your own worst enemy." In the context of this principle, our enemy will most likely be a negative thought or emotion such as sadness, frustration, or anger. Unquestionably, this is precisely the path we are going to venture on for the duration of this chapter, the concept of internal enemies. Considering the basic idea underlying this principle, the Principle of Humility may now make sense to you.

You may possibly be a bit befuddled from the above paragraph; therefore, allow me to explain further by sharing an experience I had with my own internal enemy, an adversary most common and likely shared by all humans. Also, it can seem the strongest in any given moment, for it is considered the root of most enemies, if not all of them. This experience may also answer the second question: How does it work? Let's return to my stay at the monastery in northern India. I clearly remember Master Lobsang approaching me one day while I was planting rice. He calmly and flatly made a statement, "You are going to meet a great teacher," and while looking straight into my eyes he asked, "Young man, what is your greatest fear?" Considering for a moment what I felt that would be, I looked into his twinkling eyes after a momentary silence, stating without hesitation, "Master, I fear a slow and agonizing death." He responded with another question, "Do you actually fear what humans term as death?" "No," I replied, "I just don't want it to be slow and agonizing."

He smiled thoughtfully, bowed in his humble manner, and then walked away, leaving me puzzled as I watched his graceful return to

the monastery. After a minute or two, I shrugged my shoulders and resumed my planting without giving the incident another thought. In and of itself, do you realize fear is one of – if not the greatest – enemy of all our emotions? Even to the degree of physically immobilizing us? It can instantly turn success into failure. We would readily commit to a lie if we fear the truth, in general. A person may even have a fear of losing their loved one, a situation occurring quite frequently nowadays, a fear so deep-seated they would most likely be the first one to actually leave the relationship while truly believing they can avoid what they fear! We simply cannot avoid what we fear. How do we avoid the emotion of fear? I will explain as we travel down the road. Regarding the above scenarios, even though each carries its own Karmic return action – the first associated with lying and the second with leaving – all must deal with the third principle: *What you resist persists for you.*

I continued planting when, a few days later, a runner greeted me in the field, breathlessly informing me, "The Llama wishes to see you!" Oh my, what a great honor to have an audience with the Llama, the head of a monastery, for they have such a wealth of wisdom. I knew in my heart this was going to be a very great lesson, coming from the great teacher! What I thought was absolutely correct, in a sense, but I had no clue what was in store for me. You see, when a teacher at a monastery has a lesson for you, that lesson will also contain the associated experience so it can become permanently ingrained in your mind. In other words, the lesson is first spoken, and then experientially applied in a manner and at a time unbeknownst to the student. Such non-traditional teaching creates a rather exciting and mysterious process for the neophyte, and more times than not, the arriving experience unfolds quite humorously. Generally, Master teachers use a variety of methods to carry out the lesson, from the use of words, to actions, even to the waking stick, each method being unique and extremely effective.

Entering the Llama's chamber, I remember distinctly how thrilling it was to receive an important lesson, yet having absolutely no idea what it could specifically be. My mind was deep in thought during my deep long bow. Based on previous discussions on this particular

principle with Master Lobsang, I sensed it might apply to my inner enemy, whatever that was. The Llama looked at me as I up righted myself, approached and quietly directed me, "Please go to the local village and get the items on this list," while handing me a small piece of paper along with local currency, a few rupees. I was startled as I said to myself, "What is this? I am just going shopping?" Okay, on one hand I felt let down because I was simply walking to the nearby village to get thread, spices, and some material. Big deal! On the other hand though, I was excited because this shopping trip would provide me the opportunity to practice my Hindi linguistics while on my own. I bowed in acknowledgment and quickly headed toward the outer door.

Shortly after I passed through the doorway, I shot a quick, nearly unconscious glance up from my feet to see the path ahead. Yes, there was the path alright – "Wha…? UH-OH!" – along with an adult Bengal Tiger staring right at me about a hundred yards away! I froze right where I stood as my mind was hollering, "I must run back inside!" I still could not move! Too late. My face flushed with hot blood from the adrenaline rush while my legs lost all motor function, for I just stood still, totally frozen with fear, peering into the eyes of my greatest nightmare. And the door for my safe passage stood a mere twenty feet behind me! "Run Steven!" But I absolutely could not move an inch! Why not? Nothing was physically wrong with me, except for the immobilizing emotion of fear! My eyes remained locked with the tiger's for what seemed like forever, and then he started pacing towards me. "Okay, don't move and he won't see you!" my mind informed me. My mind made no points in that moment because the big cat was now charging at me in what seemed like slow-motion. I even lost my voice as I stood there, my feet super-glued to the pathway, watching in complete terror for what was about to occur. Have you ever seen a tiger jump into a full head-on leap? As you stand *below* it? I vividly recall his graceful, silent vault into the air, each front paw the size of my head reaching forever forward, inviting me into his grip. "I am going to die" was the last thought on my mind in that moment. A slow, agonizing death, for I was going to be eaten alive, the greatest of fears I believe any one could ever have in their life!

Like all my fellow monks, my head was clean shaven. Here I am, writhing on the ground below the weight and jaws of a four-hundred pound male tiger, his hind legs constantly pawing me into position while licking my shiny head. "Oh great, he is tenderizing my skull before he takes a bite out of it!" as I waited for the impending crunch. By now my voice returned in full volume as I was screaming and wailing at the top of my lungs, pleading for the big cat to just "do it" and get it over with. Although the noisy commotion between the tiger and I could easily have filled a concert hall, I detected faint laughter in the background. I unconsciously moved the tiger's mouth from my head…wait, this is amazing. What? The tiger actually let me! I slowly turned my head to look in the direction of the merriment and there I saw Master Lobsang, Rinpoche Kiela the Llama, along with two other monks uproariously howling, hands holding their stomachs, at a sight I did not at all consider funny. The tiger remained on top of me; his legs relaxed and sprawled outward, until he heard Master Lobsang slap his thighs. To this day, I have yet to observe another fully-grown tiger spring upward and forward as fast as my so-called enemy that day, jumping onto my teacher, who began laughing while he and the big cat rolled and wrestled on the ground.

"What a minute…this is not possible!" as I entered a shock of sheer disbelief over what I was observing right in front of me. After a few minutes I noticed Master Lobsang and the tiger gingerly walk towards me as I was washing myself and my robes down at the river's edge. Lobsang looked at me with a gleam of humor in his eyes. "His mother had been poached by hunters and we found him just barely a month old at the front door to the monastery," he notified me while the humongous cat leisurely lay beside us, just looking up at me. My teacher continued, "Basically, we all raised him from a cub until he was almost full-grown and could take care of himself. This tiger sees monks as his family. We are all brothers and we are one with each other. He would not harm a monk or any other human for that matter because he has only known humans, even though he is wild. He was simply playing with you, intending no harm whatsoever." Initially, fury and embarrassment enveloped me simultaneously as I exclaimed, "I cannot believe anyone would do such a thing!" as my teacher only continued to smile quietly. "Come, sit next to me here," he requested.

As I scooted over, the cat stuck his head between my forearm and rib cage, to which I involuntarily recoiled. "He just wants his head scratched," Master Lobsang informed me. I returned to the position, and when I began scratching his head, I heard a deep, throaty rumble, a soft vibration coming from somewhere. Oh, he is purring! It is just several octaves lower than a house cat but with greater volume. Can you imagine it?

The big cat's friendly purr and contentment rubbed off on me, for I regained my composure and cleared my mind, enabling me to then listen to my teacher as he began to explain the concept of fear. "Do you remember how you reacted in total fear the moment you first saw the tiger?" he asked. "Do you now realize what your greatest fear is capable of doing?" and, "Do you realize fear, by itself, is your worst enemy?" "Yes," I responded now having the full implications of the teaching. The degree of power that a single emotion can have over us is remarkable! I knew in that moment the relaxed tiger was not my fear, as he continued his "purr" concerto next to me. Fear, along with so many things the human mind creates, is indeed our worst enemy; yet, it is exactly the one we most need to face. We are all personally responsible for what is created internally and it may literally freeze us in place. I knew in retrospect I could have raced back to the door in plenty of time, yet fear prevented it.

In truth, we must face all what we create, as each creation comes from within us. I now understood this critical concept. The magnitude of our circumstance is directly proportional to our level of resistance to an internal enemy. During my ensuing days and months at the monastery, that Bengal tiger and I forged a deep bond. I felt like "Tarzan of the Tigers," knowing there was nothing to bother me because, whether I was running through the jungle paths or walking to my favorite meditation spot, he would always show up and approach my side, either running with me or laying beside me during my meditation. Oh yes, there were many an occasion when he and I would wrestle in fun, each in a zestful manner. In fact, he initiated most matches. And he never allowed me to win even a single one! This experience showed me the true danger of any emotion if it

overpowers us. As each day passed into the next the tiger, Shanti Che was his name, taught me so many things of life by simply watching him.

Karmically speaking, if we resist fear or anything else in life, it has no other choice but to reveal itself even more strongly through a later experience and quite possibly be expanded. This may seem unreal but here is a very simple example of a physical experience that relates. What happens when you get a headache and begin to fight or resist it? You are correct; it gets stronger. Why not simply allow for it and accept it? You may be pleasantly surprised, for it will begin to dissipate and disappear. If true in this case then it would be true in all what is being offered in this principle, in fact all the principles. To be sure, this is true in all things concerning our enemies, both internally and externally, hence the reason for the Law of Humility: *What you resist persists for you.*

The Christ once stated that when your enemy strikes you on one cheek, offer them the other. I feel He was talking about this very same principle because we create our own enemies within and without. In essence, His message tells us to no longer fight anything internally, for it will merely magnify itself, gaining evermore strength to ultimately overpower us – fear the strongest of enemies. I admit I certainly and instantly metamorphosed into a human pillar, completely frozen as the cat bounded towards me on the monastery path that day; however, we must realize a truth. The tiger himself did not physically freeze me in place; rather, it was my internal enemy, my fear of the tiger which kept me transfixed. Our fear gives any enemy its power, no matter its appearance. A funny thing happened to me. My so-called enemy quickly transformed into my closest friend and teacher, all because of the power of fear and using it.

When it comes to our life-long dreams, we are actually our own worst enemy. Due only to how we feel about our dream actually becoming a reality, we stir up emotions such as our sense of unworthiness, doubt, and overwhelming fear in most cases. You see, we actually unseat ourselves innumerably more times than anyone else. And here we go,

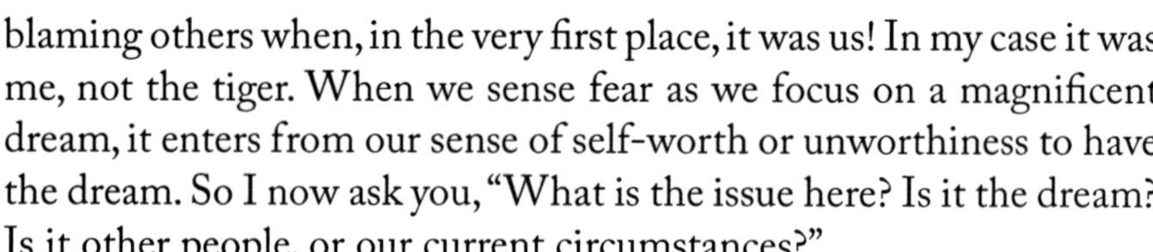

blaming others when, in the very first place, it was us! In my case it was me, not the tiger. When we sense fear as we focus on a magnificent dream, it enters from our sense of self-worth or unworthiness to have the dream. So I now ask you, "What is the issue here? Is it the dream? Is it other people, or our current circumstances?"

The true issue, our so-called enemy, is simply our sense of unworthiness, not the dream, not anyone, not anything else. Now and then, at the appropriate time, the door of opportunity opens for us to transform that seeming enemy into our internal teacher; yet, generally speaking, we continue down the path of unworthiness which significantly increases the odds that our dream shall remain unrealized. The vital key is where we place our focus. My intense introduction to Mr. Tiger transformed my fearsome enemy of a slow and agonizing death to my fun furry teacher as suggested, from which a wonderful bond and deep friendship developed. From just that one incident, no fear rises within me even to this day, and I now answer every question thoughtfully and very cautiously because my desire is to give only truth. Fear and its subsequent trauma are both great teachers, though I caution you, be absolutely ready to only use them as your teachers and to understand the reason for your fear; otherwise, do not create the fear in the first place. Why are you afraid of your dream? Does love hurt? Is this what holds it away from you? Is this what keeps success at bay? As one of my teachers once said, it is sometimes better to go ahead and climb the mountain instead of going around it.

Aside from being an excellent teacher, fear is a very dynamic tool. "Fear as a tool? What do you mean by that?" you might ask. Fear really occurs from or through what we may term as the unknown, meaning we simply do not know what the outcome will be. This is also why change is difficult as we journey from what we knew. Therefore, we hesitate or freeze-frame, becoming immobilized as I was when the tiger playfully pounced on me. Looked upon another way, the unknown can truly be an adventure when absolutely no fear is involved in the process. Just where is the adventure and personal growth when we follow the exact same path or do the exact same

thing over and over because we already know and are comfortable with both outcomes? There is an answer to this question which I will discuss in a few moments. First, let us look at how our so-called fear may be used as a tool. Because the status of material success is heavily reinforced in this part of the world, it becomes evident that harboring any fear of failure significantly increases the probability for that failure to occur. Failure, therefore, becomes the experience. If my supposition rings true for you, I offer an idea. Change your mind! Rather than fearing failure, allow yourself to harbor a fear of success, thereby increasing the probability for success to occur. This idea may certainly sound bizarre; however, it definitely has merit, does it not? In other words, if you fear failure and it happens time and again, why not simply apply the reverse by merely utilizing self-imposed reverse psychology? We obviously do this with each other, so apply it to your self in this instance.

Here is the next point: What do fear and humility have to do with each other? Their concepts appear quite the opposite, don't they? In truth, fear is one of the teachers of humility, and herein lies their relationship. If one is humble and operates from this arena they would fear very little, if at all, for a humble person is very flexible, contrary to being rigid. A rigid nature actually creates fear, Master Lobsang taught me, and it has proved itself time and again. Rigidity creates an unbending nature; whereas, humility does not. "If rigidity or inflexibility creates fear, what then do fears actually tell you?" The answer is: You are too rigid in the arena of which you harbor the fear. Does this make any sense? Imagine a stiff, rigid tree. How long would it stand in high winds, no matter its age? I would venture to say not very long. The same is true when it comes to the winds of fear, created purely by our rigidity, which means we are destined for a fall all because of an internal enemy. Even during times of change, fear can strike as the old drifts away, thus immobilizing us into a pillar of salt as we cautiously venture into the unknown, for we yearn for the comfort of the past, even when the change is for the better. And it usually is, isn't it? When the wind of change blows, it is all about humility; therefore, simply apply the greatest level of flexibility in those moments by allowing the wind to blow upon you. Accept the inevitable change; never block or get in its way because, if you do, struggle is guaranteed.

We, as individual thinkers, do not necessarily accept change with any level of grace or ease, even though the reality of life blatantly reveals change as a constant, continuous, and harmonious aspect of nature. It is most interesting to observe how the unknown can instantly block us during a time of change as our innate fear rears on its hind legs to resist it. Both personally and globally, resistance is futile, for the bottom line is, change remains constant. Change is evolution. Yes, we seem to tenaciously prefer the well-worn path and all our creature comforts because, during times of change, we become stoically rigid. If we were to instead peer into the unknown as an adventurer, and approach the change with a high level of anticipation and excitement for entering yet a new experience, we would certainly establish flexibility. In truth, it will engulf our whole being; hence, fear and the resulting emotional trauma will no longer feel at home.

Though I had never been there, when my journey began towards northern India, I was excited the whole time because of all the new adventures encountered along the way. This viewpoint remains with me much the same way to this very day, for I always look to the new events. Do you know change can bring wisdom, whereas the same thing each day can only bring entrenched limitation? Remember, struggle is the old comforts colliding with the fear of new events to come; therefore, by objectively observing our struggle, it will plainly reveal where we have become rigid, and it will derive the greatest of benefits we could ever imagine, our dreams. As we progress through this process by always looking to the new, we would begin to anticipate change and effortlessly allow it to arrive totally free of all struggle, thereby experiencing our flexible nature. At the same time, we will also head into a new direction in our personal evolution; therefore, allow nothing to hold us from our change: no one or no thing.

There is another important aspect about the Law of Humility: what we object to reflects who we are inside. You may ask, "Really? Where did this come from? How in the world does this relate to

humility?" In truth, the seat of our internal enemies rests with our outward objections or denunciations. You see, as monks suggest in their monastic teachings, if it is not in us first then we are unable to see it in another living being. In other words, it must be part of us before we see it in another. Putting it still differently, if we know nothing of it in the internal sense of the word, then we would not be capable of seeing it in the external sense of the word.

Allow me to put it yet another way. Simply because we leveled a criticism about another, that judgment had to come from or resonate within us first in order for us to even see it in the other. Does that make sense? Metaphysically, we are actually admonishing something we dislike about our own self; therefore, when we view something in another person about whom we find fault, this is Karma showing us what we are or what we have become. Herein lies the key to this aspect of the third principle. More than likely, the objection is not only something we dislike about our self, but is also an opportunity for us to acknowledge it so we may then be able to change or remove that particular character trait from within us. In truth, at the same moment our denunciation is raised, the Law of Humility is also offering us an inner resolution with the exact same trait, but only if we do not object to what we see in the other being.

My personal experience with the tiger was very humbling in so many ways, from my initial hair-raising objection of him through my fears, to my awe and appreciation for him – a huge, powerful, yet gentle creature – to my traveling companion. Keeping in mind this big cat weighed between four and five-hundred pounds, he moved in graceful silence, never hearing him in the forest unless he wanted me to, and became a great teacher to watch and observe. Aside from his natural ability as the fearless hunter, his behavior remained flexible and so gentle, very humble in each activity to the degree he seemed to actually honor life, taking only what he needed. What did I learn? Simply begin to accept my objections, and like so many other things, they will soon dissipate. Let us take a look at how this all works in our everyday interactions.

Let us first recall the last principle: *You attract to you what you are, not what you want.* Are you beginning to recognize how these principles overlap and lead into the other? As an example, let us choose an everyday interaction. Suppose you fault another person for handling themselves in a glaringly arrogant fashion. In that moment of judgment, what you may not realize is their arrogance may simply be stronger than yours, or they may be better at showing it, in which case you could feel a twinge of envy in that moment, the undercurrent. What if they are truly confident in what they do? Confidence and arrogance are two distinctly different ideas which may appear the same. The first has its basis in truth and the second is based on fear or illusion. The first is solid strength and the second is actually weakness. The first does not explain itself and the second shall do so frequently. You see, the essence of humility is when an individual is truly peaceful and loving life, when the person applies absolutely no admonishments and always allows others to solely be who they are.

Through our objection to the behavior or personality of other beings, we are essentially telling them they cannot be who they are. We have now just transformed ourselves into a rigid, inflexible mode of operation. Of course we now run the risk of creating a physical enemy, when initially there was none. In truth, it is up to the other person to decide how they choose to act, not us. In fact, we have no right to determine how another person should or should not act. The behavior exhibited by every being is theirs alone, for it has nothing to do with us. We have no reason to judge them for whom they choose to be. Consider this, if we do not initially have that internal attribute to which we strongly object, how could it ever become an issue with any other? It cannot. We could all learn to not admonish others as much as we do, and living humbly will create this for any individual while giving awe to life. There is one caveat in this. There are times when truth may appear to be judgment and the way to discern the difference is this: are you looking at the physical only through physical eyes or are you looking at it through your higher nature? Do not fool yourself by allowing your ego to answer this question.

In this part of the world, it appears we have a high level of urgency to constantly tell other people how they should or should not be in any given circumstance, a compulsion to which I believe we have been conditioned. Who are we for doing this? What right do we truly have to do this? Do we really want others to be just like us? Would that not be a bit boring? Who knows you better than you? Wisdom dictates we are better off tending our own house while leaving other homes alone. I am not surprised to see and hear so many disagreements, for we are all plowing malevolently through life, apparently behaving quite contrary to our truly humble and natural nature. Another contrary behavior is an individual's insistence for being correct in all things. This begs the question, "Is it right to impose our right on another individual?" Just because other people do not see or do things our way does not imply we are correct to object. What is the bottom line here? Remember to be *who* you are, not *what* you are. If you spend all your time listening to what others are telling you about you, and you choose to change you only to please them so they like you, you have then lost who you are. At some point, because of this, you will not be a happy individual nor shall you ever become empowered in your own life. Though you now live in this manner, Karma says at some point, you will have to learn who you are. The message is: do not give you away, and this will not have to occur in your life.

Purely as another example without any intention of stepping on toes, let us say you find fault with someone else's choice of apparel for the evening, stating that what they have chosen is inappropriate. What is being offered here? Are you not actually more concerned about your own image and fashion statement? From a Karmic perspective, you are experiencing what could easily be termed as insecurity in how you appear to others, for a secure person would dress in any way they so choose without any concern for the styles currently in vogue. That individual is truly very comfortable with who they are and what they wear. Forgive me, but as the person passing judgment on their appearance, you may have another set of circumstances to work out since you may be more about impressing others rather than truly being yourself. This is not living the Law of Humility! Perhaps you disagree with this idea, and that is definitely all right. Merely

consider that you just may have stepped out of the realm of pure equality into the realm of pure "better than" inequality, which enters the field of arrogance. Karmically speaking, if we happen to downplay another for how they look, we are now guaranteed to have a very similar experience due to the return action.

Not only are we coming from a level of insecurity, but we are also coming from a high level of arrogance, an "I know better than you" attitude, with insecurity as the undercurrent. Downplaying another person for their appearance or choice of apparel has its basis in our thinking we may possibly feel better about ourselves; the exact opposite is the truth. By doing something of this nature at the expense of another person, we realize no gain in it whatsoever; in fact, we will only experience greater Karmic returns right before our very eyes, most likely unaware of the connection as the activity unfolds. In truth, no one human behaves or dresses any better than another since this is the basis of the third principle. When a person does not bother to act according to this Law, it can essentially be promised that they will be humiliated by an upcoming experience, the greatest teacher of this principle, during which their usual fit of anger will only magnify Karmic action. Now they will have two things to work through in place of one. Are you noticing how Karma may easily compound?

Uniqueness and individuality are indeed such special attributes and is a wonderful gift of life. This may also be what creates insecurity amongst other interesting emotional impacts but these are not so insurmountable because it is our uniqueness. Personally, be open to this so that you become *you*. Apparently though, from personal observation, the majority of people feel more comfortable being like somebody else – just illusion – yet we witness it everywhere. Although we may consider it harmless to emulate a so-called hero or a mentor, the fact remains, we are actually denying our own individualism. This will subsequently draw to us other like kind people who are also living in the same form of individual denial, all in accordance with Karmic return action. If we gossip about or downplay any thing, another return action will surround us with others who gossip or downplay. Abiding by the old adage is the greatest lesson here: live and let live – complete humility.

When you envision a monastery, do you believe the monks all shave their heads and dress alike so they may be nearly identical? Your belief does have merit, though it is based only on their outward appearance. In truth, however, their presentation is all about celebrating individuality. If, instead, you are willing to see the monks as simple cells making up the whole structure, then you will understand when it is stated that their appearance actually represents the true idea of the human specie, wholly connected to the structure's consciousness while maintaining individual identity. You see, for the most part, all monks act, look, talk, weigh, and work differently without any insecurity about their attributes, solely because they realize, from their individuality without question, they are able to develop and retain their internal peacefulness and attain consciousness because of the realization of individual nature. And it follows, their acceptance is unconditional when they visit any other monastery. When our layers of insecurity are peeled back to reveal the truth to our divine distinction, our authentic nature with which we were born may then unfurl, thereby waking us up to the realization that we are not all supposed to look or act alike under any circumstance, that we are supposed to interact with each other unconditionally. Remember, we are not about what we look like. We are about who we are since our genuine internal part matters the most. Unfortunately, denial will not lead us directly to this attribute. But truth will.

As you journey with me throughout this book, you will come to understand that Karma contains many aspects when viewed through its numerous levels of meaning, similar to peering through each facet of a diamond. The Law of Humility is no exception. Before you are introduced to another aspect of this third principle, allow me to ask you a question first, "Do you create personal pain while you deny the truth about yourself?" … "No?" … "Are you so certain?" Okay, stay with me here. I am well aware most humans truly do not believe they are causing their own pain, be it emotional, mental, or physical. But as a student in monk 101, you most certainly do! Interestingly enough, we honestly think we are able to contentedly live contrary to our true authentic self. The fact is, doing so has indeed successfully induced the illusion of a false reality, an experience void of true contentment, a life filled with pain, anger, unworthiness, and disease

among others, all brought about by Karmic action. "What, Karma is doing this to us?" you may ask. No. We do it to ourselves. It is from our self-deception, our self-denial of the true self which must in turn create a life of deception solely through the mechanism of Karmic return action.

Here is another point to ponder. Perhaps living in this false reality has un-nerved us internally to the degree we genuinely feel uneasy, or ill at ease, or *dis*-eased with life. Could this unsettling feeling be a valid cause behind all human disease and illness? From my perspective, one genuinely cannot say no for certain. Living in truth, on the other hand, leads us to our authenticity, engendering our divinity by becoming who we were originally intended to be, thereby dissolving any urge or need to downplay another human, or to show arrogance to the extent that we do in this part of the world. If we live in truth, there is no denial and life becomes authentic. If we do not live in truth, life becomes unauthentic, a lie of sorts. The truth is, in our reality there is nothing wrong or in error about living a lie. We simply live life as it is not.

Imagine if you will, the human species living completely in a genuine state and in peace through the idea of true self acceptance. What kind of world would we then be living in? We could live by the truth of who we are or, while denying the truth, we could live by the deception of what we have become. Although this sounds like a choice, in the great scheme of things, there is really none on this matter, for it is simply as two sides of a coin, both sides livable, yet one side clearer than the other, one having the propensity to create greater levels of struggle while the other offers a path of peace, one side a façade, the other expressing deep humility in its finest form.

Why struggle by swimming upstream when we can effortlessly float downstream with the current? When we live as others, we do not live our life for our self, and by living in this fashion, life becomes greatly confined wherefrom some of us may never get to know who we truly are since we are so busy living for others. We will have more on the results of this in a later chapter. I have met many people in my life who were always attempting to find out who they were. How can

they, when they spend so much time being like everyone else? You know, there lies a truth behind those moments when you have the feeling you do not belong, a time when you are the square peg being pushed into the round hole. Does this ever work? Through Karmic principles, you are simply being shown that you are not living your life in truth, that you are actually attempting to fit in a life of denial. Never deny you! Be who you were born as, because only in this way you need never impress anyone or need ever figure out who you are, for you are living that truth. It is not so much about what others think as it is about what you think. Which side of the coin do you prefer, the side of denial or the side of truth?

While denying the truth of our self – most people do – we create any number of mental and emotional pains or stresses because we are living as we are not. In fact, based on personal experience in this part of the world, I have met many *dis*-eased people who deny their truth. Ironically, most of us are not aware of this; yet, it is still the truth. To use one instance let us say you just met a very angry individual; yet, when you ask them about their anger they pop off in a fit of anger, all the while denying it! How can this be, since it appears totally irrational? I mean, wouldn't an angry person realize they are an angry person? One would tend to think so; yet, it appears they are completely unaware of what they deny. And this type of reaction also holds true for those who are frustrated, hurt, impatient, judgmental, revengeful, even irrational, etc.

"Is there an answer for this?" you could ask. Yes, we will offer a simple one. If a person is angry for years, it internalizes as their very nature and they simply become accustomed to its routine; subsequently, the anger is automatically and unknowingly expressed through every spoken word and action. Believe it or not, they never intend to do so the majority of time, but after years it is purely automatic and is no longer noticeable by that individual. Living from anger or any of the above traits is quite painful, ultimately harming one's overall health.

You may have heard modern psychology suggest that if you repeat anything for twenty-one days in a row it becomes a new behavior pattern then subsequently goes into what is termed your autonomic

system. The behavior now becomes a natural mode of your day-to-day operation, hidden from your own awareness but not from others'. Put another way, as a student in a monastery, you have repeatedly followed a well-worn path for at least twenty-one days, a routine into which you have now fallen, its rut clearly blinding you to what you do. This is precisely how this sort of illusion occurs in your life, one which Master Lobsang suggested I become keenly aware of by watching my own habits, routines, and all what I do. Perhaps this is the reason why he did not walk with me on the path that day, and to think I actually rationalized it as the easiest way to go! Herein rests the dilemma of routines in mental and emotional patterns, for they have the propensity to negate levels of humility which is why we may also become so rigid in our experiences. When change arrives it is interesting for us to handle as we now must shift how we view ourselves; if not, struggle arrives on the scene.

If you suspect there could be yet another Karmic return from not living in truth, I do agree. Why do you suppose a person enters so-called depression? Although there may exist many contributions, more times than not, however, the process is based on the moment a person rejects them self or believes in their unworthiness. Without question, humans are prone to the extreme; therefore, does it not make sense to know these two denials are both extreme falsehoods? If the state of depression is allowed to continue for a lengthy period of time, the affected one must then submit to a life of prescription drugs, a regulated regimen of anti-depressants. All of this is simply caused because they went to extremes on the original idea of non-acceptance by others and they consequently slipped into perpetual self-rejection. "Steven, what you are saying is rather extreme in and of itself, you know," you may suggest. Are you so sure? There is one thing in Western culture which does not receive much consideration or importance. Our very own mind and how it is used. As was stressed in a previous chapter, our mind is the most powerful aspect we have. If allowed to gallivant aimlessly, it shall develop whatsoever character traits it deems appropriate, thus binding us to them. Do you realize what is most fascinating? The mind can actually convince us we are unworthy, not because it is the truth of us, but because we accept the mind's denial of our divine intent! The most wondrous part is, if the

mind can journey into the abysmal depths of depression, then it can also lead us out of it once we master our mind.

This makes perfect sense, for the mind is just as able to create illness as well as health; therefore, it comes down to how we use this powerful, effective, human dynamic. You see, the mind chooses our experience, which is why we must be present with it by always remaining aware and living each moment in order to know what our mind is choosing. If it chooses depression then that is exactly where our depression resides, in choice, and if left as an anchor with our emotion, the depression certainly shall affect our physical body. Generally in our current culture, the mind makes the choice for us in nearly every instance even though we adamantly think we make the choice for the mind. You may disagree. So I ask you, "Looking at world events – international finance, trade, government, monetary systems, so-called terrorism and wars – does our species really know what the mind is creating for us?" I humbly offer to all, become mindful. Learn to harness your mind. If you do, personal denial and a deceptive lifestyle shall swiftly cease. Keep in mind, we are not just the body alone; the truth is, the body is the vehicle to give us experience only.

With a harnessed mind, a mastered mind, we will have absolutely no need to downplay or criticize another, for if we do, we now must apply this to our self as well. Arrogance also will fall to the wayside once the mind is mastered. And we would never need to synthetically formulate different thought patterns, the underlying purpose for drug use. With a disciplined mind we would each return to our basic nature by expressing as divine and humble beings, living "...in our image and likeness," as our eyes open, adjusting to rediscover an awe-inspiring life.

In the East, a monk would teach by using their waking stick, reminding the student that mind is first cause in their everyday life, and to not allow the mind to control them but to focus it. At least to me, it seems if we truly want to fill our self with self-discovery, focusing the mind would be very instrumental in that discovery. Well, how else would you be able to accomplish this other than through the mind? Just what else do we actually have? Most have no clue what their mind is doing while it goes on creating each moment of their very own life. However, once the mind becomes focused, that individual shall become empowered to the infinite degree and be able to maintain implicit control of their life by simply controlling their mind and each thought it generates. They would also fully realize their infinite connection with every being and all things. I now ask you two questions. "In reality, do you believe change can come into your life from denying who you are? Do you believe your ego is so materially driven and lost in illusions that you truly deny who you actually are?" If you answer no to both, I offer the suggestion that you do some genuine introspection. If yes to both, you then have a greater opportunity of training a very powerful storehouse of energy – your mind.

What is the point of all this? Denial ultimately gains us nothing. It purely clouds and dulls the mind, at best. "So why do we resist the truth?" The answer is? "Those in the Western culture have never been taught self-truth…until now, hopefully. Instead, most are taught to be somebody other than who they are since birth." Yes, we know the truth with the outer circumstances, but we do not know the truth with our inner realm. Why is this so difficult today? First, receiving approval is vitally important during our early childhood and it grows with us into adulthood. We began to experience rejection when we learned of our acceptance in some things yet not in others, thereby avoiding the things which brought on rejection in favor of those which brought constant approval. A pivotal point to ponder over, what if most of the things from which we were rejected during our early years were truly intended to occur but only for that one moment? Yet, as a human going in the opposite extreme, we immediately denied our true self purely from our fear of another rejection as an adult.

Later in our informative years, we watch television, mesmerized with every show and commercial while each broadcast taught us to be someone else. How about those hair coloring commercials? Why do we persist in doing this? Who said we are better off to hide or deny a very natural process? On whose authority must we believe gray hair equates to an unattractive and unproductive stage in our life? Ah yes, we better do it for fear of rejection! What a grand illusion, for

aging is a natural process of life. Do you know in the Far East, the younger generation deeply respects those with gray and white hair, for the color symbolizes great wisdom and life knowledge? Again from television, do you remember watching the blondes having more fun? To make an extreme point solely from this message and if any one of us wants to eliminate rejection from our life, the television says we had better color our hair blonde in order to remain beautiful, productive and to have more fun than anyone else. What is up with this?

Sadly, if the viewer does not do what the television says, they must resign to accept denial and believe in their insecurity. Oh well, no one sees denial or insecurity; therefore, they are not real. On the contrary, they are profitable illusions at your expense! Keep this one point in mind if you may: things do not make the human; the human makes the things. With all the areas of our daily life on which external influences play, no wonder we have so many neuroses in our part of the world! Looking at the statistics for India, we might think they have a tremendous number of diseases; however, on a per capita basis, the number is quite low. Cancer, for instance, occurs in less than five percent. The United States exceeds thirty percent! The incidence of prostate cancer is virtually non-existent in China, yet is reaching new levels nearly every day in this country. Why such a high number or rampant rate of cases in a country which supposedly has the best, the brightest, and the most? Medical science will most likely and emphatically argue no on this next point. Based on Karma being exactly what it is and your own understanding of what you now know of it, can you truly disregard a potential link between these diseases and our current level of insecurity and denial? Monks know every disease has a first cause, but most are actually unknown to physical science. If there is indeed a missing link in the human evolution, perhaps it truly occurs between our relationship with our self and disease.

Again, the third principle of Karma in our series is the Law of Humility, a principle wholly designed with the imbedded purpose of creating graceful humans. It is not so much about *what we think we are*, as it is *who we really are* in life. It is best to remember, that

which we attempt to resist is going to not only stay with us, but will also become magnified through the misuse of our mind, eventually becoming our so-called internal enemy. If we are not mindful, the ego steps in to create the illusions in which most of us participate. The Principle of Humility can assist us to alleviate this potential, but we must learn to operate with it. Resistance is generally an ego issue for us to work through. We all have greater purpose than the way in which we now operate with things because we come from smallness in place of our true greatness.

These principles will lead us to that higher purpose and that divine greatness if we simply allow them to operate with the power of our knowing, not only *of* them but also in the proper *use* of them. None may be avoided, but they can be utilized. By so doing, we would gain more direct control of our life than we could ever have imagined. Today we think we have control. But there is one more question, "Do we really?" If we do, we then would not give so much energy to so many external things which in turn create our smallness! Let us shed our self from smallness as naturally as a snake sheds its skin, thus moving into the next principle which shows us how we grow and become what we do. May you internalize and utilize these wonderful dynamics of Karma in peace and grace. Once a person experiences their true nature and dynamics they arrive at a very humbling experience in their lives as they come to realize the true divinity of all of life, humbling by its very nature.

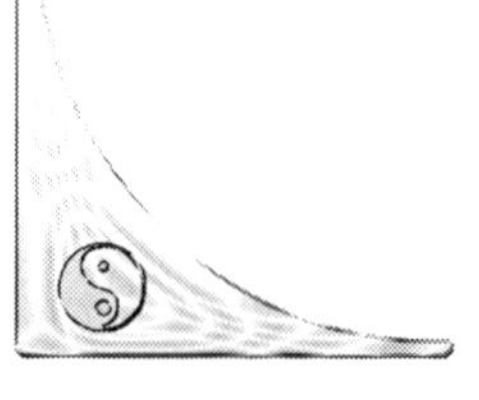

"Truth is perfect and complete in itself. It is not something newly discovered; it has always existed."
Zen Master Dogan

~ Chapter V ~
The Principle of Growth

You may be somewhat puzzled as to the reason why Karma includes a Principle which appears so glaringly obvious since growth is witnessed all around us each moment of our life. We are not talking only of the physical idea of growth, but all its aspects of the human condition, and it is unavoidable. In the last chapter we talked about the idea of change. Change is growth, so why struggle? It is quite natural. Although I feel most of us either overlook this principle in its entirety or deem it as self-evident – even trite – I humbly ask you to reconsider. In truth, the Law of Growth is infallible and absolute by its very nature as it seamlessly intertwines with the other principles, each pointing directly to our self. As an analogy, if we overlook the small stone in our path, it may be the very one we stumble over. Relating to life and our journey, we are not to overlook anything, no matter how small or innocuous it may appear to us at that moment in time. As mentioned earlier, Karma teaches us to see every thing as equal. There is no small stone, only a new discovery, a new realization, a new beginning in all moments – growth.

While walking with Master Lobsang on a particularly beautiful spring day, he suddenly stopped dead in his tracks, tilted his head forward as his gaze locked onto something. When I politely stopped a few steps behind him, as is customary for a student, he immediately waved his hand, motioning me over to his side. He subsequently

pointed his index finger towards a caterpillar crawling beside the grass, gliding noiselessly and effortlessly atop the ground as an undulating waveform in perfect phase. Turning to me he quietly asked, "Do you see it?" "Yes," I whispered my reply, along with a bewildered face screaming, "So what?" A fact about monks: they are as children with open eyes and innocent minds, surveying life with absolute amazement without any attachment to it. They approach all things and people as though for the first time, all the while displaying a deep wisdom in their childlike wonder. It is an amazing experience being around hundreds of people who live in this manner, and to think every human can wherever they live. "Young man, you do not see the truth of the creature?" he softly asked when he took notice of my perplexed expression, his eyes revealing to me the real magnificence of the worm.

As I looked down to genuinely study the hairy caterpillar, Master Lobsang continued, "All things have such great significance in our world because all life supports each other. If we do not have the precise creatures throughout the world as we do, the human would not exist." "This simple caterpillar has this capability?" I asked wide-eyed in amazement. "Yes," he firmly replied, "Even the most seemingly insignificant creature has its importance to life if for no other reason that it simply exists. All things contribute to life." Continuing, "You have the ability to realize this. The caterpillar does not." "Does it even know we are here?" I asked, intrigued now with my teacher's lesson. Master Lobsang squatted next to the caterpillar, "Yes, but not in the same sense as we know it is here. Sure it is aware of our presence, that we will not harm it; however, it does not know we are human." While pressing his hands against his knees he stood upright, and we walked again in silence.

After a short time, Master Lobsang looked over at me and described the fourth principle of Karma, beginning with, "Nothing in life is insignificant. All things have purpose." You see, this is precisely why monks will not harm any living thing, simply because they understand the magnificence and importance of its life. All of life – thought, emotion, and experience – has honor to it. Regardless of the Karmic consequence or return action, a monk will unwaveringly

and continually honor life each and every moment. "The idea is to live an honorable life," Master Lobsang offered me, "It is not so much as what you do as it is in how you live with what you do." He proceeded, "The human is the most special of all; yet, we do not fully realize this as our true nature. Your Bible gives us an idea of just how significant we are in the phrase that we have dominion over all things. It does not mean we are greater than all things, for the Divine only creates in equal terms. This purely means we have the ability to realize life, when all other living creatures do not. And because of this realization, we also have direct influence on it. Although every living thing, including the human, lives under the true Divine Law, humans will not do so until they come to understand their Divine nature. Through this realization, we in reality would have true dominion over all things! We live our lives as though we are actually above this life and for this reason we do not live in harmony with life. In truth we actually fight life, and by so doing, the realization of our divine nature remains ever in front of us instead of where it belongs, within us. This is where the experience of divine must reside, within us." I was always amazed at how he stated his ideas by unraveling their complexities so I may view their seeming simplicity. He always had a way of taking the simplest or smallest of thing and transformed it into a thing of magnificence and beauty.

Master Lobsang offered me this thought, "You in America have very little reverence for anything, most especially for yourselves; therefore, you are not able to see it in anything else. This is the way of Karma. You spend too much time being other than who you are. If you truly understand the Law of Growth, it would change your view of the world, your self, and most especially life." "What is the Law of Growth?" I asked. He simply stated, "It is about not avoiding who we are as individuals." In concept the Law of Growth is this: *Wherever you go there you are.* "Well, duh!" I laughed aloud. "This is what you do not understand," he explained. "All humans would end up traveling all over the world just to get away from their life, not ever realizing that no matter what they attempt, they do so in the reverse order." You see, we are not able to get away from either our self or our life because they both follow us wherever we go, do they not? No matter how long we search for a way, no matter how much we attempt or think we can, the fourth principle so concisely states: *Wherever you go there you are*. Wherever your travels may take you, whatever the circumstances you may be experiencing, whoever you are currently involved with, there you are, right smack in the middle of it all. Unless you can jump out of your skin, I admit the Law of Growth is absolutely and totally unavoidable. We cannot avoid our self, just as we cannot avoid the small stone in the middle of our path, over which we can easily and quickly stumble only because we failed to see it.

Do you know of anyone who excitedly informed you they were moving, perhaps as far as from one side of the country to the other? They were eager to get away from relationships and circumstances by which they were currently surrounded, and genuinely spoke of hoping to free themselves from their circumstances in order to lead a healthier life. Did you receive word some time later about how they found themselves in the same situation, surrounded by almost the same identical circumstances which inexplicably "found" them? They left a Karmic cycle! Expressed another way, even though they changed locations, they still took all their emotional and mind baggage along with their physical self, and only for a short time, feeling free and detached in the newness. What they did not realize is that they still remained exactly who they previously had been. Only the faces and places changed.

As Master Lobsang suggested, we do it in reverse order. Karma implies we are the creator of our own life, and by first changing our self, all those people, places, and things which no longer "fit" our new self shall effortlessly and forever fall to the wayside. Remember the second principle? *You attract to you what you are, not what you want.* Herein lies the reason why the circumstances remained the same in the new location. If you seek different people, first become different within your self, then all things around you shall become different. And to think this may be done without ever moving! Karma says nothing about first renting a U-Haul or moving. You see, people move in a genuine attempt to avoid; however, they overlook the most vital aspect in their current situation, them self! To prevent changing your life in the direction you prefer it to go, by all means rent a U-Haul,

in which case you will never be able to change you or your personal circumstances. If I may suggest, take the Karmic road instead; do not avoid you.

Truly, how may anyone accomplish self-avoidance? It would appear so many may be attempting avoidance, and when we blame, this is the key to this one realization. If memory serves me, I recall an earlier principle: *You attract to you what you are, not what you want*, meaning you bring into your experience what you, yourself, already are. Put another way, what is the common thread between all our experiences and relationships, knowing full well that people, places, and objects may come and go as the ocean tide? Who shows up every time in your classroom of life, constantly and continually? Just as my personal attendance record is perfect for my class, I am very certain your record is also blemish-free. We discussed self-denial in the last chapter, and I wish to take a different tact and discuss self-avoidance in this one, to which the Law of Growth pertains. Are they similar? Do they mean the same? Denial – a noun – means, "…disbelief in the existence or reality of a thing…" such as ignoring the truth as previously shared. It also means, "…an unconscious defense mechanism used to reduce anxiety by denying thoughts, feelings, or facts that are consciously intolerable." Avoid, on the other hand, is a verb, and means, "…to keep away from; keep clear of; to prevent from happening." In this context, how can any human avoid themselves? Even multiple personalities exist in the same body! Certainly we are capable of denying anything and anyone through our entire life in order to avoid their existence; however, we are not capable of keeping away from our self. Even though it appears the vast majority earnestly attempts to do this in a variety of ways, avoidance does not work. Karma shows this constantly.

The Law of Growth simply tells us we are not able to avoid our self, making its statement absolutely appropriate: *Wherever you go there you are*. If we are not able to avoid us, then reason suggests, we are also not able to avoid our experiences since we are always with us. In fact, it is precisely because of Karmic return action, created by us, that we are given these experiences in the first place. No one else can. This is the leading cause why avoidance or denial simply does not do anyone any favors in the long run, for we are the cause and truth of our life in every respect. As mentioned earlier, experiences are a reflection of us, and they actually reveal our teachers when we choose to accept them as such. The Law of Growth reveals why.

In essence, this is what Master Lobsang was teaching me that day through the simple life of the caterpillar, along with recognizing the importance and presence of all things in our world. He shared with me, "This Law is about creating our very own personal surroundings. If we do not change then our surroundings will never change either." Through this fourth principle, Karma only attempts to guide and assist us, moving us into what is required to affect the proper change(s.) If we are stuck on a path of avoidance, Karma will essentially attempt to cut that path off until we come face-to-face with what we avoid. A pivotal point here, each and every principle of Karma thus far offers one fundamental idea, the idea of our creative ability. Karma faithfully and meticulously demonstrates how we are internally creating through what we have created, called our external experience.

No matter the distance or direction they go to get away, if a person thinks they constantly have problems, those same problems come right along, just like soft gum sticking onto the sole of their shoe when stepped upon. The phrase, "When we move, we take our baggage with us," includes not only our physical possessions, but more importantly our internal ones, inevitably the most important ones. So what do we do? Stop avoiding them. Face them head-on! Learn from them so they can dissipate and go away. This is the only way we may work through anything. As Master Lobsang offered, "This Law is about our creation of our own personal surroundings, and if we do not change, then in actuality nothing around us has changed either."

As shared with you earlier, we are creators in our world, or co-creators if you will; therefore, if we prefer to create new circumstances in our life, simply change our mind. Master Lobsang looked at me one day and said, "Young man, do you like your life?" At that time my answer was no, and he said to simply *change* my mind. At first I thought he had offered sarcastic humor, but later I found out his answer was right on, especially when I slowly changed my mind in

how I saw me in my life. My life then began to change. It changed all on its own while I simply made the decision to shift my mind into a different direction and different thought streams. This in turn shifted my self-perceptions from what others told me I was to what I truly was. This is not an easy task to accomplish due to the numerous mental routines we may have established through the years, but if we remain objective with our thought forms and patterns, then it can be accomplished. It takes diligence of mind and thought for this shift of inner dynamics to take place, which in turn, affects our outer world. Now we no longer need move from where we are to attempt to become someone else. It is an inner, not outer, solution.

Only by first changing our mind can it then change us and then our life so we can change our experience. Do you now recognize the order? This may not appear so easy at times; however, the catch is to merely keep our mind focused on the new idea until it arrives, keeping it all in present time, not a future moment. Ironically, the mind itself effortlessly yields to change; yet, seemingly at the same moment, the change can manifest only with extreme difficulty, all because of our daily routine, the mental process into which we have unknowingly fallen. If this is the case, we now return to personal responsibility, trapped in our old worn grooves of routine mind as we continue to carry our old issues with us no matter our journey. Be aware of one thing though. We best not blame the new experiences and relationships or anything else for our old issues, for they belong only to us. On the other hand, if we watch for the small stones on our own path, we will avoid many of these mental routines or stumbles.

Here is a simple exercise to do. Practice being totally aware of your thoughts each moment you are in. This is mindfulness. Through awareness, the mind shifts much more readily, like wind blowing across desert dunes, effortlessly creating new patterns on their surface. Relating to our mind, new patterns of thought lift us out from the deep ruts of routine just like the path I was walking on with my teacher. This in turn shifts our patterns in life with wondrous ease. Remember, it is your mind, and the moment you grasp control of it, the mind will do whatever you desire of it, for it can no longer cling to what it had previously done. Remove the grooves and let your

life shift on its own accord. Allow it to seamlessly transform and unfold you into a different you. "What just happened to me?" You have grown.

As mentioned above, it has been suggested that we remove all blame for our relationships and circumstances. This leads us into the direction of accepting full responsibility for the people, places, and things around us, ultimately including our entire life. After all, it is ours and here is where our focus must lie. Why are people in our life in the first place? We attracted them to us for perfectly Divine reasons, and only when we understand their purpose will we then be released from the relationship, allowing it to close naturally and harmoniously. Keep in mind, however, do not attempt to figure them out for what they are, for it is not about them; instead, figure out why they apply to who you are. Only by realizing their purpose in your life at that particular time will you get to know your self completely, for every place, person, thing, and relationship, is a teacher to you. From this deeper understanding, your growth automatically occurs under this very principle, the Law of Growth. All people and the experiences they bring are teachers and bring in to your life the dynamics which show you what you create in the way of change or no change. They may be the very dynamic necessary to show you how to change in your own life. People are always there for a reason so accept it and learn to appreciate them for what they bring into your life. By approaching people in this manner then all people and the subsequent experiences become part of your personal education. From this viewpoint, all sorts of confrontations are automatically removed, for the most part. My hope is that you understand this vital concept.

For emphasis I would like to repeat a sentence from the above paragraph. "…only when we understand their purpose will we then be released from the relationship, allowing it to close naturally and harmoniously." Mind you, attempting to forcefully remove someone from your life may in reality only create immeasurable and unnecessary stress for you both. This alone may generate the high probability of a negative Karmic return, which now may require a healing for either or both of you. Ponder on this: when you force a person from your life,

you will most likely get to experience the same type of relationship all over again in order to acquire the full lesson which was originally necessary. Have you ever experienced the same or similar repeating relationships? Have you noticed repeating cycles in your experiences? The purpose of these cycles is to show us that there has been little or no forward movement in those very arenas. No growth. And there you still are.

The same holds true for all your current circumstances. Simply moving away does not remove them, they only re-move back to you! Nothing in life requires force. Ever! From a monk's perspective, allow the relationship or circumstance to close or move away from you, in their own time and by their own accord. You see, by shifting your thought patterns, by changing your mind to release them, they will automatically, effortlessly, and harmoniously move away, dissipating on their very own, allowing the shift for the new experiences to arrive in your life. This path creates a positive release, free from any future healing or cycles, free from any long-term regrets or need to look back at the past, thus allowing you to easily remain present in the moment. There is no hurry or urgency in this process, for you will have the clarity of mind to glean all things which are necessary for you from each person or event.

On the other hand, if you clamp onto what has now become an unnecessary relationship or circumstance, struggle shall most assuredly ensue and an unhealthy life will consequently develop. Allow me to ask you a question. "Now that you know how Karma can work either for or against you, knowing how it can return either a positive or negative experience based solely on your choice, in which direction do you prefer Karma to work?" If you want Karma to work for you, simply observe what you are struggling with in your life. Look through your eyes of objectivity, so you may see where adjustments can be made in your mind, hence mentally seeing the resolution. Release and let Karma handle the details for you. It is perfectly understandable how challenging this may be since we are so used to making things happen. Be assured, it is guaranteed much simpler to allow things to happen through the actions of Karma; besides, in this manner, struggle cannot occur as circumstances shift and change for you, harmoniously and automatically.

Before you feel completely overwhelmed with the onset of severe responsibility disorder, let us just stop here for a moment. Relax. Let us start at the beginning of things by first considering just one event. What exactly is an event? Personally speaking, an event is created only when a minimum of two things occur. What does 'occur' mean? "…to be met with or found; present itself; appear." In my words, therefore, an event is created only when a minimum of two things meet or find each other, or when they present themselves, or when they both appear at the same place and time. As one example, what is the event called when both cold and warm air collide? A storm. Which event is formed when cold air and a lot of moisture are combined? A snowflake. What do you call the event when you touch your index finger on the hot stovetop? Where am I going with this?! Well, every event must consist of at least two parts; therefore, as its way of learning and growing in this wonderful world of ours, the human species must interact with at least one other thing. Experience, therefore, becomes manifest only between us, and something or someone else. In light of this reasoning, is there such a thing as a one-sided argument? We may honestly think so because we genuinely believe we can argue with ourselves at times, most especially when the other person never utters a single word. This is not really the case, however, since we are actually arguing over two sides of the exact same coin, a single perception. Do we not agree with our own argument each and every time? Remember, between two points of view will an argument ensue, but only if both points of view are not allowed. If both are flexible then there is no argument necessary. It can be as simple as this.

In our reality is there such a thing as a one-sided love affair? Although a narcissist may desire it to be true, this is just the finest example of possibly pure arrogance. Have you ever known anyone having a physical love affair with them self? Based on my understanding, however, it takes at least two people to become involved in order for these two events, an argument and love affair, to take place. When played out, they develop into what is termed as their experience. If it takes more than one person to cause an event, then does it not follow that each person in that event must assume an equal share of responsibility for the occurrence? Generally speaking, when two people enter a relationship then each must accept fifty percent responsibility. For a two-person argument, they each have a fifty percent stake in the event; otherwise, when five people get pulled and become lively in the argument, then each of the five must accept twenty percent. This is true with all events, personally or globally.

What am I leading to? Only when we accept personal responsibility do we then assume full accountability for our own action, not the action taken by any other, though many times we attempt to do so. When we accept the blame and responsibility for an action taken by another, especially for our children, we just did two things: 1) we personally created a path of denial for the other person; 2) we ultimately affected our own self-worth by taking the blame for something we never did. And if we berate ourselves for doing this, or when we perform any action for that matter, we dissolve our self-worth by choosing a negative approach; hence, nearly guaranteeing we are going to do it yet again. The always-guiding Karmic return! And here is the bottom line. Although we believe we are helping others when accepting their blame, we are actually no different than a thief. "What?! No different than a thief? *Really?*" your face shows. By now this should certainly come as no surprise. When we accept the responsibility for any other, do we not take something away from them which does not belong to us? We actually take away their personal responsibility through our acceptance of it and to think that we actually believe we are avoiding a potential struggle. In reality we are not because we are actually weakening them in their life's journey and in their lessons. By doing so, we shall encumber many lessons from Karma on responsibility which means we would be placed in many uncomfortable situations. How may one have the true depth of experience if they do not have responsibility for it?

A two-part question is in order here. Do you seek growth so you do not create the same negative experiences all over again, or do you attempt to remain the same in order to avoid growth? These parts appear silly; nonetheless, they are extremely valid. They are valid because we all seem to repeat so many experiences and there is a reason for the repeats. Karma. Most people seem to desire to remain the same as opposed to allowing the natural process of growth to take place in their life. I humbly offer the suggestion that you never avoid

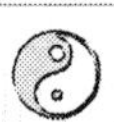

or even attempt to avoid who you truly are, for this is the best path, if not the only one, which you may take.

You see, when we assume this level of being we will face certain music of course, but it shall fade away the moment we observe it, face-to-face, only to then begin anew in another direction with greater, more empowered purpose. Interestingly enough, we cannot avoid growth because it is simply part and parcel to the process of life, even when we think we can remain static. Spiritually, we are each personally responsible for how and in which direction we grow. We are not born a thief; we grow into being one through personal choice. Forgive me, we are not born unworthy or a sinner; we grow into these traits through personal choice, just as we may do for any character trait. The Law of Growth, therefore, is paramount in its significance to all of us, on an individual basis.

Chances are you have overheard someone declare at one time or another, "I like myself just the way I am." Just what is implied here? They no longer wish to change? Life is about constant change, and when we choose to stay the same, there no longer is any forward movement or growth. The truth is, that person just accepted an illusion because there is never any way to literally stop change. It may only be slowed at best, but of course, struggle will arise. The ancient texts reveal that we are each born in this world for our soul to experience and grow. We are to grow so we may accept self-realization and enlightenment within our very own temple of life. But by attempting to remain rigidly static, we essentially place our soul in stasis wherein it's ever-loving and infinite patience will allow us to return yet again and again so it may accomplish its goal, not our physical goals. In other words, those who refuse change will become rigid, unbending, stubborn, and resistant to new things and experiences as they trudge through their timeworn road to the degree of repeating their cycles, completely ignorant of the reason. On the other hand, by allowing for change, we create more of an adventure to life as things always unfold right before us.

Generally speaking, people honestly believe both positive and negative experiences exist; however, a great teacher who lived around

two-thousand years ago once stated a Universal Principle: a house divided cannot stand. It shall simply succumb during a period of difficulty or struggle. Metaphysically speaking, we as the human cannot stand because we divide our house of experiences through either positive or negative judgment. In truth, they are simply experiences to have. The funny thing is, as co-creator, we had originally chosen them through which we may grow; yet, here we are, declaring each one as either a positive or negative, good or bad circumstance. This is most fascinating! We judge the experience; it does not judge us. If we like the experience then it is termed as a positive one. If we do not like it, the reverse becomes true as we see it as a negative one. To think we must experience so-called positive and negative events, have we not truly divided ourselves, forever remaining in surrender to illusion? Who or which institution dictates we are required to encounter both, which in truth, are generated by our own mind? When present, the mind operates properly; however, when it drifts, no one knows what it does other than to aimlessly drift in thought, never knowing exactly which seeds are planted for creation, forever wondering why things occur in the fashion they do through positive and negative experiences. A mindful human, though, always knows what their mind is generating in each present moment.

Through its infinite wisdom, the Creator formed patterns which inherently must repeat and from which we may grow, if we but guide these patterns toward another direction. Unlike any other living creature in our world, we not only can detect patterns of other creatures, but we can also detect patterns to our own life, thus enabling us to choose our own experiences and the manner in how we attain our personal growth. We may also choose how are going to experience the pattern. No other living thing has this ability. I learned this in the Far East through many observations of my great companion, the Tiger. When things take *their* time – not according to our time – changes take place automatically and we merely flow with the dynamics of those changes by accepting in full grace their place in our heart and mind, now everlastingly formed in the foundation of truth within us.

If any negative environment or experience appears in our life, the ever-present guide of Karma will remove it for us unless we prefer to remain in our cycles while holding onto them. By allowing ourselves to change as easily and naturally as life, these cycles no longer exist, for we now travel the straight and narrow path. The Zen tradition calls this songha, simply following the flowing stream of life. It is a Divine spiritual dynamic inbred within each of us which we completely ignore as we intellectually force our way hither and thither. By operating in a force-filled fashion, it completely blocks songha from our experience while our mind continues to dwell on unfocused thought streams. We can stop this type of living, and instead, experience songha because any individual may do this through a simple shift of thoughts. Songha occurs when our life simply flows as the stream and we have all had glimmers of this at different times. Imagine if this is your permanent experience. Then choose it!

When we learn and follow the principles of Karma, we indeed follow the flowing stream of life. We, therefore, easily attain and acquire songha more naturally, for it is truly our Divine state in the very first place. Simply stop interrupting and controlling the water's flow; otherwise, the pressure of return action will increase exponentially just like the pressure against a dam as the reservoir fills. Can we truly achieve songha without any personal effort? Absolutely! When we come to realize in each moment what our mind is doing, we will know precisely what we are generating; therefore, we would create a flexible and fluidic life free from seeming disasters and dramas which we have apparently learned to live with, a life free from teetering on the crests of emotional storms or drowning in the depths of anchored memories.

Can you imagine a life *totally* void of so-called negative experiences? Do you believe this life is even obtainable, that it is directly in our hands? Today we may not think so, but remember now, we are not our things. Things are the "what" we are, not the "who." Up to now we have been conditioned to define our self only by outer circumstances whereby we lost all ability to control and directly influence our life. To gain control once more, denial

and avoidance must be eliminated. We must focus instead on the truth of our self in every given moment which subsequently shall guide us in all we do. By so doing, we attract only love, peace, and synchronicity throughout our lives in an uninterrupted, harmonious flow – songha.

By introducing you to the first three principles, including now the Law of Growth, we hope you have awakened many questions concerning your self and the events of your life. Their answers will lead you to your true self and an understanding of your daily processes, guiding you to realize why your life has become the way it is. Once made clear, you will henceforth never avoid the inner truth of who you are. From acceptance and trust, you will grant your implicit self-mastery to instantly and effortlessly reveal just how to create your life in a different fashion, thereby changing its direction and releasing all attraction to negative Karmic circumstances. From my sojourn in the Far East, I can personally attest that self-truth is much more powerful than living in perpetual ignorance of our self while lingering in error. Let us now journey to the fifth principle of Karma which will show why this principle is just as vital as the caterpillar, why life constantly and continually attempts to reveal to each of us just exactly who we are in this reality. Are you ready to look in the mirror?

"If you wish to see truth
then hold no opinions for or against anything."
Seng-Tsan, Zen patriarch

~ Chapter VI ~
The Principle of the Mirrors

After painting for several days in late summer, I felt a great relief from this apparent endless but enjoyable task when Master Lobsang approached me one morning and stated, "Young man, it is time for you to learn the next principle of Karma. Come. Walk with me for awhile." I easily admit I looked forward to these walks with such a great teacher. He had such depth in his understanding of life and its intricacies, most of which we all miss in this part of the world. As informal or fascinating as they may turn out, I always gained an immense amount of information and understanding when we walked and talked. Master Lobsang turned to look at me and I remember him saying, italics are my emphasis, "Young man, your life is a direct reflection of *you. You* are always the first cause in your own life, which is true for *all* individuals," he informed me with smiling eyes. "*Every thing* in your life is attempting to tell you *who you are* in any given moment." Continuing, "What you see in another human is actually *you* looking at *your* self in the mirror of life. *All of life reflects your image of you.*" The truth is, by not knowing or understanding the Law of the Mirrors, I can now say our ignorance of this single principle can produce self-imposed slavery to our life and events. This is true because we may never know the cause of all what occurs around us unless we first look at our self in complete objectivity. We should always be objective with our own actions and activity, whether it is external or internal. Objectivity is the most important approach to

understanding and appreciating ourselves and our life. It is the only path for observing the true shape and condition of our house, the inner one we each have intimately created by mortaring in place one brick of experience at a time and shaped by every seed so planted along our way.

Master Lobsang offered, "Through all personal experiences in each and every moment, life individually reveals to each of us precisely who we are. This principle attempts to show us only our self in all its aspects, no one else's." Of course, my face once again wrinkled into a look of utter bewilderment as images of other people I have known flashed into my mind like a slide show on fast forward. "I am condemning myself? Not *them*?" as I crooked my head only slightly. He further explained, "This concept of your reflection through life is correct and is part of the reason for the Law of Attraction, the major reason. This is why we attract to us what we are and not what we may want or desire to have in our life. This is the basic idea behind the Law of the Mirrors." My teacher paused then continued, "What we see in another person or, more importantly, what we think we see as wrong about them is actually Karma's way of showing us what we do not necessarily like about our self. Whether or not we acknowledge this, is totally irrelevant." Master Lobsang concluded his thought, "Whenever you think there is something wrong, the truth is, there is something wrong in you, the very essence of this Law."

He could easily see my expression of deep contemplation about this totally new concept of life. Americans can be so completely befuddled by these principles, for I certainly was! In this part of the world, we generally look only through filters of right or wrong, good or bad, without ever considering the concept that everything and everyone is exactly as they are supposed to be right where they are, excuse the grammar! But you see, there is nothing wrong out there in this wonderful world of ours, and there is nothing wrong with any other human being because they are simply who they are. To this very day you will not hear me utter or write the words "right" or "wrong," "good" or "bad," unless used for explaining truth. These words do not exist in my or any monk's vocabulary. These are forms of judgment or opinions as stated above, nothing else. The Christ Himself stated very

succinctly to not judge, and in my sense, He was attempting to tell us that all things are precisely the way they are supposed to be, and that we have no right putting them into some form of personal concept based on judgment. Besides, the truth is, when we judge it actually has the power to blind us from what is real and not illusion.

Now a question for you, "Do you believe in coincidence?" Please do not jump right to your answer. First consider the question and acknowledge how you feel about it, for this question will assist you to understand this principle, along with the others we have looked into thus far. If your answer is no, you then believe everything has a reason or purpose attached to it. You believe all things are precisely the way and where they are supposed to be, is this correct? This reasoning further implies there are no events such as accidents, mistakes, or any failures. Further, nothing so-called wrong exists out there in our wonderful world. Bluntly put, the above events are human labels – illusions – and are not real. Perhaps without even being aware of it, this means you believe in Karma because you do not believe in coincidence!

The ever-present, guiding principles of Karma bring these events to us purely as an opportunity to become further educated and to understand the truth of who we are in those moments and to grow from them by making a different choice. I ask you, "With Karma, just where is the coincidence?" The truth is, every moment and experience in and of itself is neither right nor wrong, neither good nor bad, because they all just are. It is each of us in and of our self, on the contrary, who simply do not agree with what we are seeing in that particular moment or experience. What am I offering here? We are simply looking at life backwards, from the outside in! Does this make any sense to you? This powerful concept is simply letting us know that we need only spend our time making the necessary internal adjustments in our own mind instead of expending all our energy and effort with making external adjustments to others and our environment. If we do this, we rectify our self rather than the outer world. Master Lobsang simply stated to me, "Change you, and this changes how you see events."

Using the same analogy as mentioned in chapter one, it is best to realize the full composition of that brown silt resting at the bottom of our individual pool of consciousness rather than completely ignore it. Unfortunately, most of us do ignore it, thinking it will remain settled permanently or, worse yet, believing it will all utterly disappear through some miraculous future event. Wait! Forgive me, for I just now realize there *can* be a miraculous future event! It shall arrive when Karmic action returns to us that perfect moment of turbulence, an experience wherein our peaceful silt becomes totally agitated, swiftly bubbling towards the surface of our pool of consciousness. Because we now understand Karma is our guiding, prodding principle for personal growth, we fully realize and seize this opportunity to rid ourselves of the brown silt entirely, once and all. A miracle, indeed! Otherwise, we can choose to settle and bury the cause of the agitation once again, allowing Karma to cycle yet another event into our future experience. Perhaps this next time we will understand the healing message, for we always have the option to release all or at least part of that which had created the agitation.

Wherever you go, there you are, remember? While looking directly into my eyes, Master Lobsang softly said, "Young man, when you become angry, remember you are still there. What does your anger prove to you in that moment? It simply proves that the reflection of that mirror upon which you look reminds you of who you are. It brings to the forefront your anger rising from within. It does this because you thought you had changed; yet, you have not, so the reflection remains the same." This is precisely why the settled silt stubbornly remains within us, traveling with us like gum on a shoe, no matter the direction or distance of our journey. This is why Karma will cause the agitation to rise. It provides us the perfect experience at the perfect time to remove it forever. If we could see it through objective rather than filtered eyes, we would understand the circumstances and why they appear as they do in any given moment.

My insightful teacher asked me four questions during our walk that day, important questions intended for deep reflection regarding my path of life and impetus for a crystal clear pool of consciousness. I now pose them for *your* careful consideration regarding you and your

life: 1. Do you believe you are immune from what goes on around you? 2. Do you blame others simply saying that someone else did it, that you had nothing to do with the event? 3. Do you try to excuse yourself from the parts of life which are too difficult or hard? 4. Do you accept life with grace and see yourself as contributing or creating a difference? Remember, the Law of the Mirrors revolves around the idea that things are not necessarily the way they may appear because there is nothing "wrong" with external experience. Let us peer more deeply into the above four questions, one at a time, to find what they may reflect back to us about our self, keeping in mind there are no coincidences.

1. Do we believe we are immune from what goes on around us? If we go around thinking we are immune, then aren't we actually saying we are better than others or too good to have this kind of experience? This is an incredibly large illusion since no one is immune from any experience. By believing in personal immunity, then things only happen to others, not to us; in fact, it never becomes our fault or responsibility, correct? It is believed that a young insightful man who lived around two thousand years ago said something like, "Nothing is above the Law." It is strongly guaranteed that Karmic return action will bring an eye-opening experience directed specifically to those of us whose mind is rigidly entrenched with personal exemption, a mind stubbornly thinking all the while that the event belongs to others. In this case, do you suppose we are denying the reflection in the mirror? Repeating, no one and no thing is immune because our experience is exactly what we already are. So it is suggested that we neither deny nor avoid it. As my teacher offered, sometimes it is best to go ahead and climb over that arduous mountain, for it may be the best path, even though it appears frighteningly formidable.

2. Do we blame others by simply saying someone else did it and we had nothing to do with the event? Allow me to follow-up with more questions: "Do we blame others for our anger?" "Is it the other person's fault for the argument?" "At times, do we think another is stupid; yet, in reality, do they not think as we do and we now think they are stupid because of this?" Employing subtle expressions, blame takes on many faces, the most obvious one being the "you make me"

complex, which has already been discussed earlier in this book. Forgive my repetition on this subject; however, I feel its level of importance is worthy of repeating, especially in light of our current subject, the Law of Mirrors.

When operating under the "you make me" complex, we lay the blame on either the outer circumstance or the other individual, essentially transferring personal responsibility to an external event. By doing so, we disown our personal feelings and actions by attempting to disconnect their integral part from us. We end up actually denying our ability to control our own emotions and to properly look at our very own mirror, its glaring reflection now showing we are not in control of our own life. Just how can another person or thing, external to our self, physically control how we feel *internally* in any given moment? If we believe they can, aren't we admitting they are in control of us? Thankfully, the Law of the Mirrors will assist us to see our self in this very situation as it attempts to realign our viewpoint. Instead of what we think we are seeing as a victim of the "you make me" complex, this Law – if we accept it– will guide us to reclaim personal responsibility of our emotional energy as we objectively observe what we do in that particular moment. The truth is what we actually see and how we judge that moment, nothing more.

Perhaps another perspective may give clarity. You tell a friend, "So-and-so makes me so happy!" for example. Notice your word choice? Without ever realizing it, you have just given up or released the responsibility for your feelings – your power – over to so-and-so. Guess what? They now have the ability to also make you angry or sad as you have now given you away. Have you ever felt drained? This is why, and we shall cover this in greater detail later. And what do we generally call such an individual who "makes" us feel or do a thing, one way or the other? A manipulator perhaps? Unfortunately, I hear the following all too frequently today, "I love you because you do things for me and are so good to me." Or, "Because you never do what I want, I no longer love you." By literally giving our self away in these moments, we have just become easy to manipulate, even though we do not enjoy being manipulated at all. Certainly no one does. Why would we do this to ourselves? We have been conditioned away from personal control of our own self and our own life.

Your desire to feel empowered is very understandable; in fact, we each look for this in our life. So what does the Law of Mirrors do for us in this arena? Two things are going on here. First, it shows we have transferred our responsibility to an external source, and second, it lets us know how to accomplish the feeling or sense of empowerment by not giving ourselves away in the first place. In fact, it shows us where we are giving it up! Simply look at your reflection and it will show the cause to you. Ultimately, our personal responsibility is non-transferable, non-promotional, non-discountable, non-refundable, and never expires. To believe otherwise is an illusion. You see, when happiness is an innate part of our own nature then we are utterly happy, through and through, for it truly belongs to us. It is our nature – happiness *is* us! No other human or thing can ever give or take it away since we can only know and express the idea of happiness. We originated it for our self, correct? Such is genuine happiness, unlike its façade. If another can take it away, then 1) the happiness was not genuine in the first place, and 2) the other person has just stolen the happiness from us, which now becomes their Karmic return. Truly, this principle now sees that other person as no different as a thief, for stealing is the same action, whether taking an object or an emotion. Both are taken away unrightfully so. It is suggested we best turn things around, to objectively see our self as clearly as does the mirror right in front of us, to accept and watch the so-called manipulator – person, place, or thing – instantly transform into one of our greatest teachers. There is a simple rule of thumb here. Each time you point your index finger at a person or an event in the name of blame, notice how the three fingers below it point right back at you! As a gentle reminder, allow those three fingers to represent three aspects of your self in that moment: 1) how you are thinking, 2) how you are judging, and 3) how you are feeling. Because their source emanates from within you, they belong to you first.

3. Do we try to excuse ourselves from the parts of life which are too difficult or hard? This activity has become all too common in our part of the world. Yet it does make sense because who among us truly enjoys a difficult mental or emotional experience? Perhaps our perception and judgment make it so, nothing more. From my teachings in the Far East, life is not about personal enjoyment; rather,

it is solely about personal growth, change, and the comprehension of our true nature during which so-called difficulty may be associated at times. For the most part, our external affairs can be worked out with general ease; on the other hand, our internal affairs can be significantly more challenging to resolve due to their depth and complexity.

Are we doomed to difficulty? Not at all unless we choose this as our experience! By no longer participating in the blame game and the "you make me" complex, the burden of difficulty will lift. In truth, when anything becomes difficult, we are applying too much physical, mental, and emotional energy on that event, thereby creating resistance. And it is this very resistance which increases the level of difficulty. Why? Newton's Third Law. For every action there is an equal and opposite reaction, which by the way, works together with the third Law of Karma: *Whatever you resist persists for you.* Coincidence? Nope! No exceptions. Even the second principle of Karma concurs: *You attract to you what you are, not what you want.* This applies simply because if we resist, we actually attract more resistance. There are now three Laws working against us? No, not against us but with us. Yes, to think in reality they could work with us instead! These are just three simple and natural principles, all of them behind us, prodding and supporting our personal growth toward full realization and empowerment. This is their purpose!

What is really going on when we run into a difficult moment? Instead of throwing wide the stage curtain as we enter a multi-act drama – we generally do from the external sense – let us remain calm behind the closed curtain and rest in our internal peaceful nature as we calmly stop the chattering monkeys in the tree of our mind. There is a perfect reason for this moment to occur, right here and now, because there is no such thing as a coincidence or accident. Perhaps soul is attempting to attract our attention in the only manner it can. Could it simply be communicating that a different direction has now become necessary in our life? What if it has placed something right in front of us yet again since we successfully avoided this issue in the past. The truth is, our higher divine self works in union with Karma constantly and continually. Not to harm or punish us, please, but as its attempt to bring on a natural and complete healing to every individual involved in our so-called difficult situation.

"So if Karma and my soul are working for me, to heal me, then why so much difficulty?" you may be rightfully asking. The apparent difficulty is nothing more than your commitment to judging the situation as difficult! That is all. You see, our judgment determines whether something is easy or difficult, good or bad, pleasing or objectionable. I hear people in our Western culture declare judgmental statements nearly every moment regarding their situations each and every day. They focus purely on their judgment. Not surprisingly, the individual gets to experience through Karma exactly what they pay the most attention to, their judgment. May I offer a change in mind and heart? Let us strip away all judgment from our vocabulary as we graciously accept the alleged difficult moment as our teacher. Let us step into it full tilt so we may receive the greater understanding which is about to take place. By doing so, chances are this supposed difficulty will clear and never return because we now fully realize its true purpose. Yes, we got the message this time – finally! It is easiest to resolve and release things the moment they occur, no matter the apparent level of difficulty, then the brown silt is removed forever from your pool of consciousness. If not, it shall rise at a later time from a future agitating experience.

4. Do we accept life with grace and see ourselves as contributing or creating a difference? Most of us believe we do; however, by far the majority behaves entirely opposite, especially when it comes to the idea of grace, the first answer to this two-part question. Does this really surprise you? Listed here are a few synonyms for the word grace: balance, compassion, decency, ease, etiquette, forgiveness, nimbleness, pleasantness, tact. Are these attributes abounding all about us and through us in our world today? When truly walking or living in grace, would we ever become irritated, frustrated or angered? Would we ever be bothered by what another says or does? Living in grace means: first being grateful for life which naturally leads to grace, then becoming totally patient in life and with all people. This allows us to be utterly free of stress and prompts us to hold a door for another or give up our place in line for another who is truly in a hurry. Always be aware of honoring and treating others in a graceful manner. Also, remain calm and peaceful while driving in traffic and never being rude to another. Most importantly, being graceful is fully living to

assist others at all times, not just in those moments when it suits our fancy or appears necessary.

Once again, when judgment filters our perception of either an event or person, there remains no room for grace at any time. Why do we judge what we see? I offer this quote by Jean-Yves Leloup, author of "The Gospel of Thomas," translated by Shambhala Publications: "The eye with which I see God is the eye with which God sees me: one eye, one vision, one knowledge, one love." From a life filled with conditioning and habits, our vision has become completely prejudiced by our judging minds to the degree we no can longer see clear and true. It is like watching a blurry movie because of a dusty and oil-smudged projector lens. On the other hand, if we operate through the boundless idea of grace, then our judgments toward life are removed and life now becomes an honor. We then purely see and witness its true nature, its true beauty through the guiding principles of Karma. From the perspective of my teachers, if we are not at first graceful within our self, there is absolutely no way we can consistently behave gracefully outside us. We vacillate from being graceful externally to stumbling and mumbling within through self-condemnation, along with possible other issues. We, therefore, hopscotch between truth and error, transforming our divine greatness to unnatural smallness all because of how we operate our mind, simply by seeing through a judgmental lens, colored and opaque at the very least.

My answer to the second part of the question is the same. Although most of us believe we do contribute or create a difference, I beg to differ. I am not talking about our career choice or professional accomplishments; instead, I am talking about our personal interaction with all the people whom we encounter each and every day. I am talking about total strangers and those who truly need assistance in that moment when we just happen to appear in their space. Coincidence or chance? Do we stop to help them or to lift their spirit? "First, what is in it for me?" or "I do not have the time right now!" is written all over most everyone's face. I am not kidding because, again from personal observation, there is a tremendous number of individuals in this part of the world who will assist another, but only when there can be something gained by doing so. Do you recognize any grace in this

mindset? This approach is more self-serving and one of vanity than anything else. It is actually manipulation, truth be told.

If you wish to genuinely contribute or make a difference, it is simply suggested that you give of yourself in silence and grace, being of service to one human at a time, being genuinely humble in your nature as you do so. No need for fanfare, a ticker-tape parade, or major media coverage. If these are offered then why not? As you are now more fully aware of Karmic return, do you truly desire to toot your own brass horn at the expense of the other? Kindly reconsider these public acknowledgments, for you will not take too kindly when another toots their horn at *your* expense. Besides, these external affairs will only feed the ego by eroding your true nature, a nature of harmony, peace and synchronicity. Let us now journey forward to more fully understand our nature by looking at each of the seven separate reflections known as the Law of Mirrors.

Let us first re-introduce you to the significance of this fifth principle of Karma, so aptly stated to me by my teacher, Master Lobsang, "Whenever there is something wrong, the truth is, there is something wrong in you." Just what is the purpose of this principle, the Law of the Mirrors? While events are going on all around us, the object is to understand precisely what the mirrors are showing us – about us – to get us to remember who we are. One of the great challenges we all have in life, I fully understand, is the fact that our eyes can only physically see outward. I will give us that physical limitation, but our mind has the ability to see inwardly. No physical eyes required here. Because of the eyes, the human has become prone to only look at all the superficial things rather than those immediately in front of and staring back right at them. More importantly, we very seldom turn our eyes inward by way of inner reflection. The bottom line is, the mirrors of this principle are solely about us and our ego, along with where we stand right with our self. In the Nag Hammadi library it is stated, "When you carry the water I am there; when you lift the rock I am there; when you split the wood I am there." The Creator is literally everything-everywhere – including us! Through our experience, these seven mirrors show us just how we truly see our Creator, how we truly see our self.

Let us begin with the first mirror: it is called the Reflection of the Moment. Its parable reads: *You may read the face of the sky and earth, but have not recognized how to read this moment.* I must thank Greg Braden for bringing these to light from the Gospel of Thomas of the Nag Hammadi or Gnostic texts, yet, these are much older than the texts discovered in the deserts of Egypt. I was told they are ageless. As mentioned earlier, being in the present is the only place anyone can actually live their life, but most people do not mindfully reside there as has been shown. Life happens exclusively in the present, the moment in time when the creation of events takes place in our life and when we lay our seeds to sprout the future. When we place our focus strictly in the future, a time when our body cannot live, we accumulate a massive stack of misguided and deceptive building blocks which are not necessarily relevant to the issues staring right at us right now in the present moment. Do you genuinely believe these blocks will completely realign in order and in context once our future arrives? Unfortunately, this is not to be the case. And constantly looking into the future clearly forms a path of denial, the denial of who we are this moment. The mind is an amazing human attribute; however, it appears we have misused it way too often in our world by not keeping this powerful organ with our body, right where it belongs behind our eyes, in the present. We are generally looking into a future time or back in the past. As we do, we actually miss our life in the present as we wonder what just happened.

Looking at this idea from another perspective, our body is always right where it is, incapable of traveling into the future and unable to slip into its past. How about our emotions and feelings? Are they not also contained in our body? In fact, they are actually meant to protect our body, not our timeline. How about our soul? Time is irrelevant to the soul since it lives eternally; hence, it chooses to remain where the body is, using the body as its fingerprint to sense further understanding and experience in the physical realm. You see, there exist only two exceptions for the soul to leave our body; it is either astral projecting or it is leaving the body at our moment of final transition. How about our mind? I must say, this is the only attribute of the human not required to remain in the moment. This is glaringly revealed by way of all the trials and tribulations evident throughout our world, and is reflected to us in this mirror by the very parable and the way it is stated.

Clearly, we have easily allowed the most important part of our body and the guiding mechanism of our life to wander aimlessly out of the present moment. I ask you, "Without the mind being present, do you have a complete and true idea of what is going on all around you and within you in this moment? Do you realize this moment is the single most important moment of your life because it creates the next one?" The purpose of the first mirror, therefore, is for us to know where our mind and thoughts are actually being placed. After all, this is the mechanism which makes all the decisions affecting our life, and if we are not present with it along with our body, just how do we know of any decision genuinely being made? Most of them, therefore, are made through our subconscious mind to which few of us, if any, know what this aspect is doing. This is why it is referred to as the subconscious mind, for it is beneath conscious mind. When we become aligned with what is termed as consciousness, we would know what the whole mind is doing. This occurs through presence of mind.

While walking along the trail, Master Lobsang shared with me, "What we are looking upon is a reflection of our self in that one small moment in time. This is not only consistent but is also constant by its very nature." You see, this first mirror nudges you to ask yourself, "What do I see in the moment before me?" I am reminded of the old adage: you only hear what you want to hear. Perhaps the very same is true when it is said: you only see what you want to see. How especially true when we prefer to not necessarily see right in front of us in that moment. The Law of Mirrors can only reflect the truth; therefore, do we see the truth or do we see the error and immediately judge it, as when we see something wrong in another person? As stated earlier, if you see it in another person, then it must first be within you; else, you will simply not see it. Forgive my repetition if you feel I am pounding this principle into your mind. We were born in the moment, so let us live in the moment; otherwise, Karma will have an overwhelming and significant impact. It will not hesitate to return whatever is necessary to help us recognize the truth of who we have become by straying from the moment. The value of living in truth and being in the moment empowers us to know what we are creating, and ultimately, what will return to us by what we do each moment in time. As the human, we have to understand that the biggest thing going on is what we feel about our self while in our experience with life – at any time in the moment. Life is one big mirror and it solely and purely reflects back to us how we feel about our self.

Let us look into the second mirror: Reflection of Judgment. Its parable reads: *Recognize what is in your sight and that which is hidden from you will become plain to you.* Notice how the first two overlay each other; the first reveals to us how we only look at the obvious and the second reveals to us what we do not see. Gregg Braden states this title the best simply because our judgment, more than anything else, literally blocks us from viewing the truth in any given moment. In monastic teachings, it is known as breaking the veil of blindness which was explained to me with Master Lobsang's question – emphasis mine, "Do you see what is *truly* in front of you, or do you see what you *think* you see?" You see, most of us are seeing precisely what we think we see rather than seeing what is truly there to be seen. Silliness aside, if you do not see what I am getting at here, then we can approach this concept from a different angle. The veil of illusion blinds most of us into seeing what we think we see in every given moment in time. From whence did this veil appear? Why do we see through it all the time? In truth, this veil is pulled over the eyes by our judgmental mind, ego-generated, a mind which most of us seem to utilize each and every moment. Granted, it is not our fault in a way, for we all have the tendency to interpret our circumstances. We do this because of our personal, historical life experience. In other words, we may only see what our experiences allow us to see. Herein lies the illusion as we shall see later by what is termed as memory overlay.

We interpret what people say and do; we interpret what we see and sense. The veil of judgment creates our interpretation in the first place, and being an interpretation, the original and true meaning of the moment is swiftly swept under the rug of awareness or becomes lost in the depths of memory. Understandably, breaking this veil is most challenging because this principle is either unknown or is not

accepted; yet, it is a Universal Principle nonetheless. This means there is simply no way around it since we cannot forever avoid or deny who we ultimately are, though we constantly attempt to by evading the issue. Here is the fascinating thing about the human because, the second we see it, we still do not assume any responsibility for what we see. But we ought to. It was created for us to see us as our self in that moment! Are we henceforth forever stuck with judgment? Absolutely not! By design, this reflection urges us to break that veil of illusion, to step into our true reality by removing every nuance of judgment – to live purely in truth.

In the Western culture, we are taught to judge, beginning from early childhood all through the educational system and into the corporate world. It seems our very life depends on it! How in the world was judgment created? From God or natural Law? Neither! There is a tougher answer to consider: *judgment was taught by the human*, created through the concept of duality, fully created through the ego. Unbeknownst to us from our birth all the way until our transition, we are taught to focus on internal division, the concepts of right and wrong, good and evil, as opposed to simple truth and error. Life itself contains no division, nor is there any need for it; therefore, judgment is a non-issue. Where do you see judgment in the natural world?

During my sojourn in the Far East, I was taught that my judgment not only blinds and limits me, but also truly judges my very own self. What? I had never heard that one before. I was dumbstruck! The truth is, judging outwardly shall indeed reflect back to us through Karma, as we base both people and events on our own inner division of right and wrong, or good and evil. The veil of illusion, therefore, blinds us from the truth and confines every one and every thing to our own experience. Truth is simply truth; error is simply error. Why is this being said? We allow truth to evolve; whereas, we must individually adjust or affect a change from an error. If you indeed believe in no coincidence in life, this means there is nothing wrong, for it is simply error in motion and may be avoided.

Here is a question for you to consider: Does judgment underlie either of the following two phrases: "I agree with you," and "I disagree with you." Surprisingly, agreement and disagreement are both the biggest, blinding, judgmental circumstances which may ever occur to anyone. Do you not observe those who seek constant agreement? There exist two types: 1) the domineering individual who is never wrong, and 2) the insecure individual who seeks constant approval – agreement. You have met both types I am certain. It should come as no surprise that each type has its own Karmic return action attached to it. Must we really judge all people, places, things, or even to agree and disagree? It is right here when this one mirror attempts to reflect back to us, only so we may understand and expand our self. In truth, it is not all that important to have people agree or disagree, as we all have our very own perspectives. Perhaps it is best we merely allow every human to have their own.

Why do we not learn to accept the idea of individuality, to not interpret based on anything other than our Divine uniqueness, most especially between our fellow humans? Do we not, as an individual, have an experience which applies only to us? Where does the comparison enter? How can any comparison be made? How may we judge another or determine whether another human is wrong in what they say or do? We cannot in truth. It is most fascinating to observe how one individual easily and quickly condemns the other for what they truly believe is incorrect, even though in full light of the other's experience, such action is perfectly proper and absolutely appropriate. I remember a young man once said, in part, "Judge not lest ye be judged." Oh yes, the ever-present Karmic return action nudges again – in full force! Here is a simple plan of action one may follow. Allow Karma to handle it. It will most definitely take care of the other person, at a time most likely inconvenient to them, by the way. Watch it! If you judge or wish misfortune on others, Karma will also take care of *you* through its appropriate return action. It is best we allow every other human to simply be who they are rather than have them live under our judgment, for this path truly offers a greater level of flexibility for us while also offering a lifestyle free of pressure or stress. If we use this mirror properly, it will offer you your own experience of songha – an even flow.

We shall now offer the third reflection for you to consider: It is the Reflection of Loss. Its parable reads: "*The Kingdom of my Father is like a certain woman who is carrying a jar full of meal. While she was walking on the road, still some distance from home, the handle of the jar broke and the meal emptied out behind her on the road. She did not realize it. When she reached her house, she set the jar down and she found it empty*". The moment Master Lobsang began his introduction of this mirror to me, Rinpoche Kiela suddenly appeared from around a bend in our path. He joined our walk and on-going discussion. What an honor to have them both present! "This mirror is like giving away the self, giving away your power, something most people do all the time," Rinpoche Kiela offered. He continued, "Through life's experiences, people actually give them self away to most things on the external plane, and allow them to be in control. The purpose of this mirror attempts to get us to see this as it occurs, each and every moment. The key is being in the moment to see it. If not, we may then become drained and wonder why. This sense occurs over time and is very subtle until after it has happened."

You see, we have lost our power – no, that was not stated accurately, pardon me. Actually, we have given our power away because the outer world is now the main dynamic which is directly influencing us, and the third mirror shows us what we have given up, if we but choose to see. Although most people honestly believe they are the one in control of their life, they truly are not. Personally, if you believe you are, then why do your moods change from one side of the spectrum to the other? What makes you happy? What creates your sadness? Why do you become angry or frustrated? These are all reflections to look upon as they are messages that something is controlling you in that one simple moment in time. Generally, can we keep our power and have more influence than we could ever dream of? Absolutely, but we must simply stop giving it away to others or to our experiences constantly and continually. Allow me to repeat my intention here, and that is to offer you just as meticulous an explanation of these principles as my teachers offered me. Walking on, Master Lobsang further explained, "The reflection of loss, or the feeling of being powerless, happens over time and generally goes unnoticed until we are powerless. Our true power may be restored, but with great and

sometimes painful effort, which may be necessary to regain what we gave away in the very first place. This may involve other people or a direction we have followed for a long period of time. These may be painful in this moment; yet, in the long term, your very health may depend on this. Do you understand?"

Purely from the personal choices we make, our true power may be drained by any source in our experience, such as our careers or volunteer work, our loves or other relationships, just to name a few. Just how do we choose to lose our self, our power? As one example, we can perfectly understand how excited we feel when we are offered that new position in our career path or when we offer our services in that new volunteer position. Talk about being a go-getter and acting totally enthused at the start of work! Wow, what super energy! Understandably, we eagerly accept the new demands of these positions, replying yes to every request without hesitation or doubt until, one day, we "wake up" to find ourselves leaning all the way back in our office chair, our head tilted back facing the ceiling with our eyes closed and arms dangling totally limp by our side, exclaiming under a long exhale, "I'm worn out!"

After a significant amount of time had passed, right then we just recognized our loss of personal power, feeling exhaustively drained, realizing we no longer have any time for our partners, family, or friends, let alone our self! You no longer feel in control, do you? Does it seem your work now owns you, absolutely in control of you, whereas you were in control of it initially? You have given your whole self, your total power over to your career or volunteer work! Congratulations because you now have the opportunity to look into the mirror of truth and shift the dynamics of your drain. Maybe, just maybe, by understanding the reflection of this mirror, you will not feel the need to give up your career or volunteer position! I'm curious to know how many of you do not even take a vacation or time off from work, even if you do not go anywhere. I know many people who find themselves in this exact situation. How powerless they feel! Is there a solution? Most certainly. Simply do not forget you and the time you require for you so you may rejuvenate your energy level. A mere twenty minutes of meditation assists me greatly, and I believe this is quite doable in any profession. It merely requires us to step away from our work only for a short moment. This self-rejuvenation may be done each day. How? Leave your work at work. Hint: as previously offered, keep your mind with your body wherever it may be each moment. You now are truly meditating while in the presence.

Do you realize every single human alive has a job given to them at birth, a position from which they can never be fired at any time for any reason as long as they shall live? Talk about job security! Only a handful of individuals, though, are aware of this post. What is the title of this occupation which can never leave us, for it goes wherever we go? The divine office of *being*, a position each human holds. Wherever we are, we are *being* there, are we not? This sounds a tad familiar, like Karma déjà vu. Sadly, we have unknowingly vacated our office of *being*, simply because we do not prefer to be wherever we are. "You are going out there again, Steven," I hear your warning. Thank you, why yes I am; however, it is observed each day how we appear unable to remain focused right where our body is by not *being* in that very moment. It seems someone or something caught our mind's full attention. Away it goes, leaving our body alone at work, or alone doing most anything, even during a conversation.

If we are truly focused at work, then why do we think about all of our incomplete tasks when we arrive at home? Are they incomplete because, while at work, we thought about home or that dream vacation or the revised shopping list? It is suggested that we leave home at home and work at work. Leave home at home so in our mind we can remain focused on our work while at work. Yes it sounds funny, but does this make sense? What a wonderful impact this will have on us! By leaving our work in the office at the end of our daily schedule, we are now being with our self, taking time out and completely relaxing while being in the moment. No matter where our body goes, being at work 24/7 – in mind – will quickly build up stress in the long run, risking *dis*-ease, illness, or worse yet, leaving a perfectly great career when there is truly no need.

Let us next focus on our personal loves and why so many relationships in today's world, generally speaking, seem to come to an end all too often and at times too soon. Why or how may these become so draining to us? How can the very notion of love become so heavy? Let us offer this pivotal point: we get into our relationships because of what we feel and we leave them because of what we think. What flipped the switch from our heart to our mind? Did we not get together in the first place because we had become attracted to and thoroughly enjoyed certain innate qualities about the other person? Somewhere along the path we skipped from sharing absolutely everything with each other and doing things for each other, the relationship blossoming into love, over to taking away from each other and even doing things to each other, the relationship shriveling into unkindness. Similar to our work, we have become slowly drained over time, even overwhelmed by all of the events and memories of the relationship to the point when, somewhere along its path, we begin to blame our partner for what we have allowed our self to become, instead of looking at our reflection in the mirror.

Due to their significance, let us take you in for a closer examination of relationships. When we first begin one, are we really and truly our self? Hold just a second; think again. Actually, more times than not, we are busy attempting to impress the other, which occurs only through who we are not. To impress means we are not who we are. Although this does, indeed, spread a stronger web, it truly reveals our lack of self-worth in catching the potential relationship. Why? We fear losing their attraction to us; therefore, we dare not be who we truly are. Certainly we have all done this at some point, but in the long run, it will not work because the truth of us will eventually come out. It does every time. If we must impress the person, the mirrors have already shot a warning flare; therefore, in a sense, many people establish their relationship through levels of deception, though purely innocent they may be at first. Whether done harmlessly or through well-meaning intentions is totally irrelevant, for the underlying script of deception rings more loudly in the ears of Karma. When we develop a relationship at an unsustainable pace, we indeed drain ourselves from the very beginning; in fact, this drain unequivocally evolves from the deception we used in the budding of this new relationship. If relationships are initially based in the truth of who we are, the odds are high they will work out well, for Karmic return shall occur in kind

for each individual so involved. Live in truth and all mirrors remain harmless for they shall only show truth!

Allow us to demonstrate how this may work out by a simple fictitious example, and I have permission to use my editor and his lovely wife. By the way, thank you both! Let us say both Donald and Lorrie are single and he does not care to watch football. During their first date, both have become smitten and a wonderful relationship blossoms. One day, Lorrie approaches Donald with exciting news, "Donald, guess what?! I just got tickets for two great seats at the home game this weekend! Would you like to go with me?" "Okay," he coolly replies out of his fear of rejection or potential loss of the budding relationship. Lorrie receives tickets several times during the football season, and Donald goes each time simply to maximize his time with her, enjoying only her company, not the game. The season ends and Donald is totally relieved. Now stop and observe what he has set in motion here. What potential Karmic return did he set up for himself in the long run? By initially creating the illusion of enjoyment, he may receive such an illusion in return, will he not?

This story unfolds. The two have now had much experience and spent a lot of fun time together, thoroughly enjoying the other's companionship. What is this? Lorrie just burst into the house – they now live together – after work excitedly proclaiming, "Hey sweetie! Great news! I got a super deal! I just purchased next season's tickets for all the home football games!" Donald turns to face Lorrie with a facial expression seeming to say, "What? This is the last thing I want!" while admitting aloud, "But honey, I really do not care for football." After the initial shock, Lorrie retorts, "But I thought you love football. You don't love me anymore!" I sense you can see what is about to occur. The truth has made itself known as it always does. By not being *who* he truly is, Donald lost his power and essentially could no longer run at the pace he had initially established. As a result, they both now run the risk of feeling drained because of the certain onset of rejection and conflict. In every relationship, it is most beneficial to be precisely who you are, not who you are not. Your mirror will reveal who you are right at the beginning, ensuring the relationship is founded in truth rather than illusions created by grandstanding. If we

but notice what we place in our life every moment, we can easily see whether it is truth or illusion. Truth is always the best path to follow, even if it is the most uncomfortable at the time, because truth only reflects truth.

Let us continue with the next reflection or the fourth mirror: Reflection of Your Most Forgotten Love. Its parable reads: *That which you have will save you if you bring it forth from yourselves.* As my two teachers and I continued our walk, Master Lobsang looked over at me, asking point blank, "Do you know you?" as Rinpoche Kiela smiled on. Once again my face wrinkled in puzzlement as I slowly replied, "No… I'm not sure." He gently offered, "Young man, you have simply forgotten you, your most important attribute, only because you are too caught up in life and are used to giving your self away as the previous reflection showed you. Is it really such a surprise that you never have any idea what you are creating in your life?" You see, all ancient texts from the Buddhist traditions through the Gnostic texts tell us we have either forgotten our first love or are going to at some point since we are drawn more and more into the desires of the external world, allowing them to pull us like a magnet ever deeper into its fields of thorns and inner desolation. To me, this does not sound like an environment over which we ought to become fully mesmerized and enamored.

If we do fall in love with the world, it can only do what it knows how. It will drain us and may even suck the life force out of us over time. If we have not already forgotten, we will, simply because we have become charmed by people, places, and things which we honestly believe will give us substance, a substance we were already born with, something divine which nothing worldly can ever give back to us. Yet, we simply think it does until we are trapped by it all. The most important and only thing we require in life is our self, the truth of our very being. From this inner perspective, we can easily attain personal empowerment right along with peace and happiness with our environment. Instead, we go *out there* for what we think we require in our life. The truth is, the fourth mirror reminds you by showing that you have misaligned your priorities. You have led yourself away by the façade of the outer material world, away from

your most forgotten love. Your most forgotten love is *you*! You forgot to recognize your *true* self, the truth of your own being. As Master Lobsang offered me, "Monks require nothing external and have no desire to be led away from the most important thing in their life. Their self."

Allow me to expand on this point. When it comes to the outer world, the fourth mirror constantly reflects our departure from who we are; yet, we do not even realize this is happening in most cases! We either lead ourselves astray from our true source of power already within us, or deplete our power by focusing on the outer world and relationships, both established and having the seeming ability to diminish us. Here comes the draining part; the outer world is now in control, the root of all the reflections of self. I will grant you that our body, mind, and emotions absolutely feel drained; but the truth is, the outer world has no inherent power unless we first give our self away to it, creating the illusion of its seeming importance to us. Do not stop here, for many of us allow it to become even more important than us, all the while believing it will render us true happiness.

Sure the world can give us happiness, but only briefly at best because this type of happiness is external to us, so it is not real. Happiness is actually an internal experience only. This is the prime reason most people have no idea of who they truly are in this life, which is precisely why I was not sure who I was when Master Lobsang asked his question. We are not our position in life or our possessions; we are, in the true reality, our inner self. The external things can only create burdens since we give our energy to them rather than to our self, in which case they can actually end up controlling our life. We then have debt over them, in a general sense, and we begin to live with a sense of being trapped which is incredibly draining on the inner plane. External things ultimately give us nothing. Ask yourself, "Am I tired or feel drained at the end of each day?" If so, do not blame your life. Look into you. Also, do not blame any relationship in which you are involved; else, you are forgetting your first love yet again. I wonder, do you have the feeling this mirror may also be called: Reflection of Personal Responsibility?

Do you still wonder why so many pages have been filled to write about the importance of self? When understood, this single principle of Karma clearly states: *you are the most important thing in your life*. You see, each human in this world is important to them self, and when we each realize our self and the true power we wield each and every moment, our life transforms to a deeply humbling experience. Allowing the ego to enter, on the other hand, we can easily carry it too far by becoming entirely filled and enamored with the illusion of self-importance, even to the degree of thinking we are actually more important than any other human – a complete fabrication. This self-deception ultimately evolves into a one-way path towards a Karmic return based purely on one's ego. Remember, I am only discussing divine importance here. Every human is vitally, divinely important.

Life is an honor, an experience of individuality wherein no individual has greater significance or more importance than any other. All is equal and Karma maintains this in all respects. It is all in how we view our self, to recognize our true magnificence. Consider this: without you what would you be? Yes, that may sound like a ludicrous question, but it is one which both Masters Lobsang and Kiela had asked me. It is time to ask you the same question, "Without you what would you be? Without you what would your life be?" Rest assured, placing importance on the knowledge behind this question will guide you to who you truly are, and clearly reveal the importance of you since you are the common thread in your life and all its experiences.

As an analogy, we are each a simple grain of sand washed upon the shore of life, the universal surf gently nudging us into relationships with other grains. Although we see ourselves physically separate from all the others, our worldly beach cannot exist without including every grain, no matter their proximity, shape, or color; therefore, humankind is not complete without every single human, for each is equally vital to the whole. If, however, we treat and believe our self as insignificant, then how can we feel important to any other, let alone see others as significant? We cannot because we do not comprehend the ideas of importance and significance. How can we love or be loved by any other when we do not love our self first? We cannot. In truth, the entire basis of our experience, the guidance behind Karma

and the mirrors of reflection, are all urging us, pushing us to see our true self. To see only God!

We will now open the fifth mirror and guide you through its meaning: Reflection of Father, Mother, and Creator. Its parable as recorded in the Gospel of Thomas reads: *Whoever does not hate his father and mother as I do, cannot become a disciple to me. And whoever does not love his father and mother as I do, cannot become a disciple to me. For my mother gave me falsehood but my true Mother gave me life.* While seeming to be contradictory, this mirror concerns our relationship to family, friends, even our life and Creation. From the parable, "falsehood" is what we term as the body, the illusion of life, a warning for us to not get so caught up in the material aspects of living our life. The true Mother, our soul, the God Principle, gave us truth, the ability of life, and to choose all what we want to do while we are in it. The Father/Mother/Creator mirror attempts to reflect to us that which owns us. "Nobody and nothing owns me!" you may proclaim. There are two very significant questions to ask yourself concerning your relationship to all others, questions which you may ask at any given moment. Their answers will reveal who and what are directly controlling and influencing you in your life. 1) What do you hold onto? 2) What are you willing to let go of? Once you ask these to your self take a few moments before you continue reading and peer objectively in your life, for you may be surprised at what you see. And here is a third question, "Can you let go of the most important relationship in your life?" In truth, if you are not able to let go, then you are actually missing the true depth of love; in fact, the relationship is actually controlling not only you, but also your emotions. Otherwise, if you are willing to let it all go as an emotional experience, it actually becomes more significant than ever for you. Since there are no attachments, you have freedom within the relationship.

Allow me to share a deeper meaning of this reflection. The fifth mirror constantly reflects our level of insecurity and unwillingness over the idea of love, or the fear of being alone within the constructs of relationship. The mirror attempts to show us our relationship to life, loves, and success in any endeavor, for the reflections are all around us all the time. Interestingly enough, we do not see them

because our relationships remain more important to us than our true self. This now means that we completely miss the purpose of these reflections altogether. We have become blind, so to speak. No wonder we experience illness because illness will only occur when something gains more importance than self, for it now has complete power over us. Nothing is meant to have power over us, according to my teachings and understanding. Even in the Bible, does it not state that we have dominion over all things? Perhaps this simply means nothing should have dominion over the human, unless we have missed an exception to this life rule. It appears we have actually created an exception – hundreds of them! If we objectively observe, we see dominion enveloping us in so many ways from so many directions! No wonder we have forgotten who we are and why so many people are not at ease – excuse me, *dis*-eased!

I recall a well-known ancient Chinese proverb: If you love something, set it free. If it comes back to you, it is yours. If it does not, it never was. By approaching life from this perspective, the relationships we establish will offer us the opportunity to simply be the complete and full embodiment of precisely who we are, free of all pressure, deception, and illusion. Otherwise, if we are too busy holding onto a relationship, it will truly block our path from experiencing true love within any relationship. This is also true for any friendship which seems imposing. In truth, all relationships simply flow, free of any effort, but only if we allow for them by not attempting to control or by having them only our way. By letting go of all things, we would ultimately realize our importance to people and even careers. We would come to realize true freedom and complete empowerment. If you are afraid of letting them go or believe you are unable to release any relationship, even though it may be dragging you down or draining you, this simply reveals that you have no power in that relationship, that it is actually controlling you on all sides of your life. It truly owns you! By letting things go, there is no longer pressure upon you or any heaviness attached to any experience within any relationship.

What is the main purpose of this fifth mirror? Through its reflections, this mirror guides our eyes to see the true types of relationships we have established from the very beginning, to

understand them not from the external sense, but rather through the use of our Karmic experience. We may admit that we do not clearly see its reflections. I bet most of us have though, which can be revealed by answering this question, "Have you ever noticed the majority of your relationships seem very similar, even appearing at times that a new relationship picks up right where the old left off?" This pattern actually occurs because, in truth, they are intended to simply take care of old wounds or memories we have of our personal view of self, our physical personality which was established from the day we were born and developed by our experiences from that moment forward.

We begin life with no knowledge, and as the years pass, we expand in knowledge, growing in the direction any experience brings to us, either in truth or in error thinking. For example, a human cannot be a natural-born criminal; yet, both the education and experience can guide them in that direction. Rinpoche Kiela suggested to me, "If you tell a child enough times that they are bad, then they will surely end up that way through the relationships they attract to themselves." Most have heard the phrase: Like attracts like. So, too, are the mirrors attempting to show us who we are first. Through this level of self-knowledge, we are able to shift our self into a different mold, hence attracting the new type of relationships, ones we truly seek to experience instead of repeating those we already had. Remember the second principle: *You attract to you what you are, not what you want.* It is exemplified right here in the fifth mirror; however, if we continue to deny it, then changing it will not be possible. If, however, you totally accept what you see, then changing it becomes very real which is true for all our material circumstances.

One could easily state that our life becomes unequivocally filled with self-imposed illusions right from the very beginning. These are illusions based on our external experiences from which we are given only ill-conceived knowledge. What do I mean by this? For instance, if we grow up in a rough childhood our life becomes so-called rough. And in a general sense, we grow up seeking this very same experience in our adult relationships simply because this type of life is all we know. One day we hear that we are able to change our life, but we do not know how. In truth, we may change anything in our life through

the use of our power of creating, but we lack the awareness and tools to do so. Do we have the ability to simply create a different type of experience? Absolutely! Then how? We must first acknowledge what we are witnessing through what the Law of Mirrors is reflecting back to us, to acknowledge what we have become. Only then may we simply redirect our self into a new direction using this principle as our guide. To change our life we simply change our mind by choosing precisely how we want to live in each experience. Changing our mind may be as simple or as difficult as we decide to make it. Do not attempt to change it all at once! Work with one issue at a time. Do you realize, the most routine thing about the human is the mind itself, and as long as the mental patterns remain unchanged, our life remains unchanged? Simply see you in a different light and the difference will arrive based on Karmic Law. An angry person does not have to remain angry any more than a criminal has to remain a criminal. It all comes down to a change of thought and mind, thus leading them in a new direction while shifting their reflection in the mirrors of life.

Once this is accomplished then our life and relationships will absolutely shift, both moving us toward that new direction we have just chosen. Yes, it is all based on choice. As it was shared earlier, by first changing our mind, our Karma will instantaneously undergo a metamorphosis solely to create a return action in full alignment with our new choice. Perhaps an example would be helpful right about now. Let us say you grew up in that rough neighborhood, along with a tough family environment. Obviously, tough Karma developed over the years and now must be worked through, but only if you choose to do so. While working through it, one day you suddenly throw up your arms and proclaim from your heart, "Please, I just want to live peacefully!" What just occurred? You just let it all go while instantaneously making a new choice, right? What happens now? By developing a peaceful mind, attitude, and approach to your life, new Karmic action can only return peace to you and your life, overriding the old rough and tough mindset while obliterating all past experience.

Just remember that focus and patience will be required here, for both will keep you away from internal frustration. You already know how Karma handles frustration, and you do not wish to sling-shot back to the old well-worn path you were accustomed to walking. Well, maybe you do. This is yet another choice. The moment when all the old Karmic circumstances have been resolved, there can be only one thing left for you. Total and utterly all-abiding, encompassing, inner peace as you and your life! Such transformation holds true for *every* human's Karmic issue! Because there exists no escape nor avoidance from Karma, then I suggest we make the choice to stand right where we are, to face it and work it out, moving always forward to create a different outcome. It is not suggested in any way that we re-create our life because un-creation is not possible. Our life is exactly what it is because we created it that way, so start from where we are right now. Create a different outcome so you can move into the new direction while gaining different experiences as the process unfolds, for you are now open to and accepting of life.

Let us now begin the sixth mirror: Quest into Darkness. Its parable reads: *All are born and must walk in the two spirits that the One has created in human, the Sprit of Light and the Spirit of Darkness.* Once more I thank Gregg Braden and the Gospel of Thomas. Master Lobsang explained this reflection to me in this fashion, "You have the impression there are dual realities. While it may appear true, the fact remains there are not; there exists only one. You just live it in a dual fashion and this is not necessary as it just creates further separation in your mind and life. In your part of the world, young man, you all have been taught this since your entry into this world. As children, your parents told you that you were good or bad while you were saying or doing something which, from your perspective as the child, felt entirely innocent." He thoughtfully paused when he noticed my head bobbing up and down, for I was busy absorbing his words of wisdom, while at the same time, reflecting upon my own past. "Since childhood," he resumed, "you continued to learn through this type of modality, starting with your parents and continuing through your educational system right into your careers, seeming to abide by the mantras: this is good; that is bad. Or, this is right; that is wrong," as Master Lobsang pointed to one side and then to the other side of our pathway. "Or so you think," he concluded with a twinkle in his eye.

To assist us in understanding this reflection and the idea of separation, consider the following. The only way we can recognize daylight is because we have night time. The only way to recognize a female is because we have a male. We recognize a house simply because we have what could be termed as empty space around it. This open space is what allows us to see the house or even a tree; yet, the open space and the object are actually one. God created the idea of a dual reality from which we can learn but not to own or live by. When viewed in oneness, both light and darkness are opposite sides of the same coin, just as female and male – one coin is a day, the other is a human. Both aspects inseparably make the whole. Both are not dual; rather, they are singular since this is a Universal Principle, for it applies to all things. In the Western culture, we see all things only through this old duality filter due to our conditioning, when in truth this filter is pure illusion. So what is the bottom line? According to my Master teachers, we journey only in oneness with all of life.

As stated, duality is fine for the sake of learning and for knowledge because we utilize comparative thought in order to understand what is being taught; however, it is not the best way to live or to use as our guide in life. Living from this perspective creates division which is literally how our logic operates; yet, if we live in division, did the Christ not say that a house divided cannot stand against itself? It is this precise view of dual nature which has created what we know today as judgment, the verdict from which we apply to our everyday life. Judgment creates the illusions of alienation and isolation – both outright falsehoods! Based on monastic teachings, they are purely the reflection of duality or the two worlds. We are not soul and human as we may have been taught; more truly, we are living soul in the flesh. We are not a light body and a physical body; more accurately, we are the result of the light body in this plane, for we are already beings of light. There exists absolutely no separation between these aspects.

The Middle East calls this mirror, "Journey into Darkness." If we see dualities then we are essentially walking in illusion into darkness; therefore, the idea is to become aware of this, that when we see right or wrong, when we agree or disagree, we best allow this mirror to guide us back to seeing only oneness. If we do not live in alignment with

our own energy stream, we then get swept into duality, trapped in the "I am right and you are wrong" life. Think about this for a moment. How can this truly be in reality? How can only one person be correct all of the time, or hold the only right perspective on life? Can the rest of the world really be incorrect? You and I know each human has their own experiences which validate their own perspective. No two individuals can sense and perceive in the exact same manner. And when the reflections occur, they are as unique to the individual as the individual is to them self, for it is their reflection from which their life shows every moment, no one else's.

In essence, this mirror reveals to us that we do live through the darkness in error, rather than in the brilliant light of higher truth. Its reflection really does have the propensity to magnify the idea of duality, its sole purpose to mentally startle us as a Master teacher would with their waking stick. It is about awakening our inner realization to how we currently view this world, our experience, and our interaction with people. It constantly and continually attempts to bring out for our understanding not only what we judge, but also how we live within that judgment. Duality and all the illusions there from, are the opposite of this truth; thus, we journey into darkness, the darkness of mind and life. Living in this manner utterly blinds us to the truth through all the ways we each live, expressing our self in obedience to the constructs, beliefs, and limitations we formulate by how we judge life to be.

You may honestly think you know a person. Do you really? As was offered earlier, in most cases you do not. Why? The truth is, you know them only through how you judge them to be, and the reflection from the sixth mirror wants you to see this. Judgment confines us to live life within such a limited scope. We do not need to because life, in and of itself, is totally limitless, even expressing through a different reality in our world, which sadly goes by totally unnoticed by the vast majority of humanity. The intention of the sixth mirror is to help us dispel the myth of duality, to deliver us from a darkened mind. Many wonderful souls throughout the world – in current times, his Holiness the Dalai Lama; in ancient times, Buddha, the Christ, and Lao Tzu – work to crumble the illusion of duality by revealing its true form – a world-wide delusion! The moment we see life through our higher nature, we can only view and experience the true oneness of life as the concept of duality swiftly melts away.

Do you sense there is more to life than just the physical? Oh, but there is. Much more! In today's world, the sixth mirror clearly reflects how we are living only in the external sense, all the while ignoring the internal nature. Yes, living in duality. I, too, have lived there until I knew the difference! And we do this simply because our eyes are placed in front of our head, seeing outwardly, externally, all the while forgetting they are the windows to the soul. From the ideas and concepts shared thus far, I hope you realize to a greater extent how you can now become fully empowered each and every moment in the fullest sense of the word. To understand both the internal and external through eyes of oneness, and to create wholeness or an inner unification of your life, are the most important of all things in life – an internally unified being.

In order for this union to be achieved, there are times when the individual must apply what is termed as soul-searching, or finding one's self; hence, this mirror has been known to be called the Dark Night of the Soul. Such a title is clearly a blatant misnomer since this process more aptly relates to the dark night of our physical reality. It is simply a shedding or shredding process that strips away all the external illusions we have been unwilling to release, and potentially awakening the greatest healing we can ever encounter. The soul, in and of itself, does not – cannot – live in illusion; yet, a physically-based mind easily can. Interestingly enough, if we notice and acknowledge the reflections and then release them in the moment they occur, the so-called Dark Night need never come to pass. And even if it does, the shedding and emotional effect would be insignificant in scope versus what it can become at most times, especially in light of the way we live today.

So why do these Dark Nights occur after all? This is simple. We do not pay attention to the subtleties of life as they take place; therefore, a build-up occurs within us, called dross, which now becomes necessary to release. And this release, no matter how much or how

little, occurs all at once. Also, if this release does not occur, we begin to have physical or even mental breakdowns. It has to be stated that nature is a pretty smart energy source. For example, if we do not brush our teeth, plaque builds up to the degree that our gums may be compromised or our teeth may need removal. Similarly, our Dark Night is a natural safety mechanism which removes our soul plaque so we need not become ill. We gently suggest you be aware of this mirror of life every moment until you see *you*. Instead of waiting for this huge build-up of dross coming to pass and overwhelming you, watch what the reflection of this mirror shows you; thus, your change would swiftly and effortlessly shift. And don't forget, keep aware of what the other mirrors are showing you, for any one or more may very well help you understand why you are in *this* particular mirror, at *this* particular moment in time.

The seventh and final mirror available for us to utilize is: the Greatest Act of Compassion. Its parable reads: *Show to me the stone the builders have rejected, that one is the cornerstone*. Compassion is about empathy, not sympathy. Feeling sorry for another person is not compassion; it is actually sympathy. Through compassion – properly used – one helps others to understand themselves. When we implement sympathy, we actually block our self from true assistance, aside from the fact that it is another form of judgment. This closes us off. So how did Master Lobsang show compassion to help me understand myself? He first asked me this question, "Do you understand the compassionate side to the human?" I offered my best answer, "I think I do," to which he quickly replied, "Are you sure?" and suddenly he pushed me. Yes, I was obviously not prepared because I lost my balance, falling clumsily to the ground. I shot him a look of angered frustration while I straightened back up, nearly blowing my top as I swiped all the dust off my robes! Those softest brown eyes looked squarely into mine while he stated very politely, "Young man, you do not understand the true meaning of compassion." He offered me this thought regarding the path of the Bodhisattva, an enlightened being who, out of compassion, forgoes nirvana in order to save others, "Young man, your mind is very tight because you thought you had encountered an enemy; the truth is, you had not. On this path of true consciousness, you cannot have trash or a garbage-filled mind. Your mind will become tight, and this

is not the way." Continuing, "The mind should always be open and filled with our true compassionate higher nature where it will create a greater level of flexibility."

After a pause he shared, "Look at it this way. When the Bodhisattva encounters an enemy, they see the enemy as their teacher, and as such, they honor them as that teacher. If this is done then your enemy goes away." Since returning to the states, I have found this as the truth. On a tangent note, I vividly recall Rinpoche Kiela informing me during one conversation, "An enemy does not have to necessarily be outside of you. It may be internal just as much as external," which adds meaning to the phrase: We are our own worst enemy. We could define an inner enemy as any negative view of our self. If we choose to work with this view, honoring it as our teacher, it will help us to understand its purpose and ultimately free us from its viewpoint.

As with every principle, compassion is an action which should not be used solely for personal convenience or gain. True compassion is utilized in every moment and each situation we encounter along our path through life. Keeping in mind his use of non-traditional teaching methods, this is exactly why Master Lobsang gently shoved me, not meaning any harm but rather to show me how very little I understood the art and act of true compassion. A compassionate nature truly encounters very little resistance, for it shall only be greeted by the very same idea in return. Recall, if you will, the basic precept of Karma: *What you sow so shall you reap*, a principle naturally working with all things in life. Even in a very complex hectic world, you may enjoy a quiet life by purely living very simply. See the world and life as your teachers, because the truth is, they are. In fact, they are why we incarnate in the first place – for soul experience. The act of compassion is the path of mastery because there is only oneness when we truly live a compassionate life. Please understand, this does not mean to give yourself away. That will only drain you as explained earlier and sympathy will open the door for this to take place. True compassion takes the path of honor, always honoring life, taking nothing from it other than what we are able to personally use at any one time. True compassion is allowing life to be fluid, which it is anyways. Allow me to rephrase that. Because life is naturally fluidic,

we can choose to flow with it through our own flexibility by acting from true compassion.

Initially, this is no walk in the park because the reflections first shown to us from this mirror may not necessarily be enjoyable; in fact, through Karmic return, they may be the most difficult of all reflections since they will literally reveal just how angry, or sad, or even how selfish we may have become. Rather than fighting or denying these reflections, as we now do, choose to operate through our compassionate nature. This nature is to honor all of what we are shown as the teacher. Bow to it, and what we would subsequently experience is a very giving, flexible, compassionate-filled life in return. Truly, this can be the only reflection we would see. By the way, compassion is not about giving of money or material things, though these are a miniscule part of it. Compassion opens the door for others; it gives two additional arms for carrying things; it assists motorists stranded on a lone highway, or even smiles to simply cheer up a distraught stranger on the street corner. Material things are no match for compassion, for it is a heartfelt action to help the life of others become easier, no matter the situation in which they may find themselves. Purely from the wallet does not cut it.

With our heart as the dominate source, all reflections shift to higher purpose and they reveal the fullness or completeness within us. Compassion takes nothing, but gives all of itself to life and living. This unconditional being contains not one negative thought, and can only contribute crystal clear drops to the pool of world consciousness. This is to say, true compassion is the greatest strength any human can have, the greatest aspect any human can give. Compassion occurs only through acts of our love, kindness, and sharing in all ways we can. When we are doing compassionate things from our heart, God is there right along with us. We have the full ability to give of our love, the full ability to give the truth of our being, no matter what others give us in return. The return does not matter. They cannot hurt us. No one can.

It is my hope that some light has been shed on the reasons why your life is truly the way it is. It is my hope you now have a deeper

understanding of how life has actually been created by you – for you – so you may shift it to the very thing you desire the most, thus the importance of the second principle: *You attract to you what you are, not what you want*. At the very least, the seven mirrors reflect all of what you are bringing to you by way of Karmic activity. In a sense, they act as an early warning detection system, working for you but only when you see the mirror of life before you in each moment. No additional time, just your full attention. If you desire self-empowerment then you must first realize what you produce in your life, and from this awareness, you become a very powerful resource, not only to your self, but also to all the people whom you encounter.

Once the Principle of the Mirrors is mastered, you will instantly know whether you are placing crystal clear drops of water or brown sludgy silt into your personal pool of consciousness. You would also have the ability to shift consciousness, to filter and even clean much of the silt which has accumulated in the pool of mass consciousness of our world. By so doing, you have personally become an eraser of error thinking, if you will, as you constantly and continually focus on the clearing and filtering of the so-called super mind of our world. Your compassionate, unconditional nature will guide you to a very productive and peaceful life, filled only with great ease, all struggles slipping effortlessly to the wayside. Be cognizant of two truths: life is the school; love is the lesson. We fully realize there is much in this chapter, but it is well worth the undertaking if you truly desire to become fully realized and empowered in your life. This chapter alone may well be worth reading again so it becomes ingrained in your mind, your thoughts, your actions and awareness of them, for they are the keys to the implementation of the Law of the Mirrors. What does your life say to you, about *you*?

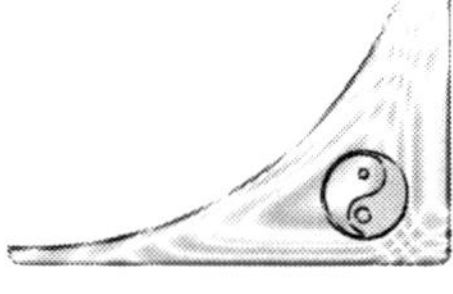

"Look within. Be still. Free from fear and attachment, know the sweet joy of living in the way."
Buddha

~ Chapter VII ~
The Principle of Synchronicity

I remember working very lovingly and diligently in the rice fields near the monastery, especially one particular day. I had spent the majority of my time after the harvest to help others bring the rice in. This was hard yet exhilarating work, for we needed to separate the rice kernels from the stalks after the plants had dried in the fields. After a wonderful swim in a nearby river I felt refreshed and sat down for the evening meal with my brothers. In the evening, Rinpoche Kiela appeared before me and asked, "Young man, have you really looked up at the stars in the night sky since you have been here in the Himalayas?" "No, Master, I have not," my voice betraying my joy over the idea, thinking it the perfect way to relax after such a long day of work. "Come with me," he openly invited.

As we walked out onto the roof I looked up and became instantly transfixed. "Whoa!," I thought as I exhaled slowly in complete awe as my peripheral vision made a futile attempt to absorb what I saw. The limitless depth and expanse of a crystal clear sea of twinkling stars seemed to envelope me. Billions of them! Never in my life had I seen so many. So *close*. "What do you see?" Master Kiela asked, breaking the infinite silence. I told him. Being always the teacher he asked a somewhat surprising question, "What else do you see in the reflection you are viewing in this night sky?" I answered somewhat easily, knowing now the implied meaning behind his questions, "I am witnessing a perfect flow or harmony in motion." He smiled while I continued, "Everything is working in complete union." He nodded and informed me, "It is time you truly learn the ideas behind the sixth Principle of Karma."

I have always enjoyed the way Masters teach in the Far East. The student never knows when the lesson appears, and when it does, the Masters use life experience as the example. Such style of teaching does make a lasting impression on the student's mind. I have attempted this same style in this part of the world; however, it apparently does not work very well, for most people do not understand the metaphors which are used. My teaching, therefore, has now become a little more direct in its manner of showing and explaining metaphors to the western mindset. In an earlier chapter I discussed how automated we generally have become, and moving people from this routine is not the easiest to accomplish, but worth every effort in all aspects of individual living. It is freeing and empowering! We are, indeed, very interesting in our lives and mannerisms. Let's continue.

Rinpoche Kiela began with this concept, "No matter where you go in life, there are many things you will do. Some will seem very special and important to you, and some will seem very insignificant and irrelevant. You must treat them all the same. Do you remember the caterpillar?" My answer was yes, fully remembering Master Lobsang pointing to the fuzzy creature and informing me of its significance. Do you realize that a vast number of people have never considered something as plain as a night sky to be such a wonderful teacher of harmony and how life can be so synchronistic? In truth, *all* things are this way, whether or not we personally agree. Here is the kicker: agreeing or disagreeing shifts harmony into disharmony. You see, the only thing separating importance and irrelevance is a judgmental mind. We tend to express a stronger commitment and perseverance towards those matters which we judge as important; whereas, we may very well become lackadaisical in what we do or even procrastinate from that which we judge as trivial. Rinpoche Kiela continued, "All things are important. In truth, no one thing is more important than another, and both should be treated with the same level of diligence,

no matter the importance or seeming insignificance. This includes each and every human in our world along with each and every experience."

He stated, "This is the basis for the next principle of Karma, the Law of Synchronicity. All things are perfectly equal." Continuing, "All of life is like this night sky," he pointed up towards our light show. "All of life is a perfect flow of harmony, and it does not matter whether a person agrees. In truth, life itself does not get out of harmony. Humans do." I was actually surprised at his last words as we sat and watched in pitch black silence, allowing the blanket of stars to embrace us. From where we sat under the expanse of the Universe, what Master Kiela said made sense because there was no discernable difference between any of the stars, each twinkling absolutely in harmony – equally. What a perfectly magnificent view of life in motion! We witnessed stars, planets, and space existing in total acceptance of each other while all moved in perfect unison. They acted as though they were totally unaware of anything else except to know there was not even one iota of insignificance about their existence. This same idea applies even when looking at a beach. Each grain is just as important as the other; else, the beach would not exist. Whether a Universe, beach, or even the mass of humanity, from these concepts we can simply flow in harmony with each other while being impervious to everything else in life.

Rinpoche Kiela softly offered, "It is time for us all to learn how to live in a very synchronistic fashion…" – living in songha as the Zen traditions call it. This simply means we can lift our self above the physical pulls of life and look through the eyes of our divine nature. This is an aspect born right along with us and is an integral part of our makeup, to see all people as our equal in all respects no matter their system of belief. Unfortunately, we have not yet accomplished this on a world-wide scale, for synchronicity still lies dormant within the majority. So how do we live our life in this fashion, in total peace and harmony, when life itself is so hectic? This question just answered itself if you had read it closely. If you think life as hectic, Karma will accept this seed from you and return its like kind – a hectic lifestyle. Life is hectic solely because you are interrupting it by possibly seeing

life as it is not, or attempting to control it which you cannot. If you are, in fact, doing these things, we suggest you let go and relax, release your grip before rigor mortis sets in. Allow life to be exactly what it is! Simply step out of the way and learn to allow. This is all what is required. Understandably, this may be most interesting to implement in this part of the world, and I personally know it is difficult to teach. But it does work.

Unlike all of nature around us and the stars above us which operate only in harmony and flow, we humans appear to hold onto our need for control, always so urgent and ever-present. We have come to believe that someone has to be in control, even if it is our self; yet, in truth, no one need be. Which world-renown philosopher, scholar, Master, Guru, or spiritual text flatly declares that some *one* must be in control? You see, in monastic living no one is in control. Yes, there is a Llama to oversee the facility, in my case Rinpoche Kiela, but he is not a so-called boss. A Master, yes. Not a boss. No monk needs to be told what they need to do because they can easily see and do what requires attention in that moment. They work in union – voluntarily – with each other without an inkling of opposition. They honor all life and each other, recognizing every thing as *awe*-fully important, no matter how seemingly small it may appear, from the tiniest insect to the entire planet. To them there is only equality. And equal with you and me.

You may certainly ask, "Yes, Steven, that may seem to be easy to do in a monastery in the remote foothills of the Himalayas, away from city life, a family, with children, a job, a car, traffic, and…, and…" Placing all judgment aside, life in a monastery is not at all a walk in the park – oh no – coming from one who lived in one for many years. But living in equality, peace, and harmony is truly not all that difficult to accomplish in this part of the world, either. You see, it all comes down to how one views the world, life, people, and more importantly, them self. So…how do *you* see the world, life, and people? Here is the key question to ask yourself, "What is important to me and what is unimportant?" Your answers may very clearly reveal how duality has slyly entered your life, a subject shared in the last chapter. All things are equal means just that. No exceptions. Yet we still do not see it that

way. God, our Father, Super Mind, the Creative Principle, no matter your personal name, cannot create with inequality built-in because, if it does, this makes God an ego-based concept. Thank Itself that It is not!

Feeling the item as insignificant, an ego-based human will pay no mind and easily step over sidewalk litter rather than take a slight moment to drop it in a nearby receptacle. This act is truly considered a compassionate move for Mother Earth and the rest of humanity. Yes, I realize this is a small gesture, but imagine *every* human picking up after themselves and what they see around them. Wouldn't the world become very clean? Seeing a cleaner environment, perhaps we would be less inclined to discard items out the car window. Is this an insignificant act? Is a clean world a small thing? From the eyes of Equality – the Law of Synchronicity – this is our natural state of living if we but only enter this level of realization.

Earlier, it was related to you my story about the tiny simple caterpillar, and if it did not have life then neither would we. One part of creation may not survive without the other. The truth is, a clean world simply requires clean people. We are not talking of physical cleanliness; we are talking of our inner nature which means we should not judge negatively or even feel this way, nor create a negative act. Let us all create harmonious acts and we have a world of harmony. This is cleanliness.

This begs the question, are we clean? It begins with a clean mind. A clean mind is free of clutter, meaning no judgments. Without judgments we now have a clean world, Karmically speaking. This also covers our emotions of current times which are filled with so many variants on life. Truly, all we really need is one emotion; the rest are unclean. To Rinpoche Kiela, if we clutter our self internally as we are wont to do then the same is going to occur in the outer world. There is no way around it. Does this all seem trivial to you? If so, then truly consider this Principle as the very stone right in front of you on your path, the one you may be overlooking in your own life. Your attention to it may very well be worth the journey.

Along with equality comes the next idea we would like to present. It is the concept of our connectedness with all things in our world. Yes, it was talked of earlier in the introduction, but we would now like to look more deeply in this concept for you as it applies to this Law. Under the Principle of Synchronicity, the notion of separation perishes from all thought, and the fervent belief that we must live in struggle or chaos silently and easily slips into oblivion. Figuratively speaking, it is my hope that all this repetition does not beat your mind to death; yet, I feel this requires a repeat. *Every thing* is connected, from the tiniest insect to the human; in fact, from a single atom to the farthest star in the farthest galaxy, for this is what Rinpoche Kiela explained to me that evening, "We are just as important as the stars in the night sky. We are the only ones in our world who have the ability to realize these stars are even there. Does any other creature realize their existence? Instead of understanding our connection *to* them, we have established the notion of separation *from* them – along with all things – which is falsehood. Not only this, but we have even separated ourselves from what we term as God, our Creator."

He continued, "No living thing is truly separate from any other, for one may not live without the other. On the other hand, you in your part of the world seem to treat everything almost as being insignificant and separate from you, except that which you individually consider and judge as most important." If I may ask, "Is your career most important?" "Is your family the most important to you?" "Or do you feel in your heart that the love of your life is the most important?" If you answer yes to any one or all of these questions, I submit to you that the last Principle of Karma, the Law of the Mirrors, is reflecting right back to you all those aspects and people of your life who are truly in control of you. Of course, it is fully understood they are a major factor in your life; yet, to have a life of synchronicity, you must find equality in every aspect of it before life can truly flow as it is meant to. What is the intended meaning here? We, as the individual human, are the most important idea in our life. This is not to say we are meant to be arrogant or filled with self-importance – remember Karma? It simply reveals the inner concept, that for any other thing to be important to us then it must be in us first. Such a mindset will actually bring things closer to us and may even give us the impression

of a closer relationship to all of life. *All* things are special – including *you.* Treat all things in this manner then separation melts from you.

Have you ever stopped for awhile to purposefully and genuinely observe wildlife in their natural habitat, to watch how they operate within their environment and with life, to notice their interactions with others in their family unit and other species? It can be both a learning and amusing experience, for I have noticed a few things about them: 1) They remain constantly present, fully in the moment and know this is the only place they are able to live, 2) their marked territory is neither smaller nor larger than is simply required to satisfy their food source and family protection, only protecting it for these reasons, not because they feel superior or inferior to their neighbor, 3) playfulness is a genuine and necessary part of growth besides building and maintaining their home, 4) they "go to work" to feed the family unit. It appears wildlife lives as we humans do, right? There exists, however, a big difference in one aspect. They live in perfect harmony, seeming utterly unconscious of any inequality and time. They interrupt nothing; we interrupt everything. Why do we do this?

We are the only living creature with the ability to truly think independently of life, and herein lies our break from synchronous flow. It is our independence of life. Have we become too independent? While studying in the Far East, it is vividly remembered how rarely I ever knew either the day of the week or time of day simply because I rose with the sun and went to bed with it at most times. No, I did not take the sun to bed with me! You have got to love English literalism, and come to think of it, this could very possibly be the whole issue for us because we are quite literal for the most part. Only my rooftop stargazing during those brilliantly clear nights interrupted bedtime. They were well worth the small interruption if one wants to term them as such.

Independent thought, in and of itself, is not at all erroneous. My point is, we utilize our thought – independence – in an extremely erroneous fashion. Those in the Western culture are taught to only focus on how and what to think with their lower thought forms. Generally speaking, these place more attention on the external environment

and physical possessions, thus allowing miniscule attention to higher, non-physical endeavors and divine thought. The key to the proper use of mind is being mindful as the Zen monastic traditions term it. Although our mind is one of the most amazing and powerful aspects we have, we take it all for granted still to this day. It seems we are treating our ability to think independently as though it is a trivial activity while it is actually not. Forgive my straightforwardness; yet, in all honestly, we genuinely believe there exists absolutely no consequence to all what goes on between our ears.

From what I have personally experienced with my Master teachers in the Far East, this body organ cannot, by any means, be labeled as inconsequential or be taken for granted since I now realize the truth of the matter. It is our very own mind which shapes our life, and we are the only creatures in this reality who are capable of accomplishing this task. Yes, we do shape our life. Do we shape it in the manner in which we choose? The reality is, is, more times than not, this is simply not the case, though many may believe otherwise. Do you recall the second Law? If not, you may possibly want to take another peek into what it offers. Look at our world today and you now see just how we use these transcendent attributes – mind and thought. The connection or even disconnection is now shown to us only because it may not be denied. This is so because of our connection to consciousness and each thought which emanates from us contributes to the idea of consciousness. This is why it is advised that we know what our mind is doing in all moments as it is our personal contribution to consciousness. As the individual thought goes, so also goes the mass thought, ultimately – positive or negative, local and global Karma, respectively.

What was learned from my teachers is that, overall, the inhabitants of our world totally misuse their ability to think. It appears the world prefers to think only for physical material success, ego-based domination and/or control, even for destruction just to prove a point. How truly fascinating! It appears we would rather use our faculty in *this* fashion rather than in the fashion for which it is truly designed, our divine nature, which has been embedded within us all along since the beginning! While on the rooftop with Rinpoche Kiela that starry

night, he said something which really surprised me. It was something I had never even considered and I believe this to be the case with most of us in this part of the world. It comes from the way we have all been taught.

Consider what he shared with me that night. "Our ability to think independently is just as our Creator is. It is divine." The ability to think and realize what we think will place the individual in overwhelming awe the moment they recognize what this truly means and the extent of it. Our mind may be material and operate in the lower realms, or it may reach much higher and operate in the divine realms. Our choice! Simple as that. The truth is, we need merely align with it and nothing more because it is already present; therefore, when we put forth only our divine nature, then according to the principles of Karma – which you are now getting to know quite well – only divine nature shall return to us, no other. On the other hand, when any thing is taken for granted we invariably overlook its significance, and the Law of Synchronicity awakens, fully illuminating its guiding reflection right at us, hoping to snap us back to attention, to remember the importance of all things.

Allow me to repeat, our most influential and indispensable attribute rests squarely between our ears, for this is what determines the human. As long as our mind is not in a synchronous flow then how can our life ever be? If our mind is the steering mechanism of our life, why do we prefer to give it total control as though driving a bumper car at the local carnival? We do just that! It is written in The Dead Sea Scrolls that unlike the rest of life, we humans do not operate under the one Law, The Law of Harmony. Nowhere does it say we are *incapable* of doing so; rather, it purely implies that we have *chosen* not to. Somehow we have separated ourselves from the one Law; yet, we do not have to – ever.

When we align with this principle it does not mean we give ourselves up or lose total control; on the contrary, we shall become more dynamic than ever. If knowing this principle could offer us harmony, then why would we not immediately and thankfully operate with it? Here is a simple answer. Frankly, we are *not taught* to live in

harmony, to fully connect and flow with the idea of self which is internally generated by our mind and extends itself into life. We have actually been taught the exact opposite of this, allowing the external environment to be our prime persuader behind how we think and feel, while we constantly attempt to find out where we fit.

Heaven forbid if we do not fit in with the crowd! Does this truly create harmony? It appears we live and operate only in a mode of constant interruption. No wonder our minds are out of synch! Unlike all the other living creatures in the world which spend their time only in the present moment, we humans seem to focus on and spend the majority of our time in the future. Simply be present with your mind! This kind of makes us wonder which one is truly utilizing their highest ability, the other creatures or humans? This is offered because at the present moment we are keeping our true dominion buried in a grave of dormancy, covered with a mind filled with chattering monkeys as Buddha once stated it.

Returning now to my extraordinary rooftop discussion with Rinpoche Kiela, I vividly remember his subtle grin when he turned to look at me, an expression that seemed to say, "Ok, young man, here is one for you." Although that evening occurred so many years ago, I can recall even to this moment the profound impact his words had on me, indeed, my eyes truly opened to a whole new level of understanding. He offered a roll reversal; the italics are mine, "What if *you* are this thing we call God or the Creator?" He explained further, "*You* created our world and all life on it. And you have the natural, innate urge to have your creation strive to be just like you. As parents, are we not precisely this way with our children?" He paused for a moment while I sat motionless, totally captivated by his every word. "Now, let us say you desire that your creations search for this ability to be like you, wanting them to look and discover for themselves the key to achieving this absolute equality." He then popped the "big one" on me, "Here is my question for you: How would you do it and where would you hide this ability?"

Only then did I realize how patient he was, for I pondered for what I felt was forever, only to blurt out my gut honest truth, "I

am not sure, Master." His answer totally astounded me, "First, you would make it so simple that *logic* would have great *difficulty* seeing and accepting it. Second, you would put it in plain sight, ensuring it would be even more difficult to accept." After a brief silence he asked, "Does this surprise you?" His question awoke me from my inner reflection, my mouth open, to which I could only form the words, "Yes it does." Not until many years later while studying the Bible, did I discover that Master Kiela was correct. From the Book of Matthew 18:3 & 4, "[3]...And said, Verily I say unto you, Except ye be converted, and become as little children, ye shall not enter into the kingdom of heaven. [4]Whosoever therefore shall humble himself as this little child, the same is greatest in the kingdom of heaven." In that moment the connection was made to what Master Kiela had intended for me to comprehend: *the absolute pure innocence of a little child* is the only key to realizing who we actually are.

You see, we are already divine and the requirement is to merely accept what we are taught we cannot be! Did that make sense? Put another way, by humbling ourselves as little children, entering that wonder-filled world of innocence which defies our adult logic, we appear in plain sight, aligning with and creating perfect symmetry between lower form and our higher divine nature, expressing perfect synchronicity within our self and with each other. Yes, we may certainly forget as we grow older; nevertheless, it remains ever-present. What a brilliant awe-inspiring gift! Imagine the Divine creating human life in divine equality, each one of us divinely equal even to the Creator Itself. Perfect! After all, don't we create our lives within each and every moment?

Do you desire to understand why your life is not as divinely synchronous as you may prefer it to be? I can only offer the tough and true answer: It is because of you and your interactions with the Principles of Karma. All of them coalesce to create the precise life you are now living. Please do not despair or shove this book between others in an obscure place in a fit of frustration. Be assured, your life is *totally* changeable through your knowledge, understanding, and use of these Principles. Mine was. Completely! We strongly suggest you stay with us through the course of this instruction manual, if you choose.

So, why do we not live our life through our divine nature as originally intended by the Creator? For one, is it really so very difficult to believe we are something totally opposite to that which we have been conditioned to believe? Also, these next questions may enlighten us as to the reasons: 1) Are you waiting for either Prince or Princess Charming, or wishing to win the lottery? 2) Are you only seeking the material rewards and accepting the ego-rewarding tasks? 3) Do you ultimately use those near and dear to you to attract the admiration and approval from others? Have you ever experienced a relationship such as this? Kindly take a moment to ponder these questions because they will help reveal why your life is the way it is. In other words, if your mind has settled into these areas then you now may realize why your divine nature remains dormant. Let us peer more closely into each question.

Question one: Are we waiting for either Prince or Princess Charming, or wishing to win the lottery? The key concepts underlying this question are the ideas of waiting and wishing, for both lure our focus away from the divine to the physical level and material aspects of life. A young man around two thousand years ago, a Master who understood and lived completely in divine nature, offered to the masses, "Take no thought for your life, what ye shall eat, or what ye shall drink; nor yet for your body, what ye shall put on…seek ye first the kingdom of God [within you], and his righteousness [truth]; and all these things shall be added unto you." Considering that waiting means the act of remaining inactive or stationary, know there is no thing worth waiting for in the lower physical realm, unless of course, you want to remain inactive or stationary. Be careful what you ask for because what you put forth returns to you. In this case, Karma will gladly help you wait – indefinitely! If you choose to wait, may we suggest you at least sit in a comfortable chair. But then, why wait when your unconditional divine nature, that inner aspect which will bring all things to you, *wants* to accept your call right now?

The second part of the question – wishful thinking – can easily diminish the reality of who we truly are. This becomes accomplished through things such as "I wish my life were different" to wishing we had more of whatever while actually accomplishing very little at best.

Wishful thinking does nothing for us because it is unfocused thought which may very well create the reverse of what we are wishing for. The truth is, it is more closely tied to the feeling of dissatisfaction with our life at present. Now this takes us all the way back to the very first principle: *What you sow so shall you reap*. Indeed, a wishful mind contains thoughts which tell us we wish our life to be different. It is actually saying, we desire to move away from what we now have. Are we not really recreating what we already have by living in the previous fashion, thus planting our own dissatisfaction with each thought? Karma agrees. Hence, we go nowhere as our mind sinks more deeply into the quicksand of wishful thinking. Within this mindset there is no room for the Law of Synchronicity or forward movement since we can only create discord while going through the motions. I beg to repeat what has already been suggested. We can always begin right where we are and move toward a different outcome. If we wish to be divine then become that which we already are. We lose nothing but gain all things. Plant divine seeds in your life and a divine life will spring forth. No waiting or wishing is ever necessary!

Question two: Are we only seeking the material rewards and accepting the ego-rewarding tasks? For the vast majority this would seem to be the case, especially in the western mindset. This question points to the material mind, a mind genuinely believing such rewards will help us feel good and bolster our self-esteem. As honorable as our intentions may be, it is suggested we quickly make a u-turn; otherwise, some one or some circumstance shall take control. Why would this occur? It is termed as Karma because living in ego returns only a greater ego and there is no other way around this idea. Seeking material rewards places our external environment in the driver's seat. This happens because we focus on performing only those tasks which have the propensity to further *inflate* our material-ego mind. Karma yet again. This now entrenches us ever more deeply in the realm of falsehood rather than the higher realm of truth.

Here is a very important question which is needed to be asked along with a major hint: Building a life on falsehood creates a Karmic return of _______? Tackling things from this perspective, we live blinded by our own self because the ego kidnaps us from our divine nature. Subsequently, it now blocks both the creation of a synchronous life and the direct involvement of consciousness. Such individuals are destined for quite a number of tumbles as will be shown to us by the next Principle of Karma. Since no thing is above the Law, can we not also include business entities, non-profit organizations and governments? Remember Enron and MCI WorldCom? Perhaps it is best we do all things which are placed in front of us, not just those which build and inflate our small self – ego. The ego desires to saturate every fiber of our being solely in material physical nature, thus expanding our difficulty in reaching higher divine nature. After all, it is the lower nature which creates and inflates the ego in the very first place.

Question three: Do we ultimately use those near and dear to us to attract the admiration and approval from others? This question should be heavily considered as it implies a manipulative mindset which we all may possess in moments. This frame of mind is something to avoid. Perhaps this is a prevalent practice and predicament throughout the Western culture; at least it appears so. Do you not see people using people, businesses using businesses, governments using governments? Notice what is going on here. People and entities actively use others for their personal benefit, only to end up never trusting any one and any thing. Never trusting others? This begs the question, "Do you hold unconditional trust for those who are using you? Perhaps we don't necessarily trust because of Karmic return! These twelve Principles are relentless in every aspect of our life; in this case, they shall guarantee our own experience of being used, just as readily as guaranteeing our own experience when we use others. Of course, the experience deepens when we somehow find ourselves amongst those who do exactly what we do, and for some "unknown reason," we become drained in life. Ever heard of: *You attract to you what you are, not what you want?* In the long run we find ourselves alone, merely moving from one individual to the next, not a one trusting us as we are unable to trust them. A perpetual, downward-spiraling cycle, indeed, until we choose to break free from it by merely reaching upward for the ever-present roots of our higher divine nature.

Allow me to bring up one last point. What happens when we actually judge some thing or some one as significant? I offer this pivotal point: The degree to which we now give the object or individual importance is directly proportional to the degree of their fall into insignificance at a later time, even to the point of being completely overlooked or taken totally for granted. You may wish to read that again. Ironically, this will come from the very person who makes these two judgments in the first place. Never place any thing or any one on a pedestal, especially your self for that matter. Have you ever felt you were being taken for granted? Doesn't this occur in our relationship with a significant other? Kindly reflect on this for a moment. The mere act of declaring a thing or person as important moves what was once before the important thing down a notch or two on the priority list, does it not? Certainly it may appear we hold equal weight to both, at least initially; however, if our heart remains focused on the "new ticket" item, the other shall easily fall to the wayside into the "has" bin. To best visualize this, we invite you to watch infant toddlers play with their toys. Do they not appear engrossed with that toy right in front of them until another comes to view, at which time they drop the first only to reach for the second? Parents call this a short attention span. Perhaps, but this does give credence to my point.

This is similar to going after the exciting new fashions or newest generation of electronics. Vital today; passé tomorrow! Most likely you agree that no human desires or wishes to be treated like this because, if they are, we both know they will go elsewhere to seek validation and worth. And here is the fascinating part, we have been *conditioned* into this, for it is the exact same way we treat our self. As our life comes to a close, as we approach our last physical breath, only then do we realize we have truly forgotten and taken totally for granted the most valuable part of our life – our *self*. This idea of self is the higher ideal known as the soul which now means, based on the Principles of Karma, we must incarnate again at a later time to learn and never forget the unseen self – our divine nature.

As are the other Laws of Karma, the Law of Synchronicity is not a punishing Law; instead, it guides us through its reflection, revealing just how and when we make the erroneous judgment of declaring

one thing more important than another. It provides us the moment to immediately take care of the situation regardless of how trite a person or thing may appear to us. Keep in mind, do not merely handle the situation with minimal effort based on personal convenience, but delve into it full tilt, giving it everything we have into it each moment. This is what the Christ intended for us to understand when He shared the story about the woman who gave her last few pennies. He, like so many other Masters, was not explaining about money in the literal sense; he was, however, offering truth through the allegory that we each give our whole self to life in all we do along our journey, giving all we have just as that woman did. Two things will absolutely happen, 1) our energy and aliveness quickens, and 2) Karma returns more unto us in like kind. The choice is entirely up to you; live all the way full tilt or just half way. And keep the following in mind. When giving your full self to life then Karmic action will return to you complete fulfillment through all what you say and do. Anything less and life will match you in all regards.

If we see and hear life through the negative filters we have placed behind our eyes and ears, we shall naturally hold back and withdraw. What will Karma do in this case? As its return action, do you suppose it would cause life to hold back and withdraw from us? On the other hand, if we solely view life simply for what it is, all our judgment and attached negativity within the constructs of our life silently slithers into a somnolent sleep. This next allows only our unconditional flowing nature to express through all our actions – songha. And what will Karma return to us now? Do you sense more of the same? I do, too. So you see, when we come right down to it, we need simply make a personal choice, the choice to live with and through our unlimited divine nature, or the choice to remain confined in the stuffy and limiting box of material reality.

Remember these words: seek first your divine higher nature and all else shall be given you. Imagine your life with all your dreams fulfilled. Imagine how crystal clear the pool of world or mass consciousness would look like when each human has only their own like kind drops to add. Where in *this* environment can inequality, judgment, or conflict arise, individually or collectively? To think this type of world

is available right now and yet witnessing how we do not choose it as a collective civilization is quite a surprise to me. Do you prefer to live fully in a very synchronous way? Perhaps your introduction to the sixth Law of Karma now inspires you to go ahead with that choice as you hold to inner discipline leading you down the path of true humility, dissolving once and for all, your world from aggression, frustration, stress, and inequity. You would enter into sublime, endless peace, a state of grace so awe-inspiring to all. Here it is, right *within* you! This is that very attainable reality wherein we each live and share our divine selves. In divine equality!

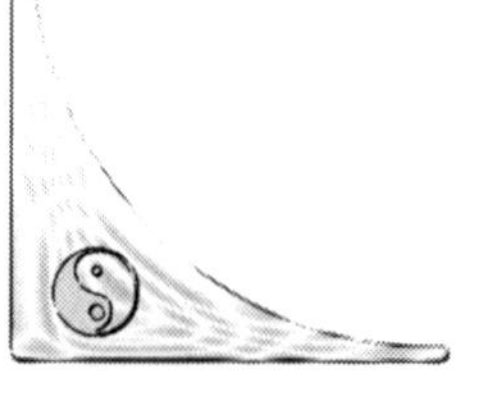

"One who is able to realize the truth within one's mind has sown the seed of buddhahood."
Buddha

~ Chapter VIII ~
The Principle of Direction and Motives

One day in late spring Masters Lobsang and Kiela approached me asking that I join them on a short journey because they both desired to show me something. Instantly perceiving my obvious change in energy, Master Lobsang queried, "Why do you always get so excited when either of us ask you to journey with us?" I exclaimed on reflex, "I always learn something new about myself and life while I'm with you, Master! This always brings joy to me," while thinking to myself, "My mind always seems to expand exponentially when I journey with you two!" Also, perhaps unconsciously, my energy level rises because these two wise and gentle souls were simply the first to greet me and purposely invited me to accompany them shortly after my arrival in India. Indeed, I have known them the longest since my arrival, and wherever they traveled they took me with them. In retrospect I realize how each of their lessons took me yet a step closer to my goal of higher divine nature. I thoroughly enjoyed my experiences while learning and accepting new concepts of life and my self. Master Lobsang smiled, "Is it really necessary for a person to learn anything from a teacher?" "Well – yeah!" I replied, adding some momentary wisdom, "I have heard many times over the years that when the student is ready the teacher would come." He shook his head ever so slightly, "Young man, the teacher never seeks out the student. It is the student who must seek out the teacher." Oh boy, here we go again.

My teacher continued, “You are your own teacher and your own student but only when you can observe and realize what it is you do, think, and feel while involved with an experience, never after. Remember, when observing, do so only through your objective self. Do not self condemn for this creates a bind within you. This is what your statement actually means. Your higher divine part educates and teaches your lower physical part, but not until the physical is ready to listen to the whisper of the soul.” He paused before adding, “A teacher who is external to you can only offer the ideas and principles which guide you in this journey. It is entirely up to your own internal teacher to filter those concepts to your lower part in order for your physical mind to understand and accept them. Do you understand this idea?” My response was a simple reflective nod as we walked.

Masters Lobsang and Kiela were merely two guides willing and able to get me to see what I already knew. “Is this true for all people?” I asked. He nodded, “Yes it is. A monk’s function is to simply open another’s mind and allow their own inner teacher do the rest.” It appears we each have this ability after all, as Master Lobsang confirmed; yet, we simply require the precepts through higher spiritual education in order to remember the basis of our divine self. You see, it is all about allowing our self to move away from the fleshly pulls of life, not about forgoing the flesh altogether. Think about this for a moment. If we do attempt to abandon our flesh, there would neither be a student nor any experience. The meaning is more aligned with our level of awareness through experiences and their subsequent impacts, all for inner growth. This is part of our wholeness, just as the body is the fingerprint of our soul and its journey, for this is how the soul senses and feels. The bottom line is, we *do* require our fleshly body in this world, but we do *not* require it to dominate our soul to the degree that it has! Besides, can you really not eat when you are nearly starving to death? Our material reality, believe it or not, is the one key ingredient for our higher knowledge. “You mean we need material reality?” I can hear you ask. Not in the “needy” sense, but as a tool. I repeat, higher spiritual knowledge filters through our inner teacher down to our physical mind, all from how and what we learn in the physical world. Our body is our soul’s vehicle in the material world. If not, why have a body at all? It is nothing more than this.

The instant Master Lobsang opened the outside gate, all our eyes fell upon my old friend, Mr. Tiger, slumbering in the shade in his regal manner; yet, as we walked out, he must have recognized our motions or scent because he immediately arose and approached us. I must tell you, there is nothing like losing my fingers in the abysmal depths of the tiger's furry coat while rubbing and petting him. I thought to myself, "This is a monstrous cat, yet so very calm and gentle-hearted." And what a purr! So deep and throaty. The monks' name for the tiger made perfect sense now – Shanti Che – for peaceful tiger. He appeared to continually flow right along with whomever whenever for whatever. I enjoyed the big cat immensely because I felt so safe and content while with him. I mean, come on now, what or who is really going to disturb you as you walk with a full-grown male Bengal tiger strolling along your side?

The four of us continued our walk in silence as was normal. As a fellow neophyte – beginner – we allow the Masters to determine when talk or silence was appropriate, for we learn early on that the student cannot learn through the chatter made from their own thinking or talking; therefore, one must wait until their lessons come. I remained in silence, simply allowing for the teachers' guidance, for the lessons always seemed to occur at the appropriate moment. We journeyed for a rather short period of time in the space of silence when suddenly Lobsang turned off the path, immediately followed by Kiela, then me and my furry companion, the leader weaving between the trees and thicket. I faintly heard the rush of water just a moment before a magnificent clearing opened right in front of us, the sun piercing through the lush canopy of foliage. Framed by trees and underbrush, directly in front of us, a waterfall cascaded into a crystal clear pool of water, completely surrounded by rich green moss. Of course I walked through it! But only after taking my sandals off. Just to feel it. So velvety cool! Master Lobsang motioned me to sit, and as I did, Shanti Che wriggled between my ribs and arm, his twenty-plus-pound head coming to rest on my thigh and closed his eyes.

Master Lobsang was the first to speak. "This is where you should come to meditate and allow your inner teacher to guide you through all the lessons," he began. "Come here to reflect on them and see how

they fit in your life. When you are here, only nature itself will offer any sound or disturbance. It is very silent and will allow deep inner reflection and inner conversation on all of your teachings." "Great suggestion!" I thought to myself. I had absolutely no idea this spot was so close to the monastery! This is the perfect place to reflect on my lessons, to commune with nature and my higher self, the rush of water near the fall or the trickle of water downstream providing my rhythmic, musical background. Along with all the green parrots. Hundreds of them. Everywhere!

The voice of Master Kiela interrupted my thoughtful planning, my attention snapping back to the gentle guides next to me. "Young man, no human has the ability to think of two things at the same time. And no one may do two things at once and remain truly effective in doing either." My face must have wrinkled in bewilderment yet again because he continued with, "Young man, you cannot daydream of the place you are already in while you are learning, both at the exact same moment. This is the Principle of Direction and Motives, and you must learn this. You must learn to keep your mind focused on what you do in any given moment," as an ever-so-slight smile crossed his face. Did he know what I was thinking, where my thoughts had gone? These two monks constantly amazed me with their acute level of intuitive sense. It was as if they could actually read my mind. Indeed, I have found they could. And don't forget, they did attract me here to this wonderful country in the first place!

Master Kiela had just introduced me to the next principle of Karma. This Law, through its simplicity, is beautiful in concept because it points us toward our God-given, higher divine nature, an aspect which most humans completely ignore. This is not surprising since it seems the majority also ignores the twelve Principles of Karma. This is why the flesh should not overpower the soul or our inner divine nature. This blinds us to higher concepts. Do you desire your life to be different? Have you ever wondered how you can arrive at a different result? Truly, this Principle will assist you should you so choose; in fact, make an earnest attempt to internalize all of them and find out for your self.

Allow me to repeat what Rinpoche Kiela offered me that day. We humans are not able to *think* of two things simultaneously, just as we are not able to *do* two things simultaneously. Did you get that? It does not matter, regardless of what you or I think we believe or have been taught. This action is simply not possible. Purely and simply, the human is able to think or do only one thing at a time. We Americans are quite humorous because the Western culture has conditioned our mindset to believe that we actually *can* multitask, as it is called. However, stop for just a minute and observe. For instance, as a passenger, do you honestly feel safe when the driver composes and sends a text message or at least talks on their cell phone, while *simultaneously* driving in heavy traffic? Or do you know of any individual who can effectively listen to two conversations at the same time, one with you personally and the other through the phone? Do you feel you have just been put on hold? Can you daydream and read a book at the exact same time, all the while remembering every detail in your dream and fully comprehending all what you are reading in the text? In doing these, the person cannot give their full attention to either, whether it is their most important task at hand or least important one. "You're not paying attention to me!" is expressed both verbally and physically all too often in this part of the world. Do we wonder why? We simply cannot do all things at once.

From this perspective alone we can understand the underlying meaning of this principle. Does it not make sense now, that when we do two things at once, we are truly divided and ineffective? Wasn't it once stated that a house divided cannot stand against itself? This would also apply to our life. If we attempt to do two things at once, we are not able to realize the seeds which we plant along the way by doing things through only partial awareness. Remember the idea of being present from the second chapter? When doing or thinking about two things at the exact same time, can we fully be 100% present in both activities? This is not possible; yet, the attempts by others are observed quite frequently. In nearly every instance, both tasks end up significantly inferior or even incomplete. Evidently, those tasks are best handled with a present mind. And do not forget the total drain on our emotional, mental, and physical well-being throughout all this, an experience which has already been discussed

in the previous chapter. Unfortunately, we live in a world very much divided, a world which cannot bring either a sense of wholeness or any level of unification, not even a level of completeness for which most humans seek. So why do we create division? It certainly cannot lead to wholeness because, in truth, the concept is opposite of what wholeness implies. More importantly, there does not exist any way for an individual to achieve their self-empowerment as long as they express or live in a divided manner.

There is another stone hiding a deeper meaning to this Law and we wish to expose what lies beneath. On the surface it appears our lives are swept in a complex and whirlwind culture, a society demanding our immediate attention on everything around us – each moment! When first studying this principle with my Master teachers in the Far East, I sensed a direct underlying idea to this principle. This Law plainly exposes a deep chasm, an abyss if you will, dividing us between spiritual – not religious – and material values. Consider for a moment, even the Christ knew of and fully understood this principle when He clearly stated this same truth, using different words of course, that we cannot worship God and mammon. He also expressed this truth through another phrase: a house divided cannot stand. Doesn't our scattered attention and constant attempts at doing two things at once validate this very principle?

Forgive me for going out on another limb here, but I feel there is no way we can positively establish higher spiritual values while, at the same time, live in division by diverting our full attention only to the lower material values. In other words, we must remain focused on only one or the other in our mind, not both at the same time as we currently believe we do. If we focus only on the spiritual, this is what we become; on the other hand, if we focus only on the material, then that is what we become. Can we effectively focus on both at the same time? I feel the words offered by the Master Christ were: Seek first the Kingdom of Heaven [higher knowledge, spiritual values] and all else is given unto us. Do we sincerely believe those words? Do we even live according to this truth? It does not appear so. Observe how we act. It is as though His statement is nothing more than mumbo-

jumbo in the Western culture, completely irrelevant to the culture's day-to-day busy life. Just stand back; simply observe people in their activities. Do you not witness the same? Ultimately, we are each measured by *spiritual* value in this world rather than by religion and material wealth, truth be told.

Now hold on for a moment and allow me to climb further out on the limb by clarifying the word "spiritual" from a monk's perspective. Spirituality has absolutely no attachment or relevance to any religious affiliation because it always was, is, and always will be an independent and individual divine aspect of *every* human. Kindly read that sentence again. Generally speaking, religion is a tax-exempt business organization displaying a symbol to which the congregants are requested to worship. Then it is cemented by human-made structure and dogma, utilizing trained missionaries to constantly seek and enlist additional members. A religion is our chosen path; spirituality is an integral, inseparable part of us, no matter the path. Allow me to add a tangent. When the Christ stated, "Seek ye first the Kingdom…," this does not at all imply our inability to have wealth or to label it as so-called evil. We certainly *can* have wealth. But here is the deeper meaning: seek the higher first then the second or all else will come of its own accord, free of struggle. If we seek only the lower then the other will never arrive. It cannot. The lower can only create division while the higher brings wholeness. This is truly an individual and personal decision.

This principle concerns itself with the creation of wholeness through our spiritual value, not our religious affiliation. From its mirror and guidance we will remove any idea of duality and its subsequent illusion of dual nature once and for all. In essence, physical form is the end result of our spiritual or light body. Put another way, if form is the end result then is not every human already whole, the same and equal with every other? Truly we are. Please keep in mind, I am not talking about religious concepts on spirituality; instead, I am talking about spirituality as a divine attribute of our inner nature. The mirrors of Karma will not reflect to us any level of spiritual value about us until we realize our split or divided nature.

Generally in this part of the world, we are conditioned that the most important attribute is the external; yet, this is simply not the case. If I am in error, please forgive me. But why do I observe so many people in our modern world feeding their external shell, only to starve their internal nature of being? By only following the external path, it is not at all surprising to observe so many people in our modern world not know where they fit in life. In truth, our inner self continually attempts to offer guidance on how we may return to our path of higher nature, a nature of being in which every human fits, through the Mirrors of Karma of course. This is totally opposite to the external perspective, in which case our ego appears to further the idea of our separation, especially from others. In this sense, higher consciousness, soul, or teacher, guides us along while we, the students, do all the searching. Here is the clincher: to find our "fit" we need only look inside in order to realize our true higher nature.

The force behind this search is simply the soul gently talking to us, "Okay, (insert your name here,) just how can you be doing two things at once right now in this one single moment? How can you focus? Your spiritual task truly contains the most important realization for you, yet you focus on a material task which is minor by comparison and reveals mostly pitfalls and mud puddles. Though there is infinite patience within me, I truly feel this is the moment for your 'Ah-ha,' but of course, it is completely your choice. This will be arrived at sooner or later, in this lifetime or another, for this is our purpose and our life together."

Any moment we choose to follow only the external or material road, it will not only lead us away from the truth of our divine being, thereby transforming us to a very shallow human, but such a road will also become much easier to follow over time. This material road will become a rutted and well-worn path, thus the ease in following this road. Its deep grooves prevent our every effort to alter course simply because we tend to follow the material mind too often. This is the well-worn road of life which most of us travel. Succinctly speaking, following the path of our ego-based mindset only leads to a dead-end, and according to my teachers, it always has.

On the other hand, pursuing our path to higher spiritual knowledge can only offer us great depth and wisdom to our character, elevating us from the physical to the divine human, our natural, spiritual, true state of being. Focusing solely on higher values, no room can exist for the attributes of greed, lust, selfishness, judgment, or any anger, manipulation, and frustration, to name just a few. Our spirituality is squeezed out to the same degree if we allow one or more of these to fester and grow within us. And dross accumulates. Spirit has absolutely no concern whatsoever with the external world, our fertile garden of materiality where these so-called wraths seem to migrate, propagate, and easily develop in our mind, only to then sprout into our life and experience.

These are merely attributes created by us from our trials and tribulations with material reality. They have nothing to do with our higher divine nature; yet, they may be teachers once we awaken to them as such. In truth, these experiences are actually a steering mechanism, a wake-up call if you will, alerting us that we have fallen off our higher path. This is precisely the reason why a monk desires nothing, for the monk realizes the very real power a simple desire may have over the true nature of a human. The pull of the lower will get us each and every time if we allow for the trap as it taunts us to follow it. Now, I do not suggest you ignore life totally and completely; what I *do* offer is that you not allow the external or materiality to be so dominant over your life because it really does not have to be. True, we must live and operate in a material world, this is for certain, but it can be done through spiritual eyes and divine being, manifesting a significantly more magnificent, peaceful, harmonious outcome.

When we were all at the waterfall that day Master Lobsang stated, "This area, your personal place for meditation, should be considered sacred ground. You should honor it as such." He continued, "By honoring it, this intimate space will teach you that all of life is a sacred space." He then dropped the bombshell on me, "Young man, the most sacred of all is the human itself because only the human [*each one of us!*] contains the very idea of divine realization. But for one to accomplish this, they must unify their self with the concept of oneness, oneness with their self and ultimately with all life. Here is

the interesting thing, we already are unified but we do not allow our minds to come to this realization. Once you become fully realized it creates sacred space, the temple of life, our body." "Wow, a simple quiet spot can have a person realize all this?" I asked myself totally amazed.

In *every* moment, truth be told, *every* one lives and resides in sacred space, the original garden from which *no one* has ever really left. That hidden waterfall and pond did, in fact, help me to understand that all space is sacred, and when a human being treats their space in this way, sacred life comes to that human, the original generator of it. This action and return action sounds rather familiar, does it not? What a great side-effect to Karmic principle. Such a divine elixir!

In truth, there is no such thing as duality while living in sacred space because we constantly and easily keep the lower path in check. We do not succumb to external pulls. In reality, there is no lower path, and the pulls of material life truly do not have a white-knuckle grasp on us at all! How can materiality pull at us when all is sacred living, when only divine life exists? Yes, the simple fact remains that we are completely surrounded by sacred space; yet, we overlook it for material things as we accumulate and throw away, as we stress and die. Such was my insight from just one simple lesson in a place so beautiful! To this day I am very grateful for being allowed to see through those eyes, to see all life and humankind as sacred. Working through this principle will give our life a whole new meaning and how to live it. In a world broiling in seeming discord, absolute harmony can easily and completely take hold of those who abide by the Law of Direction and Motives, totally free from inner division.

What are most of us focusing on? Are we in a hurry? When we awaken each day, do we take the time to be thankful? Do we make peace with our true higher source? Do we give our family love and attention before we run off for the day? Do we foster hidden agendas of personal gain and feed the compulsions of our lower carnal nature, completely ignoring the rest? Ask yourself these questions and, as before, let us view these one at a time so you understand their overall impact upon our lower and higher natures. These questions were posed

to me that day by Master Lobsang as he told me of this Principle of Direction and Motives. What is your motive? – is the intention. Keep in mind, the Law of Direction and Motives concerns itself only with the concept of whether a person is pursuing materialism or spirituality by living in truth. Both offer their own set of Karmic returns, potential life-threatening dilemmas or personal empowerment, respectively.

The idea of direction is that we are not able to go in two directions at the same time. Call me if you have seen a person literally split in two as they pursue both ways. Sincerely, I have observed people go one way or the other, though they inform me to the contrary. This principle also implies that if we momentarily choose the spiritual road only to return to our material travels, we are actually making the attempt to follow one *and* the other. "Seek ye first the kingdom…," echoes in my mind. So choose only one and go in that direction. Ask yourself, "In which direction do I travel?" Keep in mind, you will gain wonderful insight from either road, but if you find yourself in a state of discomfort or frustration at most times, then listen to your soul because this is where that particular sense is arising from. What to do? Simply shift your direction and seek the higher path, then harmony is yours.

Question 1: What are most of us focusing on? Actually this is a very critical question; therefore, please do not take it lightly. When you ask the question to yourself, how do you feel about it? Now let that feeling be your guide. Follow it, because it will point you in the direction of your focus. This question can grab your attention, awakening your awareness so you will gaze upon your priorities. Are they on your self, or your material life? More times than not it is the latter, but know that materiality is our condition, not our natural state. Remember in the first chapter where I spoke of our personal pool of consciousness? If we decided to move toward our spiritual self, our consciousness would indeed transform to an absolutely crystal clear pool with no trace of brown sludgy-silt. This is why the Law of Direction and Motives becomes so important. And to think that it is just a simple individual choice. Imagine if the masses accept and choose a direction which can potentially change the whole world!

Question 2: Are we in a hurry? While observing the vast majority of individuals in this part of the world, it could easily be stated as a resounding yes. Do you personally feel you are caught with the others, running to and fro at a high rate? Look at India for a moment. Even though there is over three times the number of people, they are not nearly as rushed as we appear to be. They merely take their time as they drive their cars, trucks, scooters, bicycles, elephants, or camels. And as a society they are actually very happy people, much more so than we are in this part of the world. Sure makes for a fascinating ride when a visitor sees all these modes of transportation on the highway at the same time – next to each other! And yet, there are significantly fewer accidents in mega-populous India than in America. Now hold on a minute, does not this country have less than one third of India's population and more room? The reason is simple. In India, they do not force each other while in traffic, or while they do anything for that matter. Their life is honored. Road rage is nonexistent and there is a significantly fewer number of fights and arguments. I am not talking about monasteries here. This is right in the thick of the general population. You see, the citizens of India simply allow for each other, whereas we do not. Their tolerance and acceptance runs higher, whereas our culture pushes for conformity – the inflexible mindset.

Consider the following phrase, going something like this: The faster I work the behinder I get. Have you ever stopped right behind the same car that had passed you by at what seemed to be the speed of light just five minutes or so ago? If we simply take our time, very seldom would we feel behind or late and we would not hurry in the fashion we do today. What a perfect immune booster since stress is directly linked to all types of illness because it hits our immune system, also perhaps a major cause of *dis*-ease. Do you suppose rocketing around all day could be a prime reason for an accident, let alone an argument? I only ask for you to consider what is being offered here, for I am attempting to help you understand that when a person hurries to and fro throughout their day, they tend to focus on the next item on their agenda, no longer paying attention to what they are saying or doing *now*. They live completely outside and away from the moment. Talk about a pressure cooker. Slow down! We all

have time and nothing more; besides, we cannot truly save time to be used at some future moment even if we think we can! Learn to allow for all the time necessary. If we operate from a spiritual perspective, our need for daily racing hither and thither vanishes. Yes, projects and appointments will still get completed, and quite possibly, in a significantly more efficient manner. Living spiritually creates optimum health which in turn elevates our energy level which in turn clears our mind which in turn intensifies our focus, which in turn…you see the pattern here. So what is your pace? All of this simply means we are living outside of ourselves and not inside where we belong.

Question 3: When we awaken each day, do we take time giving thanks? Have you ever really observed a sunrise as it splashes rich hues upon the sky and puffy clouds, as it wakes the shadows now peeking behind trees and foliage, as it nudges the early morning breeze to softly brush against your cheeks? Have you ever taken a moment to really listen to an early morning rain as the drops fall what seems very gently, splattering and glittering in delight as they stir fresh smells into the air around you? These are thankful moments indeed. On the other hand, do you immediately roll out of bed upon awakening, only to begin a race for the day, grappled by the urge to hustle about your home and office? Some food for thought is offered here. Please take a moment to consider these ideas since they may save your life through creating better health.

While living in the monastery, my fellow students, teachers, and I began each morning by quietly sitting and enjoying the idea of self, our ability to realize, and the perfection of all life. What a peaceful, conscious way to start each day, and I know the majority of humans overlook this concept entirely. Since my exodus from the Far East so many years ago, I continue this morning ritual even to this day. Its sole purpose is to create a generously more relaxed state of being and keeps my mind clear of all the events I will be involved in throughout the day. Also, both my mind and body feel consistently more energized. Just wake up a little earlier each day and dedicate this time for you. Merely being alive is something to be truly grateful for and this is shared with my wife each morning, thanking her for being in my life.

Remember, nothing is insignificant in our life. Being grateful and thanking spirit is just a way of life, a graceful life wherein all serious events are handled with greater ease. If it may be suggested, focus on thankfulness, to be grateful no matter what you are faced with in life right now because the arms of grace *will* come your way, enfolding you in peace and reverence. Yes, another form of Karma returns again and in such a positive form.

Question 4: Do we make peace with our true higher Source? This question has great importance because most of us basically ignore our true Source, thus our reason for life. Sad but true, all too often we either blame Source for our lot in life, or we are entirely too busy to pay It any mind. We all have observed when others look through eyes of blame, have we not? Yet they really do not realize they are driving themselves away from their higher Source, sliding more deeply into fleshly materiality, hence the main point of this principle: *we are not able to think of two things at once.* We simply are not able to travel the higher while focusing on the lower. This is not possible. To honestly think, to even believe, we are capable of grasping the epitome of both materiality and spirituality is astounding to me, especially when our spirituality can be clearly heard as it whispers by, yet unnoticed by the hustle-bustle of the vast majority.

"Why is spirit so important in the first place?" you may ask. Because we are spirit first, body second. No, this does not imply duality at all actually. Our body is the end result of our higher Source or spirit, and the main idea behind this Principle is to realize this, and then we are to honor it. Not to worship it, just honor it. Recognize its presence. Listen to it because it will guide you through all your experiences, alerting you to something in error just as quickly and easily as to something in truth. Additionally, it gives any individual a greater sense of purpose when acknowledged. So, if you find yourself lost or confused, listen to that higher energy base from which you and every human has been fashioned, that aspect referred to as our soul, spirit, or Source. And who actually listens to it? *Very* few, sadly but true. Just look around you. Even better, ask people. The answers I receive run close to, "Who has time for that sort of mumbo-jumbo?!" It is suggested that we simply make the time to honor it in special moments, such as when we rise before our day's hustle-bustle schedule, listening to what it tells us about our day. Or, if preferable, we may do this before we go to sleep at the end of our day, but doing it at this time is a little more difficult as our minds remain very busy. But if this is the path of choice, simply listen to your impressions then drift off to sleep. It will only offer very wise counsel, *never* steering you in an improper direction. Source is important. We would not have life without It. It's that simple.

Question 5: Do we give our family love and attention before we run off for the day? If we do, perhaps we now understand more clearly the purpose of this seventh principle, for it knows how to perfectly reveal our direction of focus to us if we pay attention. You see, materiality thrives on one's own ego and intention for personal gain; on the other hand, spirituality thrives and expands simply from our own recognition of it as we come to remember our true unconditional nature. Karmically speaking, is our family truly an accident or coincidence in our life? This would have to be stated as a no because each member serves a very significant purpose for us. Read question number three again. Therefore, from a Karmic point of view, which is the better and less stressful of the two: 1) thanking, loving, being grateful for, and attending to our family and to those close to us, each of whom are present in our life to help us understand who we are, or 2) criticizing, condemning, or ignoring our family as we focus on personal material gain? We sense you have read enough by now to know that Karma will purely and simply return to you more of what you ask for, all in accordance to your direction of focus and motives. There also would be another side benefit from being grateful for our family. It could reduce gang and crime activities, possibly even drug abuse. Perhaps a short moment in time to give an encouraging look, a hug, or word may change many things in our lives.

Question 6: Do we foster hidden agendas of personal gain and feed the compulsions of our lower carnal nature, completely ignoring the rest? This question clearly reveals one of the two directions every human has a choice of making and the short answer is offered here. If we have chosen this path, we know Karma will reflect to us all what we ask for. And we are not necessarily talking about a million-dollar return here! Yes, we could very well achieve a substantial material gain, initially at most. But ultimately, what are we truly asking for? Doesn't this path reveal deep-seated selfishness, inflexibility, and control? Therefore, two questions are offered: 1) True or false: the attributes just mentioned take from others, and 2) based on all the information offered in previous chapters, what is the Karmic return for *takers*? Keep this in mind as a perspective of truth and it matters not how you live your life. We came into this world at birth with nothing; we leave this world with nothing. We entered empty-handed and we will leave the same way. There is nothing we may do except to keep the following two questions in mind: "How did you leave your world?" and "Did you leave it a better place?" This is important regarding your next entry into this world since Karma determines your next experience. This is what the Master Christ referred to when we, "...lay up in Heaven that which is within you..." What we lay up is precisely what preordains what our next life shall be for us.

In all the ancient texts I have ever read, each one reveals two paths, the material and the spiritual. Their words of wisdom unanimously declare that the spiritual path would give us a deeply fulfilling life in every respect, steering us only into the direction of positive Karmic flow. Can we really be forewarned of our developing extramarital love affair? Do we feel funny internally before we take something which does not belong to us? Does our face flush with guilt before we spit out words of anger or judgment? This is observed all the time as people know when they are doing something improper or inappropriate. It is called our voice of conscience, our divine counselor, who advises us to release our attempt to control, who changes our physiology when we do anything in error, regardless of intent. It does so one hundred percent of the time. No exception!

To the same degree as our ego grows into total dominance, we listen less to this voice, a still small voice ever whispering in the back of our mind, an inner voice to which very few humans now have the ability to hear or listen above the roaring din of their chattering monkeys. We all can, most definitely, but only when we take the time to nurture it back to strength. Attend to it. Listen to it. Only by doing these can every human reconnect, not only to their own soul, spirit, or Source, but also to each others', and then to consciousness itself. At this level of awareness, we will know exactly what we place into mass consciousness, each and every moment. Perhaps we can end the very thought of inner and outer conflict once and for all. Life would henceforth have more value than ever before in the history of our world.

This has been the principle of direction and motives that we have been sharing with you and would like to leave you with more food for thought before moving on to the next Principle. If you truly seek within for your sacred nature, then by the very Principles of Karma your life will change in this process as you come to know the real you. By so doing you invoke the second principle into your reality, the Principle of Creation: *You attract to you what you are, not what you want*, and there is no way around this. The truth is, *every* human does this anyway. The reality is, we now are able to take full control of this principle in this new sacred dynamic of life because now we know.

One may only seek one or the other in this life – materiality or spirituality – in which we all live. If we look around, things are changing, but are they changing to higher dynamics or lower ones? The outcome of this obviously remains to be seen. One thing is clearly certain, life is changing. The questions for you now become, "How do I want to change me in this life? How may I, as an individual, impact our world into a greater and more sacred dynamic?" Simple. Shift *you*! And others just may follow. Buddha was only one human. The Christ was just one human. The ancient texts tell us it only takes *one* to shift the *entire* face of humanity! Although the world is ready for a new paradigm, we must wait for the shift to unfold this new paradigm, the birth of the divine human in the flesh. Are you prepared for this higher shift of dynamics? What is your direction and what is your motive? Do you choose materiality or do you choose *your sacred self?*

"Look within. Be still.
Live free from fear and attachment,
Know the sweet joy of the way. Live
In joy, in love amongst all things."
Buddha

~ Chapter IX ~
The Principle of Willingness

This one Law itself can shift the face of American society along with *all* societies. When fully understood, it will simply and easily change all civilization. Yes, these are two very strong claims, but consider, the lesson of this Law is contained within its very name, the willingness to not only share what we have learned in life, but also the willingness to show it. This equals living it! Willingness ultimately promotes flexibility with our self and all life. In that moment when *every* individual lives in this fashion, we would be sharing and learning in an incredibly tolerant society. There exists a big however, though. From what is felt and observed, most societies have sprinted in the completely opposite direction by evolving into an extremely intolerant, materialistic lifestyle. And its citizens these days have become so darn stubborn with each other! Could this be caused from the influences of Western culture? Do you not feel the same? In chapter one it was shared how rigidity, control, and dominance influence our physical nature, and right here in front of us we now have the Law of Willingness, perfectly designed to assist us exclusively in this arena, imagine that! What is truly remarkable, over twenty five hundred years ago Buddha taught not only the Principle of Willingness, but also the eleven other Principles of Karma to a society that truly listened, for they exist and are practiced in existence

in the Eastern part of the world today – the country of India. Here in *our* area we have somehow missed these greatest of all teachings, which is why this book is written.

If memory serves me well, when I introduced the Law of the Mirrors to you it was discussed how much we actually avoid our self. Most may not realize, avoidance is yet another form of resistance; therefore, Karma will oblige by creating more of the same. Naturally, this brings up a fascinating question: Just how does one go about sharing and living willingly when they avoid or resist life? In the end, we cannot avoid our self, no matter our effort, even though we all seem to believe that the most difficult thing in life is to know our self for who we truly are. May we gently remind you, difficulty is merely a belief. The truth is, by understanding both the Law of the Mirrors and the Law of Willingness, our so-called difficulty slips effortlessly into oblivion as we willingly step up to the plate to observe what the mirrors reflect back to us about us and our lives.

Rinpoche Kiela approached me one winter day and softly announced, "Young man, we are journeying into Tibet." This would be my first sojourn to this ancient land, the seat of Tibetan Buddhism, and the magnificent, unyielding beauty of the Himalayas. "Aren't the borders closed?" I posed, understanding that Red China was in control at the time. I finished with another question, "How are we going to get me, an American, across the border?" He replied instantly, as though he had known my questions even before they came to me, "There is much for you to learn during this journey. Everything will be fine. You are to act as a deaf-mute." I wrinkled my brows, "Is there a need for deception?" He replied, "We are going anyway. You can do whatever you want, but if you say that you are an American, you may be shot or imprisoned." Uh, okay-wait. The image struck my tongue with a funny taste; yet, I felt it best to just play along for now. After preparations had been made for our winter trek and shrouding myself with numerous coats and furs, two Master teachers, twelve monks, and I set out on our journey into Tibet with my single thought tagging right along behind us, "All of us can be easily killed!" Master Kiela expressed not the slightest concern. In that moment I realized the concern was mine only, and that it was best for me to work it through as we journeyed. Although my willingness to make this journey waivered several times, I sensed there was much for me to learn; therefore, I continued in complete trust.

As we walked along in single file, I grew deeply disconcerted over the idea of being deceptive. You would too after learning so much about it and the importance of living the path of truth! Sure, I knew then that the world was filled with deceit, but wait just a minute here; my deep desire was to live in complete Truth just as the Buddha suggested to us in his Sutras. During a momentary rest with our noon meal, Master Kiela motioned me over to sit by him. Looking at me straight in the eye, he asked, "Young man, why are you so troubled?" I blurted out, "Karma and the idea of deception!" He smiled at me of all things and answered, "Good." After a moment he continued, "But this is the Chinese Karmic return. Fourteen monks and an American crossing their borders are actually equal to their Karmic return for taking our country." What? I found his comment rather humorous and felt that the other monks had thought so, too. "Play your role," he cautioned me once more. And I was utterly taken by surprise to hear him state, "Deception is the teacher of Truth just as impatience is the teacher of patience. So, too, is anger the teacher of peace. If you are having a difficult moment, look toward the opposite of your experience and this is your lesson." Hold on. I must read that again. I remember smiling after he shared those thoughts. My teachers always had a way of making a lesson out of any situation. In addition to merely the words, they also give experience to their teachings. It can come from the smallest of events up to the greatest one, for there is always something to grow through and learn from while a student with these kind gentle people, let alone being a human ensconced in everyday experiences. Non-traditional teaching is totally fascinating!

Even though I was buried under coats and furs, sure enough, my intense nervousness attracted attention as our single file approached the snowy border. The Chinese guards stiffly approached me, asking a question to which I simply could not respond. I was literally a deaf-mute in that moment. I was totally dumbfounded. I really could not speak! All the monks swiftly jumped and huddled around me, I suppose to reassure the guards that I was so nervous purely because I

was a deaf-mute. The guards slowly settled down, believing what my friends had said, and waived us onward. "Oh man, we will have to do this again upon our return," my body trembled with the thought. The border incident raised many concepts to the forefront of my mind and I became deeply concerned again. I just *had* to ask my teachers, "What is the impact of Karma on me for not being in truth?" Master Kiela responded, "Young man, when you become a monk, nationality is never an issue, and the guards saw that you were simply a Tibetan monk. No lie was perpetrated by anyone." I thought I noticed a twinkle in his eye as he concluded, "Besides, in that moment you were quite frightened. You were truly a deaf-mute!" So he *knew* this would happen! I just shook my head in wonder and chuckled aloud. Wow! What an adventure!

Like a sponge, all my senses intensified as they absorbed the surrounding landscape, dwarfed by the majestic, towering Himalayas, when suddenly, Rinpoche Kiela turned around during our walk and gently said to me, "Young man, come up here with me as it is time to begin the next principle of Karma, the Law of Willingness. This Law was demonstrated for you through everyone's actions at the border in how they were all willing to offer themselves for you. Only the truth was spoken and shown, and the guards did not pursue it." He paused then offered, "This Law's basic precept is merely this: *If you believe something to be true then at some point you must be able to demonstrate that truth.*" Looking at me straight in the eye, he affirmed, "Only that particular truth in that moment was fully demonstrated because we were simple monks and you could not say a word, nothing less." Master Kiela was right on target, of course. The Chinese guards were truly only interested in knowing where we were headed, nothing more. Again, monks are not viewed as having a nationality to speak of, for they are just individuals traveling the path of consciousness, all studying Truth. This had all been demonstrated, and I had not considered any of it when we departed on this journey.

Have you either heard of or said the following two phrases? "I do it the same way as my Mom (or Dad)," or "our family has *always* done it this way." These statements are heard countless of times, escaping from the mouths of people from every direction and all walks of life.

Apparently most people in this part of the world really do stick to another's belief. They do this so frequently, they will not only clutch it tightly and never consider changing it, but they will also fight over that belief. This is most fascinating! Whose belief is it in the first place? Is there any growth in this? Why do we do this? When viewed from the perspective of truth, there occurs little growth from doing this, if any at all. When an individual believes in the belief of another, are they not actually living by the other's belief, the other's life, rather than their own? It can be pretty near guaranteed that by doing this the individual will not fully know themselves and they will truly operate out of the past rather than the present. Ideas and beliefs change with time like truth as it ever expands and grows. One path is limiting and the other is not, and I realized this during my journey into the Himalayas.

Allow me to repeat this Principle's primary point: *If you believe something to be true then at some point you must be able to demonstrate that truth*. Even though it has worked for others in the past, perhaps many times, do let me know what happens when *their* truth no longer works for *you*. What do you do now? Would you like the short answer? Change how you operate in your life because that belief no longer works with the present. The purpose of that belief is to head you into another direction; therefore, do not struggle with it as most people will do. Things have simply changed and the old is being replaced by new thought and or direction. Move toward the present truth, *your* truth. Obviously, the old one no longer operates as it did before. This is more akin to a change of mind or viewpoint in how a person sees their life and it changes into the new direction. Beliefs are guide posts, not stop signs. They merely reveal our direction and growth without ever intending to cement us in place. Life is about discovering and traveling the higher road of Universal Truth, not necessarily our personal truths. Oh yes, there *is* a difference between them! Look at the entire world. Even though nothing seems to be truly working, we are all still attempting to stay in the same direction. This does not work as higher truth is now exerting itself on us all. Let us all move forward in faith toward this shift in dynamics.

Let us for a moment reintroduce the idea of Universal Truth.

Universal Truth overrides our personal truths simply because our ego has no involvement in Universal concept and action; on the other hand, ego just loves to poke around and into all our personal perspectives on truth. Why does it do this? Because we do not focus the mind and we allow it to intervene in our thoughts and the tempter steps in to have us prove our truth. Universal Truth always demonstrates itself; whereas, our personal truth may not. Now what do I mean by this? Well, who said, "Change is inevitable?" Actually, it does not matter since "change" is the only *constant* in life. Put another way, if the demonstration of a belief does not work out the same today as it did yesterday, change has obviously occurred. Yet, generally speaking, individuals in Western culture prefer to clench onto that belief with the white knuckles of their mind, even though the belief no longer works and its resultant path can no longer be followed. I stand corrected here, for a person actually *can* continue to follow their well-worn, comfortable, childhood convictions – technically speaking – but when they do, they should not be taken by surprise or become so upset when struggle and hardship occur. This experience is purely the natural Karmic return for their inflexibility. And all this occurs merely because of their unyielding resistance, their *un*-willingness to allow for change. Utilizing the Law of Willingness, this is a very simple dynamic to work through.

If change is a Universal constant then do you suppose it includes personal truth? Can our truth really alter? Is the truth, as you knew and understood it as a child, the same or different, now that you are older and more experienced? If Universal principles apply, the concept of personal truth must be changeable, no exceptions or extensions. This is why our truths can and do shift, while on the other hand, Universal Truth does not necessarily. It does not change per se, but it does expand, and within its expansion, the seed of the original Universal Truth remains constant. This happens because we are able to realize greater levels of truth, always changing as we expand our knowledge and realizations; yet, the original seed remains ever-present. Karma nudges us in order to accomplish this shift through the proper use of truth. *Everyone* experiences this shift toward higher truth only when it comes time to demonstrate what their personal truth is, and if it no longer works for them, their lives have then shifted in dynamics, the perfect moment to release an old belief.

Do you recall when it was suggested, "There is no such thing as good, bad, right, or wrong in truth?" While reading that earlier chapter, you may have personally admitted to not believing in coincidences or accidents. Perhaps you may have also admitted that everything happens with intent for a purpose; therefore, from such a viewpoint, only truth and error exist, correct? Good. Only from this perspective, error now merely becomes a steering mechanism. This is true because what we thought was true now comes out as error which signals us to shift with it into a new understanding of our self. You simply are not today who you were yesterday, and what worked yesterday may not work today. Such is change and growth. How we acted as children is not how we act or respond as adults, in most cases I quickly admit. We have more depth and experience from which to draw which naturally changes the way we see the dynamics of truth over time. This is Universal. It is suggested that we let go of our old perception of the truth in order to allow for the new one. This denotes growth.

Let us offer a question, and please, *really* consider your answer: "Are you afraid to change and grow?" It is sensed that you would answer in the form of, "No, Steven, because my whole life has revolved around change and growth." Yes, and so has mine and every other human's life. If the majority so easily admits to their personal change and growth, then why do we struggle through them each time? Looking for the deeper answer as another stone is overturned, allow me to offer that our struggle occurs solely because we truly and genuinely have an innate fear of change and growth. This occurs because we have an innate fear of the unknown as we step into this shift. It seems we instinctively whirl around, grasping for the old dynamics – our comfort zone – which no longer fits us now. Although the old way is what we have always known as the truth, all things and beings experience change and some discomfort for a short while until the shift settles in. The pivotal point in the previous phrase is, "what we have always known." What we have known and what we now know may differ at times; here is where the shift is ready and necessary. Our personal resistance or inflexibility is partly the reason for such struggle purely because of our internal conflict. Metaphysically speaking, this is the underlying concept to what Christ offered [Mark 2:22, New American Standard Bible], "No one puts new wine into old wine skins."

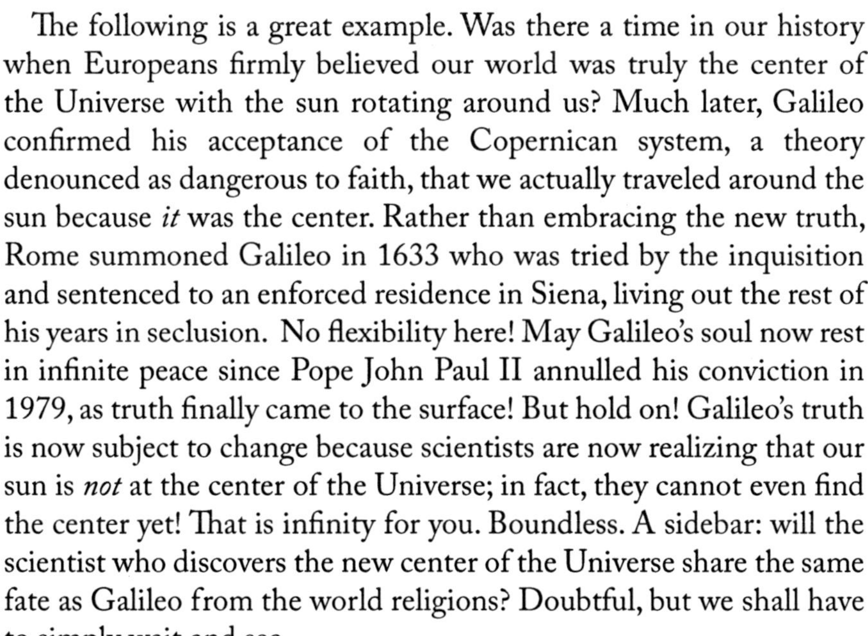

The following is a great example. Was there a time in our history when Europeans firmly believed our world was truly the center of the Universe with the sun rotating around us? Much later, Galileo confirmed his acceptance of the Copernican system, a theory denounced as dangerous to faith, that we actually traveled around the sun because *it* was the center. Rather than embracing the new truth, Rome summoned Galileo in 1633 who was tried by the inquisition and sentenced to an enforced residence in Siena, living out the rest of his years in seclusion. No flexibility here! May Galileo's soul now rest in infinite peace since Pope John Paul II annulled his conviction in 1979, as truth finally came to the surface! But hold on! Galileo's truth is now subject to change because scientists are now realizing that our sun is *not* at the center of the Universe; in fact, they cannot even find the center yet! That is infinity for you. Boundless. A sidebar: will the scientist who discovers the new center of the Universe share the same fate as Galileo from the world religions? Doubtful, but we shall have to simply wait and see.

In truth, the key is to realize the Universal seed, the reason why this principle is so important. *We* are that seed. If we believe something to be true, at some point we must demonstrate that truth when the seed blossoms into us. Put another way, it is all about what you have learned in life and your willingness to show what you have learned. It is the truth about your self, not life itself. It is about how you fit in *you*, not how you fit in your life. You are here to not only learn about life, but to also learn and realize *you* in the process. You are the common thread through it all, behind every single event which has occurred in your life. Heck, you cannot even get away from you – ever! Each experience comes down to this: are you demonstrating truth or error? That is all. If truth, then wonderful, your individual struggles are fewer in number; otherwise, shift the error toward truth so life smoothes out for you. Let Karma assist you. The truth is, it constantly attempts to in all you do!

While the monks and I forged ahead on the snowy trail alongside the Himalayas, my mind began to reflect on all my teachings since my arrival in India. My fascination deepened with respect to the Principles of Karma, for they literally have such a far-reaching effect on every human. Now think about this, not until that very moment did I ever realize just how my life had been truly shaped. It had been molded in such a fashion that my *whole life* had been *precisely* designed to bring me *exactly* where I found myself right up to this moment on *this* particular trail, alongside *these* twelve monks and *these* two Masters, walking single file beside the tallest mountain range in the world. This realization overwhelmed me, for I began to feel as though I really did have purpose after all, a life filled with intention. A warm wave of honor and humility swept over me. With impeccable timing yet again, Master Lobsang gently jolted me away from my inner reflection and subsequent epiphany by asking, "Do you understand the ideas of 'when' and 'if'?" "What?" I said to myself as I replied, "No, what do you mean, ideas of 'when' and 'if'?" Yes, I had that look yet again when Master Lobsang continued, "Good, you speak the truth. Most people do not realize the significance of these two words. They seem small and insignificant, but they can deeply affect an individual's perspective on reality, and therefore, create all sorts of Karmic returns without ever realizing it."

Can two seemingly innocuous words deeply affect our perspective? Apparently so. If we stop to listen closely, our ears will pick up on these two words all around us each day, nearly constantly! What is so bad or wrong about them? Remember, these two words are merely used in metaphor and to illustrate a point in this discussion because, in truth, bad or wrong do not exist, only truth and error. These two words are based on human judgment. Back to the discussion, what is so bad or wrong about them? *Nothing*, since both words cannot be judged as either bad or wrong in their *literal* usage: however, in their meaning, *everything* because they introduce *error thinking* to our mind. When utilizing these words so frequently, we literally enter a dream state. They cleverly yank us right out from the present.

For example, consider what is meant when we remark, "When (or if) I win the lottery I will purchase _______, give to _______, and do _______ with the money." Another example may be, "I will purchase _______ when (or if) they have another sale." Or, "When (or if) I lose weight, I will buy new clothes." I have a concern here, just *where* are these events taking place? Certainly not right here immediately in our

present moment! In fact, are we not keeping these desires perpetually in the future, dangling on a stick in front of us just out of our reach? The precise same thing occurs when these two words are used for past experiences or issues. "I remember when gasoline cost just one dollar a gallon," works well as one example. Are the emotions created by this statement truly helpful to anyone *today*? Perhaps we casually mouthed out the following phrase, "If only I had not said _______ or done_______ then this situation would never have happened." Another example, "If I had bought stock in_______ I would be rich now." Or, "If I had my life to do over, I would _______." Where is the true value in any of these types of thought processes?

The habitual use of these two words potentially moves us away from being present in our personal reality, most especially when our remark is expressed with an emotion. 'When' and 'if' can never occur according to Karmic principle simply because each implies a future or a past moment. Karma cannot go there, for it acts only when we stay in the present moment with our desires focused and with the purest of intention. Regarding the above examples, what do you suppose Karma will do? Well, have you ever had incidences seemingly repeat themselves, though the names, dates, and places have changed? Now you know why! Karma returns these past experiences for our full attention yet again, over and over as many times as necessary, in order for us to see the seeds we are planting so we will finally release the issue. In other words, I surmise your own 'when' and 'if' scenarios will continually repeat until you finally *get* it. If I may suggest, go ahead and eliminate the words '*when*' and '*if*' from your vocabulary starting this moment, though I may use them solely as an aid for this continuing discussion.

It is realized that the topic of self-deception has already been discussed; yet, due to its especially profound effects in this part of the world, I would like to discuss it from the viewpoint of the Law of Willingness. Remember, this Law is about the ability to demonstrate the truth; on the other hand, 'when' and 'if' reside in the realm of self-deception, the opposite of truth. Are they really this powerful? Absolutely! Their alluring power can very easily snatch us away from our present reality as our ego quickly entwines with them, both

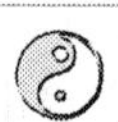

rippling through our mind while ego enjoys creating self-doubt, a game I like to call 'What-If,' no pun intended. Additionally, these both indicate dissatisfaction in who we are and in how we are living. In reality, they can move us even further away from who we are! If you feel any dissatisfaction in your life, by all means lift this particular stone in your path and look for its underlying message.

Utilizing 'when' or 'if' while sharing our past, we get all caught up in the attempt to change what has already occurred. Changing the past is not possible. On the other side of the coin, utilizing these two words while futurizing will simply keep those events dangling in our future indefinitely as an unfulfilled wish. This is self-deception and it will not hesitate to rob us of all what we have in the present. From either direction, past or future, we therefore remove ourselves from objectivity. Wait a minute … where did we just go? Doesn't objectivity *keep us away* from the clutching hands of judgment?

I have used the phrases, "in this part of the world," and, "in Western culture," many times throughout this book, tying both to deception or self-deception. During my sojourn in India and Nepal, I never experienced – at any time – one word or action of deceit, nor did I witness others deceive. No, I am not talking about only the monks and their activities inside the monasteries. I am talking specifically about the general population. You see, the people stand for and believe in truth. They understand Karma and its relationship to deception; therefore, they remain in truth by turning totally away from deception. Now imagine a society without deception. What a thrill to experience, and what a treat to take groups of people to India, journeying with them in areas still free from deception to this day! The funny thing is, when we operate from truth, this makes deceit or untruth much easier to see, and we would always know when deception is confronting us. On the other hand, when we deceive others, especially ourselves, we somehow find it amazingly more difficult to recognize. I wonder why? An example may provide us a clue.

Have you ever met a human appearing to live in a constant state of anger? Working as an intuitive life coach, trust me, I have met many.

When questioned, they whiplash their answer all over me with the likes of, "What do you mean, angry?! I am not angry!!" as I feel their voice rising in pitch, volume, and temperature. Okay. Solves *that* mystery. It is found to be totally fascinating to sense how the individual has grown into and consequently shaped their entire life around a particular physical personality. It is a trait which is actually formed by the physical representation of their ego, instead of their true nature. From the above example, anger has become this person's way of life, and it is obviously clear they have simply become so accustomed to this personality trait that they do not recognize it for them self – *as* them self. The truth is, our personality is actually determined by how other people judge us to be, and if we accept it, we grow into their judgment, a deception and gross error indeed. This is the reason why we may find it so difficult to know our true self, for we simply live full time in how we are judged by others. Here is the greatest influence of this principle and the demonstration of truth.

It takes deep objective introspection to locate these weeds of false traits in our mind and self which have been conditioned by others, especially when we have become so comfortable living with those traits. We truly become numb to these false personalities, genuinely believing this is the way we are without ever realizing that *every* dynamic and emotion in our mind and heart can be shifted or changed to the truth. Yes, it is realized the level of effort and discipline involved. Believe me, it was no walk in the park for me, either, during my *own* teachings with the Masters! But it *can* be accomplished. Instead of remaining stuck in the status quo, perhaps we can choose to lovingly understand how others may come from a position of judgment rather than of truth, for they are just following their *own* life conditioning. Let us take a calm stance as we listen to their words while telling us what they see and know. Aren't they sharing with us *their* words of truth, not ours? Allow them that. Whose life do you wish to live? Are you really living and demonstrating the idea of *your* truth as you live someone *else's* idea of life?

When you find a trait you do not like about your self, please do not dislike or hate it! Because if you put this much emotion into it, then from Karma's constant reply, "Thank you for your input!" that

trait will return with more intensity and sink more deeply within you. And nothing changes. It is to your advantage that you continuously remain as the objective observer, to merely realize the trait is there and then be grateful for the realization. Watch for it, and when it rears up, do or say something different this time around. From the above example, as the person's anger rises during a situation, perhaps they can do the opposite by becoming as peaceful as possible in that moment. Do not wait! Change your behavioral response *during* the incident. Remember, Karma is our personal abiding guide to a higher understanding of who we truly are, but only to the degree we choose to realize and implement its Principles.

Stay with me here, as there are more stones to turn over on deception and self-deception. Yes, I am fully aware that no human truly cares for deception even though it is going on constantly and continually, in one form or another in many so-called civilized cultures. What an oxymoron! Both ideas can easily affect our personal Karma, so what do we do? What armor shall we wear? In a nutshell, do not take external deception personally. Easier said than done, admittedly, but very much doable. As you may very well understand by now, when others deceive you they have just set themselves up for being deceived in their own life, hence creating their own Karmic return! Simply offer them the humility and compassion to have their own consequences from their words and actions. After all, the seeds had been sowed and reaped from *their* garden, not yours.

Though you may feel their comments are personal, they truly are not in reality. They live in illusion; therefore, do not follow it. It is their deceptive nature, not yours; it is their Karma to work through, not yours! If you choose to remain in such an environment from a personal standpoint of benevolent compassion, then so be it. But it is suggested that you first acquire a mind so deeply and thoroughly disciplined in truth that all deceit aimed toward you will instantly fizzle to oblivion even before its action touches you. Yes, such personal empowerment is very much possible, for it is our divine nature, a nature which lovingly transforms everything and everyone around us. It is truly a wondrous and very humbling event!

If, on the other hand, you have yet to attain such a level of empowerment, perhaps it would be in your best interest to simply move away from any such individual or environment. Otherwise, you may run the risk of taking the deception personally, connecting with it, and ultimately slipping into the throws of deception yourself. Becoming bound to the deceptive nature of another, you enter self-deception, the worst kind there is because you are pulled from the truth of your own divine being while being absorbed into their Karma. The moment you connect with it through your emotional body, the deception now grows exponentially because you have genuinely internalized it. The path of struggle now opens because deception has been personalized *and* internalized. The hard truth is, falling into this trap was, all along, a choice. And the good news? Climbing out of it is also a choice. But can it really be done? Utilizing the Principles of Karma, there is no doubt you can. If we get caught in another's life, we have merely carried the Law of Willingness too far in our own life while not paying attention to demonstrating truth, the crux of this divine principle.

When we live in the illusion of deception we no longer live consciously as a divine being, which we truly always are regardless of personal belief. We simply have chosen to not live in this simple construct in our own life. The Law of Willingness continually demonstrates for us what we believe to be the truth. When we are being deceptive, we can choose to realize it at any moment, and not until that moment arrives will Karma further guide us toward the truth of our being. Although self-deception is a grave error wherein we actually can destroy the truth of our very own nature, even this error can guide us toward truth: ***if we remain aware.*** Unfortunately, there are many people in Western culture who genuinely live in this manner, and the truth is, most remain oblivious of doing it until their life or health begins failing.

Self-deception can so thoroughly permeate a person's life; they turn utterly blind to the truth of their divine self and life, all the while earnestly believing they live in truth! It is suggested that we make a different choice, and this is simple to do. That's all. If we choose to live and express through higher divine nature, our ego subsides

and now operates from the truth in a divine sense. Does this idea surprise you? Operating from higher reasoning, we cannot possibly be or become deceptive, nor ever entertain the idea because the ego no longer is in control! Unless we choose to hide from the truth, the ego now has the opportunity to step more into direct influence in life. This begs the question, just how can a human hide from them self? Good question; yet, I really do observe people living this way. Nearly every human according to Buddha!

Nearly every one of us? "Steven, you better be able to back up that statement," you may ask. Yes I can. And it is all perfectly spelled out in just one word. *Conditioning!* We have been *conditioned* from the moment of our birth to the moment we depart. Wow, that is a long time! Conditioning gives birth to manipulation and deception, ultimately leading to our self-deception, a masterful opponent of our true being.

Allow me to provide an example which covers a lifetime, using my editor once again. Purely out of curiosity, Donald innocently touches a hot burner one morning as a very young child. Immediately his first response might be a blood-curdling scream because the intense heat shocks every nerve ending. An older adult is interrupted by Donald's world-wide broadcast and instantly, literally, drops whatever they are in the middle of doing in order to rush to his aid. Upon noticing either red fingers or a palm, they react with a rather stern declaration, "Oh, Donald, what did you *do*?! I told you to *never-ever* touch the stove! *Bad* boy!" To add insult to injury, his older sibling saunters into the kitchen only to add their two cents worth, "Boy, you're *stupid*!" More likely than not, even all his innumerable, harmless actions in the future may evoke this same response. This is just the beginning.

The impact of these two words is unfathomable, for Donald has now just begun the self-deception process by believing he is truly bad and stupid, after all his parents and others keep reinforcing this throughout his childhood. Even so, they must know better than him, right? I must say, this is the original "fall" of humankind because we begin to forget who we are by deceiving ourselves into believing who we are not! You may read that again. Before I continue, forgive me, I

am not singling out parents here, for I can also justifiably add all the siblings, extended family members, neighbors, friends, the school and business environments. Oh my, the school environment itself can be ruthless! The point is, Donald is being led away from his true nature by believing others and their descriptions of him. At some point he must demonstrate this truth so let us continue.

How about his continued conditioning during his educational years, being told to look, act, and learn as all the other students under the threat of a pass and fail grading system? Then we add to this all the constant mockery, insults, and jeers aimed at him if he is the least bit different. It should now be clearly understood how and why self-deception will seep evermore deeply into his young heart and mind. Oh, do not stop here, for he is strongly encouraged to attend higher education only to continue under the same or similar grading system, and is actually expected to select a major in support of an appropriate career choice. Oh no, he is told by an authority figure just before his interview that he is too skinny, too fat, or his grade point average is too low to qualify for his dream career, which further reinforces his self-deception to the degree he now believes he is not good enough. He now begins to genuinely believe only the perceptions and judgments offered by others regarding all what he should say and do. But wait, there is even more!

Donald now steps into the real business world, and generally speaking, the rest of his innocence is now sucked from him, if any remains. Even witnessing unethical behavior, unwarranted office practices, and cut-throat competition no longer shock him simply because he needs to earn a living since he is now expected to behave as a loyal employee and consumer. Is this lifetime conditioning or what?! Don't most people go through this type of life? I feel I have aged ten years just from writing this example! And I compassionately understand why I can hear Donald and others whisper in despair, "This is too much to bear! Who am I? Where do I *fit*?!" Conditioning utterly devoured his divine nature, and only a fraction of his full lifetime was given in this example!

I sense most of you think you know who you are, but do you *really*? In Western culture, it has apparently become important for each of us to always know how others see us. Slowly over time, sadly enough, we seem to have naturally grown into *their* judgments and condemnations to the point where we now can only see our self in the exact same way, knowing just physical personalities. Having learned to solely judge how we see ourselves has literally blocked us from knowing our true self, our higher personality, the only attribute we now completely ignore or find so difficult to locate. This is conditioned nature, not our true nature. Have you ever wondered or asked yourself where you fit in? We all search for our niche in life and it is hoped that you now realize why. In truth you may only fit in *you* once you discover who that is, and your higher personality will then be able to demonstrate that through the Principle of Willingness.

We have become such external creatures from focusing only on physical materiality, when all the while, we are actually *internal* creatures who live within our *self* and wherefrom our true growth and understanding arise. This is to say, although our every experience is internalized, most live an external life and apparently look to the outside for internal answers. Kindly help me understand this! By living this way, no wonder we cannot locate our true self because it is not even outside us! We are each unique; yet, we are each conditioned to resemble everyone else in our actions and approach to life. I understand most do not want to be different. This is fine. But the truth is we are.

If it may be suggested, do not take to heart and mind what others actually think of you. Personally accepting what others think of you will only whisk you down the slippery slopes of self-deception, leading to manipulation by others and ultimately losing control over your own life. Sadly, from all what has been observed, this happens each moment in our Western culture; however, I offer reassurance because you can absolutely overcome all your lifelong conditioning by simply shifting your self-perception! It's that simple. The path to self-empowerment will awaken your true nature as you realize your own thoughts are the ones most valuable to you, no one else's. Furthermore, choosing to accept and utilize the guiding, ever-present

principles of Karma will truly transform your life more effectively and permanently. Your burden is lifted, knowing you can just as easily come from a genuine perspective because genuineness breeds truth and is so easy to demonstrate. This in truth is exactly who you are! Living truth!

Life is and always has been about self-discovery. Unfortunately, as we continue to literally look outward, we seem to require that *every* aspect of our experience be defined which fosters a very critical mind filled with judgment. With such a mind, we are incapable of discovering our true nature unless, of course, we first recognize our true self inwardly, and learn how to use the outer environment – our experience. It is here that our eyes and mind may look inward to seek the higher divine nature of being, residing only in truth, and to begin the journey of self-discovery and true empowerment. As we discover, we demonstrate what we have learned of the truth and our self, only to step into a different realm of life.

The Law of Willingness, the eighth Principle of Karma, is designed to assist us in this endeavor of self-knowledge. From the Tao-Te Ching, Lao-tzu offers the following idea from which we may operate, "Knowing others is wisdom; knowing the self is enlightenment." These are very wise words and his statement truly echoes the Law of Willingness in its entire presentation. As we demonstrate who we are, we operate from authenticity each and every moment; otherwise, we may be operating in error. Remember, error is neither good nor bad! It is simply the steering mechanism to guide us back onto our true path of life and self. What a glorious relief! So always be true to you. Do not live for others. Always live for you first then you are able to give others all what you have. And you will accomplish all desires in a fearless fashion. May your journey come to a natural peaceful state of being as you learn to realize you and then know you as the unique being ***you truly are***.

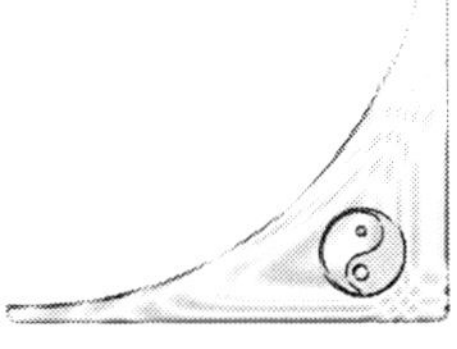

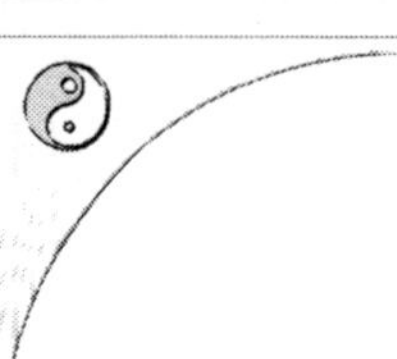

"With a free mind, in no debt,
enjoy what has been given you."
Buddha

~ Chapter X ~
The Principle of Be Here and Now

Where are you right this second? Where are your thoughts in *this* moment? Are you seeing each word your eyes come upon while reading *this* sentence? If so, your mind is exactly where it ought to be, right behind your eyes, recognizing and interpreting each word your eyes focus on as you continue to read this sentence. Otherwise, where *is* your mind? Is it contemplating that "to-do" list lying on the kitchen counter? Is it scheduling the rest of your day beginning the moment you place this book down? Perhaps you are answering a question for someone either on the phone or in person right now. Are you even here on this page in this sentence with me?

We have shared many times the importance of being constantly and continually present with our body. A Master teacher constantly stresses this concept, and will not hesitate to utilize the "waking" stick. The present is all what we have to truly contend with. The future will take care of itself – stay out. Also stay away from the past – unless using your objective self – as these points on the timeline are never as important as the present moment – the point of creation. I feel the greatest so-called "pitfall" for humankind is that we do not yet grasp this truth, and we therefore remain oblivious to everything we create each and every moment in our life. Let us offer a pivotal point in a nutshell. Being present means always keeping our mind right behind our eyes. And upon whatever, wherever, and whomever our

eyes fall, or whichever direction our head turns, our mind remains right there, behind our eyes. This simply cannot be stressed enough. Yes, of course, it is realized our mind rests behind the eyes physically; however, our answers to the questions posed above may reveal a rest-*less* mind, a mind flailing every which way, past or future. From the mental sense of the concept, I remind you, there is neither a past nor future since all thought rests purely in the present. Put another way, when our present mind turns to face the past, we then bind with the past. Ironically, we have just created the very cycle we genuinely attempt to rid ourselves of! This ninth principle of Karma, the Law of Be Here and Now, is the Karmic return arising out of our past solely because we give it so much attention and emotion. This principle can guide us to consciously apply the idea of presence – *right now*.

In late fall, I remember sitting in the main chamber of Gyuto Monastery in Nepal, about 75 miles north of Katmandu. While in a semi-meditative state, I simply watched the snow outside, keenly observing it fall so lightly and so absolutely, perfectly straight down. I felt something approach me from behind. Indeed my sense was confirmed as Master Lobsang walked up and softly asked, "May I join you?" "Sure," I replied, and we both settled into continued silence for what seemed forever. Out of the blue, his emotionless, matter-of-fact statement broke the forever part, "Young man, you cannot go home again but you must attempt to." I turned to look at him, inwardly thinking, "Huh? Of course I can! I can return home any time I want," only to see that smile on his face. He clarified, "I am not really talking about where you grew up or where your family resides." Okay, he got me again, and I knew he knew it. The silence returned as I sat, allowing my mind to figure this one out. I posed my first question, "Does this have something to do with my past?" "Yes, that is part of it," he answered smiling, "We should go up onto the roof to feel and listen to the silence of the snowfall." As we approached the top he remarked, "It is time for you to learn the ninth principle of Karma. It is termed as the Law of Be Here and Now."

We stepped onto the roof, and I felt as though we had just entered a vacuum of incomprehensible calm, a depth of tranquility so overwhelming that every worldly distraction around us had been

completely covered by the thickening blanket of falling flakes. My senses were allowed to reach out only as far as the space filled by my physical being. What a spellbinding silence! Who dare disturb such serenity? Well, I did, posing another question, "Master, what did you mean when you said to me that I cannot go home? I am certain you did not mean my home in the U.S. because I feel I am home now." He smiled with an invitation, "Let us begin the journey into the ninth Principle of Karma."

In retrospect, this wonderful Principle gave me a great depth of understanding about my self and how my life was not handled truthfully. Before we go into its details, though, I share a personal story. As a child, I was my father's single favorite target, no matter what I or any of my siblings said or did. My dad was indeed a true tyrant, a severe abuser. According to dad, it was *always my* fault, and as I grew older, I constantly looked forward to the second I was old enough to leave! Because my scholastic achievement was nearly nonexistent, my only way out at that time was the military; therefore, I enlisted on the day of my eighteenth birthday. As you already know, I found myself as an Army recruit bound for Vietnam, essentially hopping out of the frying pan right into the fire! Obviously, after my discharge, innumerable mental and emotional scars were imbedded in my mind, not only from the war but also from my childhood. I became a very bitter, angry young man, not caring one iota whether I lived or hurt others. Think for a moment, do you sort of feel I was caught up in my past, chained to bygone experiences with a battleship anchor? Yes, it is true these events and emotions took place and developed back in that period of my life; however, understanding these Principles through the teachings offered by my Master teachers, the past is now exactly that and my memories are no longer charged with emotion. In truth, they became my best teachers, as will be explained.

Master Lobsang chimed right into his wisdom which never ceased to amaze me, "Young man, when you first arrived in India you were a very angry human. The reason you were angry is simply because of your memories of life, and looking back, do you now realize how you actually preferred to be around others who were just as angry as you?" Less than a second skipped before I knew its truth, no denying it.

Also, it did not matter to me whether the person was male or female, for there was just all this fighting and arguing going on, back and forth and back and forth. It was all I knew in those times. Master Lobsang continued, italics mine, "Young man, *all* things in life have their time, place, and purpose. *Every single experience* you have had in your life has its divine and perfect function on the path of knowledge, and it has been laid out *just for you.* If you have what you judge a bad experience, you will hold onto it and carry it with you every day for the rest of your life. If you have what you judge a good experience, you – like everyone else – will simply release it and let it go, no questions asked, no second thought. I now ask you, why not release *every* experience? Once you have gone through the experience and learned from it there is no need for it to repeat or cycle back to you unless, of course, you do not release it. This is how Karma works with each human and their events, simply because the dominant thing on their mind will come to them as the next experience. If it is a negative of your past then it shall surely return in like kind. It *has* to. It is best to always have a clear mind, one which has *nothing* to do with the past, but has *everything* to do with the present. The present is where we each create our life. If our past is in the present then we are recreating our past. Steven, it is *you* who is creating these seeming cycles within your life. It is you and every human who brings these events back to yourselves, no one else. This is how this Law works. These are personal dynamics for us to work through and then release. Simply let them go. I am not saying to forget them because this you cannot do. But it is all in how you view them personally."

Suddenly, almost every principle which had been introduced began to align for me. Imagine if you will that you are seeing *your* life and each of *your* experiences in *vivid* replay. In the next instant you "see" the manner in which every event had been orchestrated, all the way down to its exact place, time, and detail, along with the perfect people. In the next instant your mind jolts to the full realization that each circumstance was merely attempting to "wake" you up, patiently urging you to change your mind and direction. Returning to my own situation right there on the roof with my teacher, was all of this because of *me* and how *I* viewed life through the filters of *my* angry mind? I sense you know the answer. The next moment for me, in

fact, was the most amazing emotional release and healing I had ever experienced to this day!

Here is a simple question for you. Do you genuinely believe that what had just happened to me was divine purpose, or simply an accident or coincidence? Now turn your personal attention to *your* case. Take as much time as you care, but go ahead and step back to observe all the repeating experiences spinning over and over in *your* life. Do you suppose you created them, just as I created all of mine? Only one answer is proper! In that moment, I fully realized that *every human is personally responsible for all of their own events!* I am deeply grateful to Master Lobsang for sharing his wisdom and counsel with me that day. And just within a few short years ago while visiting the family, my younger brother took me aside, looking right at me, “Hey bro, thanks!” I replied, “For what?” His answer took me completely by surprise, “When *you* were around, the rest of the family felt totally safe.” Apparently my placement had purpose for others, too. It brought them the sense of being safe and all I could do in that moment was to simply smile and thank him for noticing. I realized, just then, it had not all been in vain. It all had purpose! *All* things in life which include our experiences have purpose.

With the temperature decreasing, Master Lobsang and I returned to the warm interior of the monastery, all the while the cogwheels of my mind were spinning in overdrive. I asked about the issues with my dad, and as always, he provided a provocative answer, smiling warmly while answering my question with his question, “Does he hurt you today, right now?” “Uh … no,” I replied. “Where is your pain?” he probed. I had to think about this for a moment or two. “It is in my memories,” I answered smartly. He then informed me of the truth, “Young man, you are then *bound* to that memory because of the pain you have associated with that memory.” Essentially, I was concretized to the memory as inflexibly as a lion choking its prey, and from what I constantly observe in current times, the majority of other humans also allow this in one form or another. Then he offered two more ideas. First, “Young man, why do you carry your dad along with you in each present moment?” I did not fully realize that I was actually carrying around my dad with me all the time! Second, “Does your

dad create the pain today, or do you?" I did not know I was actually walking around everywhere creating my own emotional pain! So, two strikes against me: 1) clutching an old memory, and 2) carrying its emotional pain wherever I go. Then I knew. This simply must cease if I were to ever live fully in this world while knowing in some manner I would finally be free.

Really now, how could my dad literally be responsible for who I was during my sojourn in India, let alone for who I am today so many years later? This realization very much surprised me. All this time it was *me* repeating the events of my early childhood – in my own mind. My dad truly had absolutely nothing to do with my own internal anger and beating! We all seem to carry around with us our dad, our mother, our siblings, the molester, boss, co-workers, including broken relationships and perceived failures, to name just a few memory sources – constantly and continually! Watch out for this as it binds us to repetition and the cycles we fall into! Not paying attention to their purpose and lesson, we will unknowingly allow these types of memories to physically create and define our personalities as we grow and mature. Herein lies the crux behind this principle's idea: *You cannot go home again, but you must attempt it.* You see, our innocence had been taken. "Home" in this context means our *divine* innocence, the *who* we are in our perceived spiritual self, our true divine psychological and emotional self, the resting place of our memory. Be always aware of your deep emotional attachment to any memory; otherwise, it can easily, slyly slam the door shut to your higher nature as long as it resides in you! That day I realized no one in life is actually short-changed since we are all given a true gift, until we become blind to it by our past. The human cannot physically live in the past, but they can certainly be fully present, living right here and right now.

We entered the main chamber and joined the other monks, all sitting and enjoying the blanketing warmth radiating from the huge fireplace in front of us all. I looked at Master Lobsang, "If there are no accidents, why do you feel my dad treated me the way he did?" Overhearing my question, another monk chimed in, "He is your teacher on the subject of peace and a peaceful nature which is only

found within. And as long as you allow it, your dad will block this from you in your mind. It is not about him; it is about you." Master Lobsang added with a soft smile, "Because of *him* you have gone on the search for meaning in your life. In a sense you owe him your gratitude for where you are this moment, sitting in a monastery with fourteen monks, learning about Truth, life and self." What? Hold on a second! I owe my dad *thanks*? I have never looked at my relationship with him from *this* perspective! Could it be this simple?

Reflecting on this point of view, I felt a smile grow on my face. Yes, the monks were right on, and to think the solution to every painful memory can truly be as simple as seeing its event as our teacher in life and nothing more. After all, isn't this why we have come into life in the first place, for individual soul growth? In that moment, the compressed spring of my inner turmoil slowly relaxed, uncoiled, and dissolved into oblivion. Life appeared so much easier and simpler than what I had previously known and believed it to be. Now I knew what the mirrors are truly for. I could see me in that one reflection! The pain I had clutched onto for so long fell away effortlessly; in fact, I slept deeply, so peacefully, all that night.

Teachers come into our lives in all different shapes and sizes, each one unveiling a different lesson through a different function. Do you realize one of our teachers can even be how our memory remembers past events, either viewing them subjectively with an anchored emotion or viewing them objectively with a truth-filled eye? This question bears reading again because its truth is not only entirely possible, but is also the most profound idea I learned from this principle. Of course our memory and past events are fine and certainly have purpose, but we must be fully aware of our degree of attachment to them. The more attached we are, the deeper emotional effect they have on us today, which is one of the prime reasons why we have developed such multiple physical personalities in place of a single spiritual one. Over the years I have overheard so many individuals declare that each of us is the sum total or accumulation of all our memories. For them and perhaps the vast majority, this statement will hold true. Why? They have confirmed their attachment to *all* memories, and shall subsequently live and act from *them* – their emotional past. But they

do not have to, for even this is a choice! We do not have to be because life and growth are constantly ever-changing, because who we were yesterday is not necessarily who we are today, unless Karmic recycles the bygone memory back into our present with yet a stronger nudge, asking with infinite patience, "Do you get it yet?"

Here is a bold statement for you: life is an illusion. How can this be when it seems so real? Easy. We live out of our past! A perfect example comes to mind. One afternoon, while we gingerly walked on a pathway, Rinpoche Kiela turned to me, "Do you see the coiled snake?" Startled, I quickly glanced up ahead and, sure enough, there it lay on the edge of the path. "Yes!" I replied quite uneasily, not knowing which species of snake it was, as we skirted past following a wide berth. Several days later, as I walked to my private meditation site, something caught my eye up ahead. *Instantly*, I knew it was another snake coiled alongside the path; however, as I cautiously walked closer, something seemed different about it. I chuckled aloud. It transformed into a coil of rope! My laughter of relief caught the attention of Master Kiela who happened to be nearby and he immediately scurried over. "What did you think you saw?" he asked. After my adrenalin dropped I admitted, "At first I thought it was a coiled snake until I got closer." Leaning over to pick up the coil I stated, "Then I realized it is just this piece of harmless rope." He listened intently to my explanation then offered, "Young man, your memory of our first encounter with a coiled snake several days ago had literally created the illusion of the same snake on your path today. I suggest you not operate out of memory, for it only creates an illusion today based solely on the past, just as it did with this rope." I ask you, do you see the snake or a coiled rope on your path of life today? Regardless of your belief, this is a very important concept to fully realize on your journey in this world because, on one side of the coin, the experience is an illusion, the snake of your past; whereas, on the other side of the coin, the experience is very real, the rope of your present.

Each experience above has both far-reaching implications and Karmic consequences, the degree of which is purely dependent on the level of attachment. I personally realized this with the snake

and rope encounters. As Master Kiela and I walked around the real snake, I instantly felt unsettled and vigilantly observant since India has extremely lethal species, some of which actually having the ability to spit their venom great distances. When I came upon the rope a few days later, the deep-seated and emotionally-charged memory of the snake overwhelmed my physical sight of the rope. You see, memory actually can drive how we see or visualize what we think we see; therefore, by looking objectively into your memories, perhaps you can now understand why you act and behave precisely in the manner you do. For example, if you anger easily, perhaps your past is now driving what you think you see. As another example, if you are a people-pleaser, this behavior may also have been created by your past from the need of acceptance or approval developed throughout your early years from rejection. Or, you might have a negative mindset, in which case your past applies yet again, driving all you think through a colored lens of emotion clouding your vision. These individuals are each driven by their memories rather than what is truly present. Perhaps you now realize why life may be an illusion and why I have written so much on the importance of being constantly present in life. Yes, memory is certainly an important tool, but not to the degree it drives our life! Unfortunately, when it does, our *true* life is whizzing by each and every moment as we live in illusion based on the past.

In our defense, it is entirely feasible that we subconsciously recreate our past in order to see whether we left an emotional value in that relevant memory. Ponder on this idea for a moment. Read the sentence again if so moved. Do you remember me asking whether you had repeating cycles in your life? I am talking about our memories and how they steer us into the cycles created from the past while the principles of Karma recreate the experiences all over again for us, time after time. While I was on the monastery roof with my Master teacher, my newfound realization changed all of my cycles in one simple lesson: I must attempt to go home to my true nature. This can also work for every human. Simply *un*-attach our self from the memory by releasing all emotional value anchored to it. This is exactly the reason behind my seeing the rope as a snake because I had attached an emotional value to the memory of the snake.

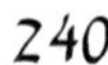

I repeat, do not forget the memory because you cannot, but merely let go of the emotion behind it, and do not allow it to drive or control you in any way. This will take some practice but is worth everything since you will be free today from the past. Whether you are conscious or unconscious of any memory, simply allow for them because they *are* permanent. And if you genuinely like yourself today, then honor and acknowledge the memories for what they have given you in the name of learning experiences. Give them a toast, for they created who you are today right now this moment! If, on the other hand, you believe the emotional attachment too overwhelming, please do not feel you are stuck in a rut. You can work this out by merely looking at your past through the eyes of objectivity, for objectivity gives you the advantage of seeing yesteryear as your guiding teacher.

Allow me to offer another story revealing the subtleties of attachment, for they can be so simple and automatic. One weekend day, I was preparing to jog in the mountains of Northern India. Master Lobsang approached and observed me for a short while then casually mentioned, "Young man, if memory is held too tightly then it has the ability to form our habits, and habits are what we each operate from." While watching me put on and tie my tennis shoes, he asked, "Do you always place your right shoe on first?" Bent over, I exhaled, "Yes, my mom taught me, and I have done it this way my whole life." Master Lobsang gently commanded, "Take them off." I did so. "Now put the left shoe on first," he suggested. Sitting on a small three-legged stool, I picked up the left tennis shoe, and as I began to put it on my foot, I leaned back too far, tipped over the stool, and fell on the floor. What happened here in this moment?

As I was laughing incredulously in total surprise, he explained, "Any time we operate from habit we are completely out of balance, in a sense. This is why you easily fell off the stool. Clearly, you are not at all accustomed to putting on your left shoe first." Okay, wait a minute! Something as simple as putting the same shoe on first, day in and day out, can actually create such an imbalance that I will immediately stumble and fall when I choose to first put the other shoe on instead? Does this not clearly show the level of power a routine memory can hold over the human? Sure, on the surface it sounds so simple; yet,

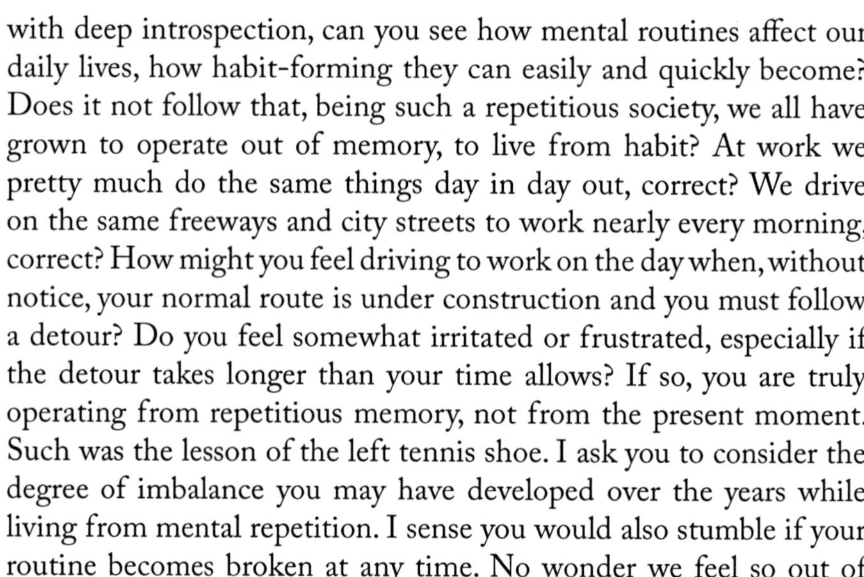

with deep introspection, can you see how mental routines affect our daily lives, how habit-forming they can easily and quickly become? Does it not follow that, being such a repetitious society, we all have grown to operate out of memory, to live from habit? At work we pretty much do the same things day in day out, correct? We drive on the same freeways and city streets to work nearly every morning, correct? How might you feel driving to work on the day when, without notice, your normal route is under construction and you must follow a detour? Do you feel somewhat irritated or frustrated, especially if the detour takes longer than your time allows? If so, you are truly operating from repetitious memory, not from the present moment. Such was the lesson of the left tennis shoe. I ask you to consider the degree of imbalance you may have developed over the years while living from mental repetition. I sense you would also stumble if your routine becomes broken at any time. No wonder we feel so out of balance and take a fall! It's all *new*.

Memories are truly a wonderful aspect of our being and an insightful guiding tool, unless we allow them to superimpose their anchored emotion(s) over our present day situation, just as my snake memory completely overrode my vision and emotion when I initially caught sight of the rope days later. As sure as we have an urge to eat, our memories have an urge to override our current affairs. For instance, let us say you experienced an emotionally charged or traumatic incident at the age of, say, twelve years old. Today you are a middle-aged adult. If you are faced with the same or similar circumstance at this time in your life, modern psychology confirms that you stand a significant chance of responding from exactly the same emotion as you had when you were twelve, not as a middle-aged adult.

Most likely your senses will pique as the memory instantly pulls you back into it full tilt. Your face flushes. Your hair stands straight out. You speak or stammer the same, or you run away or avoid the incident, exactly the same as you did the first time. Do you really find this so surprising? Have you ever witnessed a full-grown adult act in a childish manner from time to time? Up until my teachings and understanding of these Karmic Principles I *never* believed what others were attempting to tell me about me. Behind a firm and stubborn

defensive stance, I always pointed a finger at and firmly believed it was everybody else, totally blind from seeing or recognizing my anger and how I responded in those situations. Talk about memories overlaying my present! I saw my dad everywhere I went, never realizing he was not really there! I had been avoiding me and saw me through *his* vision in place of my own. One was illusion, the other reality, and the illusion had buried my true nature.

Until my teachings began with the monks in Vietnam, India, Nepal and Tibet, I was never aware of the fact that our life is actually more deeply controlled by the subconscious rather than conscious mind. Not only had the memories with my dad superimposed my present being with anger, but they had also nearly devastated my career in higher education. You see, he reminded me at least once a day, "Steven, you're stupid. You're just really stupid!" and I wholeheartedly believed him all the way into my early twenties. Certainly he must know better because I always seemed to struggle with school. While attending college to get my bachelor's degree, one day my professor called me into his office and laid down a short booklet on his desk in front of me and said, "Steven, I want you to take this I.Q. test." The first thoughts that struck my mind were, "I must be stupid because they want to test my level of stupidity."

Notice my immediate response to the professor's request. Talk about operating out of my past! Clearly, this memory overlay had profound power over me even though I was taught metaphysics by Buddhist monks in Vietnam. No matter, I resigned to take the test. A few weeks later the professor again calls me into his office only to request, "Now I want you to take another one." I flipped! My mind berated me as I thought, "Now this just proves my dad was absolutely correct. I'm so stupid that he has to give me a test for stupid people." Even though I had become a Zen and supposedly created a clear mind, notice all this stuff going through my head. I took the second test. I again got called into the professor's office a short time thereafter and I reasoned, "Okay, I'm going to get kicked out of school because it has been such a struggle." We sat down together and he began with, "I've noticed you have a level of difficulty in expressing yourself and I had a hunch. That's the reason why I asked you to take this second test."

Spinning it around in front of me, he smiled, "Steven, we aren't sure how smart you are!" You see, the issue was not my level of intelligence, but rather my ability to express what was there.

Both Master Lobsang and Rinpoche Kiela helped me to realize that my struggles in school were purely due to the superimposed memories of my dad's constant exclamations which had literally replaced my true scholastic abilities. I am here to tell you, my continuing education progresses and flows much more easily today because I am no longer attached to all those memories with my dad. Take a moment to consider these questions: do you realize how much and how frequently you operate out of your past? What do you see? What do you remember? Is your past controlling your present? You can go "home" again. While listening to your responses to these questions, you can feel totally safe as you stand in their revealing truth. No other can hear! And it is entirely up to you to release and allow the past to educate you – today.

I would like to offer a reason behind two other physical characteristics, shyness and hesitancy, because these traits are witnessed much more frequently today. A few individuals naturally exhibit one or both personalities and this is no error, of course; however, for the vast majority of humans who do not, it has come to my realization that these two personalities, along with anger and stupidity, also develop from overlaid memory. If you believe yourself to be a shy person, do you know which memory overlays your present? Perhaps you were made fun of as a young child, or ridiculed, or poked at relentlessly to the degree those memories deeply affected you. This is certainly understandable; yet, it need not remain permanent. Not for any human.

Our magnificent mind also contains the capability to recognize the precise memory and experience from which the shyness originally formed. Through our diligent awareness and presence while working with these principles, this particular trait may truly be removed with the direct result of becoming more outgoing and confident in our self and our abilities. Do you trust you? Now what about those forgotten memories? Perhaps there were people who denounced you as short,

skinny, or even ugly with their corresponding memories seated deeply in the recesses of your mind, long neglected. So it appears. Memories can exert decisive power, most especially in the subconscious level, to totally override your life very easily because their Karma perpetuates daily and automatically.

The same concept applies if you believe yourself to be a hesitant person. Which memory is overlaying your present? Perhaps you were questioned incessantly at an early age. Do you continue questioning yourself today? If so, do not resign to its permanency because, once again, memory overlay is simply pressing upon you; yet, this is not the real you or even necessary. From my observation and counseling, it seems that individuals become hesitant merely because they overlay the past and question themselves in the present due to conditioning at an earlier age. It is agreed, though, there are moments in our life when it is in our best interest to objectively question what we say or do. However, as the creator of our life, when we ask questions constantly and continuously, life will question and become hesitant toward us through Karmic return. And the cycle begins as we further develop uncertainty over our direction and self. But wait; there truly *is* a way out! When we live consciously, fully aware and in the moment, we literally intuit every reason behind our behavior and actions. From personal experience, presence brings awareness with a very clear mind. Living in this manner removes unnecessary mental clutter, thus freeing our minds to the present circumstances in which we may find ourselves. Release and let go of the past due to the binds created in the present.

One afternoon Master Lobsang and I were traveling through the forest. While I walked on the path, I noticed he was meandering beside it; in fact, I observed him traipsing around plants, bushes and trees. I thought to myself, "Walking on the pathway is much more efficient and a whole lot easier than walking around everything." I shrugged, continuing in my silence. As though he heard me, he glanced back with that little grin of his. A moment later he asked while looking straight ahead, "Young man, why do you follow the path as you do?" I pondered his question while thinking at the same time, "How does he *do* that? How does he always seem to know what

I am thinking?" and answered aloud, "It seems simpler and much easier to follow as I walk, Master." He appeared to thoughtfully consider my answer as he sidestepped another bush with his typical grace and ease.

As we continued in silence I noticed how the path began to form a deepening channel, its edge rising higher. "Why did you ask me that question?" I asked him. He thought for a few moments before answering my question with a question, "Why do you think I would rather walk around trees and plants instead of on the path?" He is going to drop another lesson on me, knowing I could only answer with, "I do not know." He led me forward, "Have you noticed the path which you are following is getting a little deeper?" "Yes!" I instantly replied, relieved over the easy question. "Young man, this path is very much like your mind in that you find it simpler and easier to follow your well-worn grooves of thought. Your mind is very repetitious in the way it operates." I was stunned because he was correct. But this does not stop my teacher, "I walk to the side because doing so is purely spontaneous. It is not routine." And he adds, "If you continue in your fashion, you will get in so deep that you will be unable to climb out, just as this path is getting deeper and deeper until it would soon be over your head." I got the message.

The Principle of Be Here and Now guides us to mind each moment, to live fully present, and to delight in spontaneous activity, guiding our return to innocence – home – which is totally opposite to what most of us in the Western world have been taught – inflexible routine and repetition. Be aware, a routine mind controls a life and can only add repeating cycles to it; therefore, make an earnest attempt to free your mind. Open it to more flowing, spontaneous thought. This will free you from the mundane repetitious mind under which we all seem to operate. Spontaneous thought will spill into your experiences, giving you the inner sense of freedom and flexibility while developing absolute balance with most things in life.

What am I attempting to reveal here? As a person performs mental repetitions, habits develop which essentially bind the person, hence confining their behavior. In this part of the world, we perform mental

repetitions entirely too much throughout our daily life, so much so that we become totally accustomed to them. We do not recognize them as the very seeds which bring to us so many repeating circumstances through Karmic return. It seems we have a fatal attraction for our mental familiarities, when in reality, we simply do not realize our life can change by simply shifting our minds to new concepts, new understandings, even new thoughts. The question is, do we truly enjoy mental repetition in our reality or are we merely used to it? In truth, if we deeply desire to attain personal empowerment, this is a key factor in the journey.

Every habit must come under our *conscious* control, mental or otherwise, in order to realize whether we are operating through that habit or operating from the spontaneous present. Remember my snake story? If something as trivial as a rope had this level of impact on my mind, consider the level of impact the whole mind has on me, and likewise on you! Our habits, whether proper or improper, actually develop into second nature, and once they become second nature they now have a powerful tendency to form a physical characteristic. If allowed, as they are way too often in Western culture, habits completely dominate the action and activity behind our responses to issues of life. During unguarded or unconscious moments, we often lapse into our habitual mental mindset. Unfortunately, there is no way around this occurrence unless we are present with our self and our mind, completely aware of its entire myriad of thoughts being emitted each moment of our life.

By returning to our higher consciousness and spiritual innocence, we are actually coming home to the ultimate discovery of our peace with self, life, and all its guiding experience. One of my teachers suggested, "There are times when the best path in life is to go straight ahead and climb the mountain, no matter how high it may appear." In this case, the mountain stands for all those accumulated, piled up memories of so-called disasters and failures which have befallen us throughout our lifetime. Forgive me, are they truly disasters and failures, or do we perceive them as such through our personal judgment of "good" and "bad," or "right" and "wrong?" Yes, I climbed my own mountain. I walked through every mud puddle and slime pit

ever produced in my own mind and memories without analyzing, but simply and objectively looking at my patterns. You see, here is what was realized from my dad in reality. He actually pushed me forward and upward toward that mountain peak. It was *he* who gave me the drive to search for meaning in my life and to understand what life is all about. It was *he* who actually gifted me the love and compassion to realize the Creative Principle in my own being. Oh I know, physical abuse was never an enjoyable experience at any time for me, but I had cut the chain of my emotional anchor to those memories and released all judgment originally attached to them. In the end, I have become very grateful for what he gave to me in my younger years! Memory may be a teacher and a wonderful guide to greater awareness if we simply allow it, rather than clutching onto it ever so tightly with judgment as we currently do. Memory has the power to literally block our life, even formidably hide us from our true nature! When I released my judgmental lens, I saw my dad's *true* purpose, resulting in the release of all internal anger and frustration, and I returned home to my true self. I also understood that he *never once* took away my innocence. How could he? My innocence, along with the innocence within *every* human, merely becomes blocked or hidden from view due to self-perceptions. In that moment, an incomparable wave of deep inner peace replaced all the turmoil of my life.

It is important for each of us to fully realize the dominion our memory may have in driving our life. One of the many things that fascinates me about the Western world compared to the Eastern world is how much time we actually spend operating our lives from the past, seeing our today from the yesterdays. It is as though we walk and drive forward while looking behind us. Does this really work for you? How about for our culture? See around you. Keeping the mind always behind the eyes and with our body performs the act of presence and is part of the path we may each take to help us return to our true, divine, innocent, soul nature. Only by learning to be constantly vigilant and aware of what our mind is doing will we develop the habit of being present. And this is certainly doable! Now I am not suggesting we must forget our past altogether because this is not possible. Think about it, how can we *un*-know what we know or *un*-learn what we have learned? How can we *un*-experience what we

have already experienced? We simply are not capable of doing this. Simply realize that memory, in and of itself, is nothing more than the past coming into the present in order to be understood, thus releasing us from its bind.

To the degree you operate out of your past, meaning you operate from your attachment to memories, your journey into consciousness will be filled with the same degree of struggle and difficulty. Superimposing or overlaying a memory on your life today will push you out of synch with present day reality, without question. This is not living! This is simply regurgitating or recycling your past, and will continue until you choose to accept it as part of your spiritual growth and Karmic process. Until that snowy day in Nepal, I realized I was not living in the true reality of life since I had totally missed my earlier life in all respects. I had only been repeating cycles of anger, drawing to me the only kind of people who could live with me – unfriendly angry people. And this was no accident because, through the principles of Karma, I originated the cycle, albeit I had done so unknowingly. If you desire to express from your true nature and to live as a divine being, then make every attempt to return home. Unveil your true inner nature which the past has merely hidden. Change your mind and this will shift your personal perceptions of *you*. And it will occur in a single moment. Our true nature has never been lost, and there is nothing to find. It has simply, quietly been lying under the rubble of illusion.

We have journeyed far on the path, one filled with many stones, and yet there is another to peer under. One of the primary monastic teachings reveals that life is truly made up of subtleties and memory actually blinds us from these. My snake and rope experience is one example. As another, let us look at a brick house. Considering how we live in current times, we do not recognize how each individual brick has been mortared in place which shaped the house to how it currently stands. You see, our own life is built in the same fashion, one experience at a time, but we do not pay any attention to the manner or timing in which each experience has been placed until our life is done. I would like to offer a quote from *The Power of Your Subconscious Mind* by Joseph Murphy: "Be careful of your thoughts, they become words. Be careful of your words, they become actions. Be careful of your actions, they become habits. Be careful of your habits, they become character. Be careful of your character, it becomes your destiny."

By focusing on the orientation of each brick, we would understand the reason for the shape of the house. The same applies to our life. By focusing on the subtleties of each experience, we would fully comprehend and see *how* every event unfolds – *as* it unfolds – right before our eyes. Is there an advantage for doing this? Absolutely! We would know the exact end result, our destiny, just as the above quote suggests. Have you observed how people in this part of the world generally pay little, if any, attention to the small things along their road of life? Be always aware! Those seeming inconsequential things can suddenly arise as sharp stones which can easily cause a stumble. In this light, it is best we follow the subtle internal actions and activities of our very own soul nature in order to find our way home again to our higher innocence. What do they suggest to us? Where do they guide us? Simply use your intuition on these understandings as you progress. Unfortunately, their messages remain hidden while we choose to wander along our current path, habitually allowing our well-worn memories of the past to collide with our present as we travel through cycle after cycle, ad nauseam, going nowhere in life.

Forgive me for what I am about to say. What is the human race telling the principles of Karma each time we create and erect a war memorial? Or an effigy of a fallen hero? Or a museum and interpretive center established out of deep respect for victims of a national or world disaster? The material intent may be informative and honorable; however, aren't they built as constant reminders of the underlying *past* event? Even holidays have been decreed in honor and memory of a person or event. Has anyone paid any attention to their *emotional* message? Generally speaking, how does the majority feel when exposed to these icons, uplifted or heavy? Consider, just within the past several years our world has been pummeled by a phenomenal increase in international wars, border skirmishes, economic uncertainty, and destructive weather patterns. The following is not a trick question. Karmic return is confirming which set of emotions to

our species: 1) upliftment of peace, love, forgiveness, or 2) heaviness of anger, frustration, blame? Please look at all those around you including what *you* have become today. If you predominantly witness the emotions of anger, frustration or blame, you are now facing your teachers and know your path. The instant we realize how every person, circumstance, and experience has entered our life solely as a teacher, we can easily forgive them, thereby releasing once and for all our anchor to their impact and emotional memory which we have stubbornly kept alive. It is our choice, pure and simple. We may all return to our divine nature should we ever make the decision to accept rather than fight our previous circumstances. We fight them because we have held onto their emotions. These emotions not only prevent an individual from moving forward, but they also prevent the whole human race from moving forward! The cycles are self-evident and clearly seen.

While sitting on the monastery rooftop that snowy day with Master Lobsang, I came to realize a few things about what the monks had taught me. We do not have to be our memories or allow them to continue to shape our present in the manner they do, and our memory has the power to completely shape our personality the second we become too attached to it. What I now realize is that I truly do like me and have allowed many levels of childlike wonder to re-enter my life, all because I chose to develop a truly spontaneous nature by practicing presence perpetually. Monastic teachings call this a return to innocence. If you do not like you, then your memories have shaped this about you and imply that you may be holding onto them much too tightly. It also means you are living your life through these same memories. By living in this manner, do you realize your present and true life is actually passing you by?

The importance of the first and second principles of Karma cannot be overemphasized. The first is: *what you sow so shall you reap*, and the second one is: *you attract to you what you are, not what you want*. The ninth principle, the Law of Be Here and Now, actually works as one of the driving forces behind these two. First, if we continue to sow thoughts based on emotionally-charged memories instead of being present, then without question, we shall reap those past events back

into our life. Second, if we remain emotionally attached to our past, then without question, we shall attract to us what we are, drawing our past back into current experiences. Now, compounding this with the Law of the Mirrors, Karma is purely showing showing us what we have become, mirrored by every person and circumstance we experience each and every day.

If you desire to change your life into a different direction then, through the Law of Willingness, be flexible enough to look into those mirrors always before you and Karma will gently steer you toward another direction, but only as long as you accept each reflection as your teacher, not adversary. Your life will magically, effortlessly move on its own accord into the direction of your desires because you have allowed Karma to shift you into what you want. This is personal empowerment! Transform into who you were always meant to be, a divine human living in the higher consciousness of your true self, your divine nature, your very own Christhood. Allow me to leave you with food for thought. If you, as the majority, hide from your self long enough, allowing your past to superimpose itself in your mind, you end up creating a false you. Life is not about *what* you have become; it is only about *who* you have always been and *who* you are right now. Hiding is not a required or necessary move in this game of life; therefore, let *who* you are shine forth in truth for humanity to behold. Be the light of the city on the hill as the Christ suggested to us.

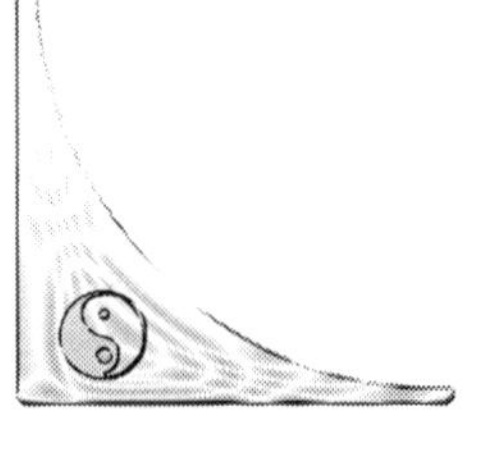

"By your own efforts waken yourself,
Watch yourself, and live joyfully."
Buddha

~ Chapter XI ~
The Principle of Change

"Young man, come walk with me," Master Lobsang greeted me one day in late August, "I want to show you a waterfall we both can sit next to." How can I say no to such an inspiring and gentle human? Besides, our walks have always been pleasant and completely informative by their nature. As we strolled along a path he thoughtfully asked, "How are your studies and understanding of Sanskrit coming along?" I held back my full rush of enthusiasm, "At first I was shocked, but now I am totally fascinated by what I am reading and learning!" Come to find out, my Master teachers and fellow monks intentionally smuggled me across China's border so I may visit the Holy Cross Monastery, essentially a granite vault deep in the Himalayas with chambers filled with documents and ancient scrolls detailing the journeys, lives, and teachings of all the Masters. Not by accident, I became one of only a handful of humans from the "outside" world ever given access to them. The monks here are the world's best and most *meticulous* record keepers since time immemorial, fiercely keeping safe and secure the knowledge and wisdom developed through *all* generations from *every* great mind for future use. Such a priceless wealth of Truth may only be found here, as far as I know!

My visit to this monastery and part of the world was no less than a mind-bending, astounding experience! My thirst to know God ultimately led me to understand my own true nature, and along the

way as part of my journey, here I sat in a chamber of this monastery, reading about the life and teachings of a man named Issa as he is known in India, Nepal, and Tibet, so I may now share this knowledge with the world. How utterly astonishing as my young eyes gazed upon hundreds of ancient documents and scrolls while my mind just seemed to effortlessly comprehend the Sanskrit writings chronicling his life, travels and teachings! While I understood and absorbed the texts, I felt deeply humbled and honored to know He had *also* traveled here to the monastery – over two thousand years ago! Yes, the rest of the world knows this Master as Jesus Christ.

While there, I also studied the life of another Master, the one who came to be known as Buddha. The records indicated that he was also here among many other Masters and teachers of the ancient world. And do you know what I find so utterly amazing? *Every human*, this includes you, your family and friends, co-workers, strangers, me, *even enemies, is exactly like them in every respect except for just one single thing*. One thing! They chose to understand and completely accept Universal Principles, some of which are contained in the Laws of Karma. They chose to fully realize how these Laws operated in their reality – so can you! This is their only difference from every other human. Forgive me, but from the explicit records I thoroughly read in this monastery and subsequent research, Jesus and Buddha are not the exceptions or idols over whom we must worship. They simply awakened to their human divinity and held out their hands inviting all to, "Come with us if you choose."

The moment Master Lobsang and I rounded a bend on our narrow pathway, I was not so much overwhelmed with the sound of the waterfall as I was with the full head-on rush of air pulsating over my whole body, to the degree that we had to work walking forward. The instant I saw the water rushing in fast free-fall, I just stood there speechless. I lost my vocabulary except for one word, "Whoa!" and my mouth remained open as my eyes actually needed several full seconds to take in its full expanse, while my mind attempted to comprehend just how far the ocean of water had to descend before exploding into the river below. I could not believe how tall this gorgeous waterfall actually was! But then again, the Himalayas comprise the tallest

mountain chain in the world. What a completely inspiring place to behold! And I can easily understand why many other Masters besides Issa and Buddha had journeyed precisely to this spot. "Sit down here!" I heard Master Lobsang whisper to me with a very loud voice, as he motioned me over to a ledge near the waterfall's center. "Let us close our eyes and simply listen to the sound around us! Allow it to lift us into a higher form of meditation!" he softly instructed through the roar of the water.

I lost all reference to time as I drifted into myself. Unlike any other, this meditation was more out of body for me and I am certain I would have remained this way if it had not been for my teacher's gentle voice asking me to return. For all I know, he could have been yelling for me! "It is time for you to learn the next principle of Karma," he offered, "we shall begin today and continue as we journey toward Ladakh." Rinpoche Kiela and Master Lobsang had mentioned this destination the day before and how I would act as a deaf-mute once again when our small band of monks cross the border toward Hemis Monastery back into Northern India. I also remember them suggesting, "Young man, enjoy these mountains and this place as much as possible because this may be your only visit here, at least as a monk." I found this very easy to do simply because of the other-worldly beauty of the surrounding landscape, the strikingly rich sunsets I have ever witnessed even to this day, and the stars. Oh my, the hemisphere was stuffed with stars each night, as though each had jockeyed into place so I may see it. I swear the Earth's atmosphere acted as a telescopic lens because my hands found themselves naturally reaching out to touch them just above my head, and I believed the full moon had altered its orbit by a few hundred thousand miles, for it slowly rose from just over that ridge so very close to me, its diameter, craters, and dry sea beds magnified ten-fold and fully detailed.

Master Lobsang asked, "Look at the water flowing over the sheer granite. Do you see any change?" Scrutinizing the falls I replied, "No, I don't, except for the falling pattern of the water itself." He acknowledged with, "Even though it looks the same, it is always in a state of change." I wanted to scratch my head on this one; however, I knew by now that my teachers never left me without further explanation. As always, though, he must have sensed my puzzlement for he continued as if on cue, "This fall has been in existence possibly since the very birth of this mountain millions of years ago, and the changes taking place with it are extremely slow, not to be seen with the naked eye, no matter the frequency of my visits. This next Principle of Karma is precisely about this. It is the Principle of Change and is observed in this manner: *the more things change, the more they seem to stay the same.*"

Generally speaking, you would be correct in saying that human evolution and the appearance of our world has changed a significant degree; yet, in some respects they seem to stay the same. The truth is, even to this day, we do the same things by following our same well-worn mental paths throughout the millennia. When we look at the world, we declare it as more civilized today than at any point in history, but I ask you, is every human and culture and nation around the world really as civilized as we proclaim? Are you so certain? Objectively observing the human condition, I continue to witness and hear of skirmishes, conflicts, wars and acts of terrorism, along with the so-called need for power and control, all on a personal, societal, and national level. Just what is going on here?! The truth is, we seek only outward change because we give so much power and attention to our external environment; therefore, we can only magnify and emphasize our outward circumstances, to which Karma infinitely and lovingly replies, "Yes, my beloved!" returning to us yet more of the same or similar experiences.

So, do things truly ever change? Absolutely! But here is the reality, only when we make a different choice by shifting our mental repetitions, or mental habits, or self-perceptions, each one an internal attribute. After this shift, the path we currently follow changes direction automatically for us through Karmic return, pointing us to a new, exciting dynamic. This Principle, the Law of Change, entwines very nicely with the previous Principle, the Law of be Here and Now, because until we finally release our old wounds to which we ferociously clasp onto and through which we seem to operate, we cannot truly begin to change and shift into our individual divine nature. There are in reality no short-cuts allowed on our path for there is only the path

of life. Even those who seek higher consciousness must overcome their grasp with physical reality and the illusions there from. This is a basic precept of the Buddha and his realization of the eight-fold path to consciousness.

Allow me to offer another piece as food for thought with this principle. Master Lobsang once told me that most of us are pretty much like our parents. This, of course, brings up two old pearls of wisdom, 1) like mother like daughter, and 2) like father like son. As much as we believe in our total independence when it comes to what and how we think about life, consider just how eerily close our choices and decisions are to those made by our parents when we are placed in the same situation. Are we really independent? Consider also where we have chosen to live, both geographically and nationally. Also, we think like Americans, not necessarily the same way as the Chinese or Europeans do. Additionally, Californians think differently than do New Yorkers and Iowans. When, where, how, and by whom we were brought up pretty much determine how we think of our self and life. What I am attempting to offer here is that if you would genuinely like to manifest a permanent change, allow your true individual nature to surface rather than simply repeating what everyone else is saying and doing. There is no such thing as peer pressure here in this realm, only individuality!

Master Lobsang looked over at me and asked right out of the blue, "Young man, do you like yourself?" Since my experiential learning with the previous principle, the Law of Be Here and Now, had yet to sink from my intellect down to my heart, the only plausible answer available for me to use in response to his intriguing question was, "Why no, Master, I do not." He laughed aloud, "Well, change your mind!" Feeling it in my best interest to not belt him one, I instead relaxed from my initial fluster, realizing he was actually chuckling over the simplistic answer rather than putting me down. The moment I chose to shift my mental habits and self-perceptions, my direction changed over time and I found that I not only began to like me, but I also felt great joy and a sense of awe for simply being alive and learning from all my experiences. After all, this is the purpose of having life, to learn from and with our experiences. The funny thing is, learning can only be accomplished by having the experience and then releasing it so a new one may come to us. To learn, to grow, and to change, we simply must release the past for what it is, the past.

How much more simple can it be? All of my teachers taught me that all things are simple and to look for the simplicity in whatever I was to do, a very valuable message. Just change your mind – now! Make a different choice about you and your life, and then Karma will automatically return wonderful things to you as you proceed along your new path. It is observed around me every day, that by far, the majority of humans truly do not fully realize that their mind is the most potent, influential, active organ they have, a Karmic generator if you will, a lifetime and dedicated caretaker which plants, tends, and energizes our thought-filled seed garden, 24/7. Watering with impure emotion, our mind still becomes a magnetic force beyond comprehension as we unconsciously allow it to go along in its daily flailing routine of creating every circumstance, every experience, every individual and teacher throughout our life. We are categorically told this in many ancient texts! So, if we ever desire to truly break away from Karmic recycling, then we must fully realize the power behind this magnetic power plant – our mind. Simply shift and suggest a new direction. Thoughts and things will change. Guaranteed!

Looking back now, I could very easily have turned out just like my dad; in fact, I was actually going full steam ahead in that direction until I listened to and followed my urges to India. From the non-traditional teachings and patient guidance offered by my Master teachers, my path altered course, simply by learning to change my mind in how I viewed my self in relation to all others and life. Mind you, this is not comparing my self to others for that will not work. If you may recall, up until my lesson in the last Principle of Karma with Master Lobsang, angry people seemed to constantly enter my life and I had no clue as to the reason for their attraction to me. Why, the truth is, they were just like me! Before my journey into India, I knew my life had to change or it was headed toward certain self-destruction, so I sincerely sought to change my circumstances, searching all over for meaning and a peaceful existence in life. And that has been found as may we all if we simply look into ourselves with pure objectivity. Then and only then may your Karma shift its power.

Yes, at first I was running away from it all; however, this led me to understand that wherever I escaped to I still found an angry young man right there with me. The moment my teachers began revealing the Laws of Karma to me, I slowly realized that I did indeed have every necessary tool to make those changes permanent in my life. I offer a perfect point for your consideration. Outside circumstances are exactly that. Either escaping from or changing them is neither a permanent solution nor an avenue for growth. I suggest you come to realize that it is your mind which not only creates these circumstances in the first place, but also keeps recycling them. This is why the Law of Change has so much significance in our life, for it reveals the idea that we must first create internal change. So long as we focus on the outer in the fashion we do, the external cycle cannot be broken because we only see the same thing, no matter the level of daily effort we put forth each moment. No wonder people are so worn out! Your cycles can vanish as did mine. And to think I only shifted my self-perceptions and to forgivingly release my dad! Any one may do this by forgiving all things in their past and then leave them there. Once again, this does not mean to forget them because this is truly not possible. Merely view them differently.

The next morning, a light tapping at my door awoke me from a deep slumber in the middle of the night, or so it appeared. Master Lobsang stood smiling at me in front of the predawn sky, "Good morning young man. We are going to have an early meal before we begin our journey to Ladakh today." Upon our departure I was reminded once more of my posture as a deaf-mute and to not say a word when we arrived at the border. How interesting to not feel any anxiety or nervousness this time! Should I have any concern? That thought vaporized instantly the second I witnessed the dramatic Himalayan sunrise in all of its radiant glory! For a short while we all journeyed in silence before word wandered back that Rinpoche Kiela wanted me up front with him. Yes! After I fell in step with him, he asked thoughtfully, "Are you ready for this long and arduous journey through the very high mountains and low valleys which we shall pass through?" I smiled, "Yes Master, I'm looking forward to it!" He continued, "I understand that Lobsang has begun talking with you about the tenth Principle of Karma, the Law of Change." I beamed,

"Yes, he has." Then his stunning statement, "I know of the pain you are in over your father," followed by his bombshell question, "Young man, have you ever considered the degree of pain your father must have been experiencing in order to treat your family the way he had?" I asked how he knew my dad was in pain. He replied, "Your dad was constantly repeating his cycles and could not break them. He could not change, because to him, each time he flew into his rage Karma was squeezing that much tighter."

I reflected upon my teacher's stunning insight and, after a short while, I felt a surge of compassion for my dad for the first time in my life. The many years of anger were replaced by a completely different energy towards him. There was such freedom which accompanied it as I no longer felt bound. I looked over to my teacher who wore a slight smile on his face; as though he "knew" I was feeling nothing but compassion for dad and his pain. "Master," I asked, "is it this way for all people and their cycles? Am I the cause of his pain?" He immediately offered reassurance to my second question, "Definitely not! You are not the cause for his pain; you have been the recipient because of his pain," then offered an answer to my first question, "Young man, it is similar with all people because Karma is indiscriminate in its activity. It is based on equality and on our individual cause which we create in each moment of our life. As long as we continue on the same path, there is no chance for anything to change. No human is above the natural Laws of Karma, for they are unbreakable and every human is bound to them. Yes, we are each able to directly influence those Laws into a positive direction, but we must first break our old, well-worn, mental cycles before our direction can ever change."

He continued, "This is the primary reason for this one Principle, to help us recognize and realize our cycles and then to allow them to teach or show us the necessary internal changes for us to work with. Once we become the observer in our life, cycles are easily revealed to us and then we are fully able to shift them into a new dynamic. This then moves us into a new outward direction." His manner suddenly transformed as he quickly whispered, "Please say no more and move into the middle of the line, head down." My heart pounded with adrenalin as I scurried away, thinking to myself, "Uh-oh, something is

happening!" Upon rounding the next curve in the path just moments later, our line of monks encountered a Chinese patrol! Of course they halted us, only to stiffly ask where we were headed, all the while looking up and down our whole lineup while Rinpoche Kiela calmly responded. They allowed us to pass asking no more than that one query and we moved away from them very slowly. Funny, I felt myself calming down for some reason.

After we traveled a bit Master Kiela motioned me to return next to him. "You must be very careful and aware of how nervous you get when the soldiers are with our group. It can very well bring you precisely what you do not want." "What? How so?" my eyes widened. We continued walking while he considered a response to my question. Out it came, "Young man, all things have the seed of Karma attached to them, whether a thought, an act, or an emotion. If your nervousness continues, especially when we reach the border, the soldiers will surely notice, and our ruse of your being a deaf-mute shall become more difficult to make work." Silence fell and I thought about his words, recalling my first time with the soldiers. That time I had no experience. Now I did. Oh, I see, I was acting from a memory overlay, just as I did with the snake which I shared with you in the previous chapter. Man, these overlays are so very subtle in how they impact our very actions in life! Imagine how many overlays must constantly be playing out for people without these teachings! I asked Master Kiela about this and he nodded, "Yes that is correct. It is also why your country has such difficulty with life and why its own cycles are constantly ever-present."

Only after walking for what seemed many miles, our humble group of monks decided to stop for a noonday meal and rest near a large, swift stream. One of the monks casually turned to me, "This stream flows into Northern Nepal many miles ahead and forms a lake known as Lake Issa." My eyes widened with astonishment, "There is a lake named after Master Jesus?" "Yes," came the reply, "He spent many days on the shores of this lake, and it was named in his honor." Master Lobsang looked over to me, only to continue my lesson, "One of the most difficult things about changing our mind and resulting cycles is how we judge things to be, which of course, includes our self." I asked,

"Is this why we should not place our judgments on anything in the very first place?" He nodded, "Yes." You see, we humans seem to find it most difficult to break a judgmental mind, which is the sole cause of so many illusions in our world along with the Karma associated with them. What? Illusions?! Well, think about it. An illusion can be mass created just through this one vehicle because, by judging something or someone, we then only see and understand what we judge rather than the true reality of the object or person right in front of us.

Master Lobsang continued, italics mine, "*There is nothing wrong in our world. All things are exactly as they are supposed to be.*" I offered another question, "How does judging interfere?" "Young man," he responded, "When we judge something we actually allow our memory to overlay the present moment, just like your experience with the snake a few weeks ago. Judgment comes from past experience, and if left uncontrolled, it will drive our experience today." He offered a slight smile, "There is actually nothing to judge in the present because each moment is brand new." After a short pause he continued, "We not only have to be aware of our past for what it was, but we must also be aware of how we judge our present through this particular filter of mind." Let me see if I have this straight. From my emotional response to the snake, my memory overlay drove me to later see the rope as a snake; in other words, the judgment created from my past snake experience actually drove me to see a snake again in my new experience with the rope. Does judgment, therefore, keep things the same? Could this simply be my ego not willing to shift, not wanting to create change?

I have witnessed countless numbers of people fight for their judgments – ego – because they are so grooved into the way things are. In truth, they do not need to, nor are they required to judge anything and anyone, even when they think they must! Keep this in mind; we are able to see life only through what we have experienced. This is true with every person. When two people look at a flower they actually see two different things because of their personal experiences. There is no way around this, which implies judgment is truly inaccurate. It is your experience that filters what you think and what you see, yet it does not have to. Simply do not limit things only to your experience.

Allow your life to become more expansive in every thing – including people – and it opens for you to receive a greater life. Judgment can only limit your experience, even that which you judge.

My Master teacher had more to share on this subject, "When viewed with objectivity, the past itself is simple to overcome. However, the judgments we establish from the past are an entirely different matter because our mental habits lie beneath those judgments being placed. As it turns out, these mental habits – mental repetitions – produce the very cycles we encounter along the road of life." This sounds like the workings of Karma; in fact, the Law of Change becomes even more significant because we are talking about Karma. If we desire to shift our Karma into a positive impact we must become aware of the cycles, at least in the sense of what they are attempting to reveal or teach us about our self and life. According to my teachers, if we observe these cycles and notice their timing, they would show us a great deal about how we are personally responsible for creating them. Do they not appear to exhibit a particular timing, appearing in our experience nearly at the same time interval? Consider this question for a moment because this is how the cycles show up in order to deliver the same or extremely similar experiences, even attracting the same types of people. To think we are the one driving or creating them!

For example, let me use the idea of love relationships and the reason why we have so many, at least for most of us. Generally speaking, the relationships end up somewhat disappointing. We can certainly ask our self, "Why?" "Did we choose improperly?" For a handful of situations, yes; however, this is not at all the case for most people. You see, for the majority, the choice is based on the subconscious rather than conscious mind, a choice based more from memories rather than the present moment, a choice based solely on Karma. Because our memories reside in the subconscious, the place from which we tend to operate, Karma ends up returning all our judgments of people, places, things, and situations. But, as you may remember, Karma does not punish, for it reveals and guides us in our growth through return action constantly and consistently through every moment of our life. Therefore, when we choose what we feel is the right person in that moment of time, we are actually attempting to heal something from our past through a Karmic return, perhaps to forgive an abusive parent or to replace a long lost love as two instances. Life is for you, not against you! We hope you are realizing this.

If I may suggest, while being gentle on yourself, take a step back to observe all the types of relationships you have chosen throughout your life. Do not analyze. Simply view each relationship without any emotional attachment. Now look for any similarities. Do you see a pattern or cycle going on? It can appear very obvious when the experiences are viewed objectively. If repetition is revealed, you may now learn from it and know what it is you are attempting to heal within you. And from this new understanding about you, the cycle or pattern is fully released, no longer retaining its need to cycle back to you – ever again! Allow me to offer food for thought here. By simply allowing a relationship to enter your life as a learning experience, then allowing your self to receive its lesson and then allowing it to close naturally, the potential for a repeat relationship and emotional upheaval at any time is greatly diminished. However, the more intense your emotional upheaval in any relationship, the greater the odds a similar one will repeat. Do you wish to continue in this pattern? Lifetimes are available if you do.

"It is time to move on." Master Lobsang announced. As was customary, we began the journey in silence for a short while. He then looked over at me, "In our reality, do you realize we are fully responsible for recreating our issues with only one thing changing? And that one thing is our location." Oh-yes, this certainly rang true for me! I remember earlier in my life when I continued to attract the exact same type of people and circumstances from which I was fighting to avoid, no matter my specific location or the number of moves I had made. Self-avoidance never really works, and as long as a person does, the cycles become ever tighter and repeat more often. Our memories and belief systems go with us no matter where we go, when we go, or how we go. Remember the Law of Growth? *Wherever you go there you are.*

From every page of this book, I have been offering you a path to

create true change in your life. This is accomplished by becoming aware of both what you create and how you create it. It is done by accepting personal responsibility for every thought, emotion, and action in your life. Understand how the principles of Karma work for you constantly and continually. And realize how all things come to fruition based on the seeds you perpetually plant during each waking moment of your life. Trust yourself, for you are the only sower of seeds along your own path of life – no one else is. Know yourself, for it is entirely up to you to create the new dynamics you so desire to have and experience – this is your journey. With greater awareness, you can choose differently.

In the late afternoon, we hiked towards a small village and a monastery nestled in a valley where we would spend the night. A flank of fifty monks welcomed us with kindness, all surprised and eager to know what I was doing with the group. Rinpoche Kiela informed them, "This young man came from America to learn about the Buddhist traditions and Saint Issa." I sensed joy and gratitude since they realized an American had chosen to travel such a great distance to learn about their Eastern philosophy and the Master. While we settled in, I felt safe and very comfortable here for some reason, knowing full well that accidents and coincidences do not exist. After the evening meal we all sat in the great room and began a discussion on how complex the world had become. Master Kiela made a comment to the whole group, "All of us must realize that human history always repeats itself due to global Karma created by how every human treats each other and by how every human interacts in each moment. The physical rewards of material gain are now the focus in lieu of the reverence for life," he revealed, adding a slight pause before continuing, "In a global view, Americans do not know how to share what they have as do monks between every different monastery." He added, "It will all remain the way it is until the human begins to realize other ways to accomplish things in our world. Right now, humans remain asleep and are not aware of anything other than personal ownership and the idea of material gain. Every Master throughout time has carried this same message to the masses. When we all fully awaken to the truth of the higher ideals then our world would truly unite and be in service from one to the other with no need for greed or gain at the expense of any other."

It is mind boggling to me how their message has gone unheard and been thoroughly neglected for thousands of years! Global Karma has evolved to become exactly the way it is in order to teach and guide us back to our path of higher thinking and being. I asked my teacher, "I often wonder if this was done with human intention and the desire for control over the masses." He replied shaking his head ever so slightly, "Young man, it is not important whether it is done with a deceitful purpose because, only if we choose to see it as our teacher leading us in the higher direction does it then all become part of the path to higher awareness. When every human realizes what they seek is not the truth, they will begin to seek on their own for a different way of life, ultimately returning once again to live in truth." It now appears this is, indeed, coming to pass as more people are seeking higher truth than ever before.

Master Lobsang explained to me how our differing belief systems are the root cause of the world situations now being witnessed today. He continued, "We are on a collision course with all our Karmic debt because of these rock hard beliefs which all humans carry. Unless we start seeking higher divine purpose, the physical world will respond in like kind, just as hard and inflexible if not more so. This is already taking shape if we but look around us." I now wonder, could this be the true cause behind the severe weather anomalies, the rise in seismic and volcanic activity, wars and seeming acts of terrorism, the total disarray of the global financial system, and the constant daily affairs tugging and pulling at us every which way? Do you suppose unrest is blanketing the world right now? Are we stuck with these events? Is this direction set in stone? Or is all this changeable right this moment? Genuinely ponder the following question: If you fervently know you could affect change in our wonderful planet, would you? The truth is, every human has this level of power and choice of direction. We can use our divine empowerment, choosing instead a reverential, loving direction, and Karma shall return to our Earth more of its like kind. We can all travel on this path!

The peace within the walls of this tiny monastery completely saturated my whole being inside and out. Master Lobsang looked at me, and of course, knew what I sensed when he explained, "We are

this way in a monastery because of the primary principles of Karma, the ones you are learning." He continued, "There are twelve principles by which we live, not so much in an intellectual sense but in a practical sense where we are aware and constantly utilize them during every waking moment, for they have become an integral aspect of our self. All monks live in this fashion. This is why we are the way we are." He offered a suggestion for the evening, "Let us now get some rest before tomorrow's passage out of Tibet and continue our journey toward Ladakh."

After another early rise and meal, our group of monks departed the lovely valley, fully rested for the day's journey. Once again Rinpoche Kiela motioned me forward to walk with him after a short spell of silence. These were truly awesome and inspiring people to be with! What with all their wisdom and unbelievable endurance, I mean, "Master, how is it that even the older monks seem to walk so free of any effort?" He replied with a one-word smile, "Karma." "Huh?" I thought while asking, "What do you mean?" He began, "Young man, Karma is everywhere. Life itself is Karma because it is divine Karma and we are the result of it. When monks do anything it is done with this idea in mind and includes everything physical, mental, and emotional. In your Bible, does it not say the human has dominion over all things? This is what it means – Karma. As long as we operate with and through these principles, we truly do have absolute dominion because we act more naturally, more harmoniously with a deeper connection with our environment. Walking, in fact, is a perfect physical teacher to reveal how the Laws operate. As we walk it shows the outer world what we are internally. Peaceful fluid motion is a true peaceful human as they operate within their own personal dynamics." I thought this over and realized I never really knew how I walked; so, I began to focus on the nuances of my movement. I shot a quick glance at Master Kiela, long enough to notice his smile. Yes, he knew what I was doing. A few walk-filled moments passed before he turned to me, "Move back into the center of the group. We are approaching the border once more just a few miles ahead." Noticing my concentration he concluded, "Good, continue your practice; allow it to become your teacher as it guides you into more fluid movement in your motion. Such motion, in fact, requires less energy."

Maintaining focus only on my walking, I began to feel how my feet touched the earthen path while my awareness spread to the length of my stride, the swing of my arms, the manner of my hip movement, and my deep rhythmic breathing, all the while digesting what they were each teaching me. Have you ever truly paid attention to your walk? What a wonderful teacher of self, an active meditation to increase your power of self-awareness. As I practiced, I began to physically notice how my movements were made with less effort. They became even more so as I engaged a synchronous rhythm, fluidic with my stride and breathing. I barely heard Master Lobsang say to me, "Good. You are now in moving meditation with awareness of all what you do. Now, observe your mind as you are moving."

We approached and proceeded through the border crossing back into Nepal without any fuss or delay from the soldiers, as if they had no care for simple monks. Continuing my walking meditation, I noticed a growing awareness of my whole way of thinking, and realized why my teacher had asked me to do this. As I observed my thoughts, I now completely understood why our lives do not actually change very much. Have you ever looked at the simple movement of walking as a teacher and how it can expand your awareness? Do you realize as your awareness expands so does your life? As this occurs, things truly reshape in your life, the cycles melt away as change – true change – settles in. A smile settled on my face as I realized something. Life is just a process as long as we simply allow all things to teach us who we truly are. If you accept and realize this, watch out, for you will grow in many directions! In hindsight, I now honestly feel my walking meditation revealed tremendously more to me about myself, life, and Karma than any other lesson during this leg of my journey.

We hope you better understand just how the cycles of life can deeply affect each one of us, but imagine having absolutely no cycles? Talk about the fast-track to empowerment and enlightenment! Without cycles, our journey in life would proceed in a straight line, narrow and strong as a waterfall, and we would experience positive growth as things change through time while moving only forward. "This is another reason why we have cycles," Master Lobsang commented, "so we may fully see the direction in which we are

headed." "What does that mean?" I asked myself then turned, asking my teacher, "How does that work?" He replied, "Getting caught in the routine for every cycle helps us think we know where we are going in life, but in truth it does not because we are operating in cycles or in repetitions that seem familiar. When our life travels in a straight line, doubt and fear have the propensity to swell in our mind." "Why?" I asked. "We truly enter unknown or unfamiliar territory each new moment," he explained, "so, to avoid this we create cycles throughout our life, all filled with their familiar, comfortable routines." He stated, "This is so powerfully true in America." He paused for a moment, "Do you know where we are traveling?" "No, I do not," I replied. He added another question, "Are you in doubt or fear?" to which I responded, "I trust you all to know the direction." He smiled. Although the answer was easy, his comments evoked a deep reflection as I looked back at my life, only to realize just how true his words are.

Breaking my train of thought, Master Lobsang had more to say, "If we become filled with doubt or fear, it automatically creates the same Karmic return, does it not? Doubt only creates doubt; the same holds true for fear. One is sown; therefore, it is the only thing we can reap." He suggested, "By staying present in our journey, doubt and fear do not arise because we are not living ahead of ourselves," then adding, "We will not arrive at Hemis Monastery until we actually arrive there. If, instead, we focus only on the distance, such thoughts will drain us and will make the journey more physically difficult." His analogy made total sense because doubt and fear also create a struggling mind, which of course, now becomes a way of life as the individual wrestles with these two emotions. "Consider this," my teacher offered, "interestingly enough, confidence is also tied to our cycles since it is developed through repetition. This may be fine in some things; however, it is a false confidence with life, nonetheless, because this type is based on the outer world, not the inner self. The reason false confidence is offered is because, once one moves away from their cycles, the confidence may not remain since they are now in unfamiliar territory. They are away from their comfortable cycles, just like the experience with your left shoe. One may also establish confidence when their life travels in the idea of a straight line simply because they are accustomed to the unknown. This would now be genuine confidence as they rely only on themselves." I had never once thought of it this way before! "Ponder these ideas as you walk on this journey," he suggested then fell silent.

His words continued to resonate through my mind as I reflected on their meaning. As we traveled to Ladakh, my focus remained only on my walking and breathing, nothing else in my life, and oh so slowly, all the fears and doubts I had been carrying seeped into my awareness. No wonder I question and second-guess myself nearly all the time, for it all began in my childhood! And right here was my answer, brilliantly revealed through my teacher's message, his words still resonating so strongly within my wary mind. The truth is, I am the one recreating childhood experiences, not my dad. My mind still entangles with and validates long-ago emotions, bringing to me a circle of angry people each day – not my dad – until that moment of realization. And to think these emotions are totally irrelevant today! I merely got caught in a cycle, a very large and all-consuming cycle. Even as I desperately sought different circumstances, an altered life, no true change had occurred in my reality. Not until now. You see, permanent change must begin within each human, then spreads to the outer world, then spills into their life. Not until we understand our life and circumstances in a truthful sense will we ever know what to change and be able to create within us; otherwise, nothing will ever really shift. It cannot. This is our only requirement. Just shift our self-perception or how we view our self in our own life and then change occurs automatically.

No human is born broken. We have never been, nor are we broken now. We simply have a broad diversity of experiences, all solely intended to lead us to full self-awareness through how we handle or not handle our life. No victims exist unless we choose or believe it so. No perpetrators exist, only teachers along our path of life. Personally speaking, I feel the greatest and most important teacher is change, for we can understand our self more from new experiences than from repeating the same-o same-o day in and day out throughout our entire life. Unfortunately, most people do this as they seek change. In truth, growth withers and dies in a repetitive life. Change is a Universal Truth because every aspect of life, both animate and inanimate, constantly shifts, even the waterfall. We can choose to either value and honor change or fight tooth and nail resisting it. I offer one last food for thought here. Resistance even changes you! This principle encourages our growth and forward movement through experience, the ultimate purpose of life.

Can you avoid change? No. Can you resist it? It may appear so only at first. Ultimately, the understanding upon which you shall arrive says no. It is suggested that we each simply allow for it and remain flexible when it arrives. This is your life moving in evolutional change, ever forward and never backward, even though at times this may seem so. If you choose to live in this manner, your life shall evolve into ever greater experiences through this awakening principle, the Law of Change. Your life is now journeying more closely to a straight line and forever ending the cycles of repetition. This now creates a divine flow in each experience because you are now aware of what you create, from and through Karma. Life for me now reveals only wonderful experiences, no more inner pain or doubt, only happiness and joy. This is nothing more than a simple choice we each have, always before us in every moment. We can simply choose to live in this manner. Now we move ever forward from one changing moment as it unfolds into the next, forever flowing with the changing tides of time.

"If you wish to know truth then
hold no opinion for or against anything
truth then is obvious to an open mind."
Zen Proverb

~ Chapter XII ~
The Principle of Patience and Reward

Nearly a year had passed before our small band of monks returned to northern India, completing my round-trip odyssey from northern India through Nepal, then Tibet, only to return by way of Ladakh and heavenly Kashmir. What a totally mind-bending and extra-sensory journey! My physical sensations burst in astonishment from every sight, sound, taste, and touch while my mind expanded exponentially. This trip taught me the most about the true nature residing in each one of us, every human on this world. I realized I had been given an extraordinary opportunity, a brief moment in my total lifespan, to listen and learn from Master teachers and fellow monks who ensured that I receive both the oral teachings and proper studies from the ancient texts. How many people actually travel, completely aware of their inward journey? Believe when I say it is the most eye-opening and amazing journey of all, an inner path leading straight to self-realization, if you so choose. More food for thought is offered here. We must always be ever vigilant concerning our inner being, our feelings, our thoughts, and our external expressions because they each generate their return action in the outer world. In truth, each human is first cause in their life; therefore, blame really does not apply – ever. Blame only knows to negate all of our personal responsibility, an attribute which comes in with us at birth and grows as we do.

Guess who first greeted us as we approached my home monastery? Yes, Shanti Che! My furry companion sauntered over to our single file of travelers. How nice of him to greet us from our journey! Of course, I just had to express my immense appreciation and joy by losing my fingers in his thick coat, rustling my hands freely all over. What a purr!

Only a few days had passed when I suddenly felt a strong urge one late afternoon to meditate at my private pond, and to reflect on my recent journey and life direction. Upon the completion of my chores, I approached Master Lobsang, informing him what I had in mind. "May I join you?" he replied with approving eyes. Absolutely always for sure a pleasure! There is such insight in the minds of these wonderful teachers of life, and they have such a huge impact on people. All people! Master Lobsang replied to my thought, "It is because we revere life and honor all things. Even the tiniest creatures are held with great significance. Life is in all things, as all things have life. Most do not cherish this enough in our world, but they easily could."

As we walked the short distance to the pool, Shanti Che suddenly strode out from the pathway thicket only to walk beside us, purring away. My teacher looked at me, "Your stride has become very efficient as you move. This is a sign that you fully comprehend the many lessons we have been sharing with you over the months." I glowed with inward pleasure and bowed with a smile of gratitude. After a moment he asked, "What are you pondering?" I shared with him all of what was floating through my mind, "Master, the majority of us Americans has absolutely no concept of these teachings. Americans do not fully realize the level of structure, discipline, and open-mindedness required to be a monk. We do not comprehend the tremendous amount of effort involved to understand the true meaning and purpose of our life through proper use of perception. We all must become objective and passive with our self. Each of us must free our self of all internal, self-imposed judgments – what a very freeing experience just by itself! The real truth of our inward journey is to fully understand our self through all the illusions taking place in our societies." He replied with a smile and nod, "Yes." I share

these principles with you because we Americans are actually very adaptable; yet, it does take personal commitment and effort to master the principles in a cohesive foundation. Oh-yes, even while we take on a life which appears entirely filled with hectic, day-to-day affairs in a complex, dizzyingly fast part of the world!

Our walk continued as did the sharing by my insightful teacher, "Young man, when you or any person focuses on life from the idea of truth, paying attention to all things both internal and external, you create a positive Karmic flow with which to operate, and by so doing, good things simply unfold for you. On the other hand, when you become cluttered or unfocused you create the opposite, and positive flow seemingly appears to become cut off and impossible to achieve, let alone maintain. Learn to constantly stay present, focusing only on this moment, and allow tomorrow to take care of itself. Your Jesus also said this." I immediately understood his intention and meaning. As I imagined in that moment while walking next to my teacher, I ask you to now imagine a life without any internal and external distractions, a life in which you are completely aware of your steering mechanism – your wonderfully unlimited mind – still and emptied of every chattering monkey, utterly free from all past and future clutter, constantly knowing all what it is generating for you to experience. This is attainable. It merely takes dedicated and disciplined practice. And positive things do happen! Sure your mind may be as a giant banyan tree, each limb overflowing with raucous monkeys and thoughts as free and flailing as a wild stallion, but just hold on for a moment. Stop! Slow your breath and still that mind of yours. Stop paying attention to those obnoxious baboons in your mind! Rein in and corral that undisciplined horse! All this simply takes time, nothing more; otherwise, we will continue to miss the vast majority of our life – without ever realizing it!

The gentle voice of Master Lobsang appeared in my flowing streams of thoughts, bringing my reflective mind back to where my body was walking, "Young man, it is time for you to understand the eleventh principle of Karma, known as the Law of Patience and Reward. Steven, the moment Kiela and I first met you at the roadside hut where you were having your tea, we felt you would be a somewhat

difficult student because your mind was so unfocused, so very rigid; yet, we also sensed your higher energy, something entirely unknown to you at that time. Initially, you were locked up tight in your American beliefs; however, we knew you contained great potential to become a good student. This is why we focused on your potential, to help you realize it for yourself through a full understanding of your blockages. Everyone had been hindering you in so many ways throughout your life." He continued after a perfectly timed pause, "It was also your impatience." Another pause, "And today, we are very pleased at the expanse of knowledge you have attained." I offered, "Master, all of this has been an honor for me. No one is more fortunate than I to learn in the manner which has been taught me. This has completely shifted my perspective of my own self and life." Again, this is very achievable for every human, and it all boils down to how you see you. True, we each have a different perspective of how we view this, but the journey must be walked by our self. A teacher can only act as our guide. There exists no other way to bring change, a permanent positive change, into our life. We must do it. This reminds me of an old Chinese proverb, "If we don't change our direction we are sure to wind up in the direction we are headed." These are wonderful words to ponder over for a moment.

My wise teacher had more to say, "If all people focus on their own life instead of on others, many inner realizations would appear. Life is not a struggle unless, of course, we choose it. I realize this may not be agreeable to some, but neither agreeing nor disagreeing can change the truth. Life evolves into a struggle because we stay focused only on our outer environment, which means we do not pay any attention to our inner life, and we end up planting negative, judgmental seeds haphazardly all over our path. These very same seeds sprout and grow right in front of us, creating personal struggles, like walking through a thorny thicket. If, on the other hand, we focus on our life, observing both the internal and external aspects, we shall clearly realize and understand what we do in any given moment, the part which actually creates the second half of this Principle: *...and good things happen.*"

As the three of us approached my meditation pool, the soft rush of falling water and the ocean of bubbles popping on the pond's

surface were music to my ears as I had not been here since we left for our journey. My thoughts filled our silent walk, pondering just how a specific rhythm becomes established when I focus only on my walking. In fact, by focusing only on this one single activity during my travels with my teachers and fellow monks, my life appeared to follow this same rhythm. It must follow, therefore, that a rhythm or pattern unfolds for every action in the life of every single human. Can we truly know what befalls us long before it ever shows up in our life, merely by focusing on what we are doing now? The truth is, we must only focus on the moment we are in. "What the…?" I wailed when I suddenly felt the big cat firmly nudge me off balance into the pond and immediately jumped in after me. "Yes, tigers like water and have no fear of it!" Master Lobsang called out in hysterical laughter. Surprisingly, Shanti Che was actually a very efficient swimmer. Ever play with a wet tiger? The next instant, my mouth gaped wide open as I watched my teacher jump into the water with us! Talk about spontaneity! After a short spell of splashing and swimming, my teacher and I climbed while Shanti Che jumped out of the pond so we could all stretch out to dry. Besides our two smiles, I do believe I also recognized a sly smile etched on the tiger's muzzle as though pleased for pushing me into the water!

My loud chuckling caught my teacher's look, expecting a question, "Master, did Shanti Che have anything to do with the lesson about my focusing on my life?" He replied, "Yes, in a sense. While we were walking alongside the pool, you were absorbed in your head thinking about something and never once noticed how he moved closer to you until you found yourself freefalling into the water. Tigers, like all animals for that matter, remain constantly aware, unable to think as we do. They only know how to stay in the present. The human, on the other hand, thinks entirely differently. We have the ability to experience free thought. On one hand, when we choose to focus in the present, this becomes our greatest talent and life dynamic; on the other hand, when we allow our thoughts and mind to wander every which way, this becomes our greatest challenge and struggle. If you had been focusing on your life and on what you were doing in that moment, you would have instantly noticed the tiger's movement towards you and quickly given him more space. Instead, you fell

off balance, which very well has become your lesson. Now, he still may have continued pressing against you, forcing you into the water anyway." At this thought my teacher laughed, "He probably wanted us to join him for a quick swim! He paused for a moment, "This experience, indeed, is a good example of focus and mindfulness, or the lack of it." He offered more insight, "You will now remember this experience in joy, and it shall be easier to understand just how subtle a lesson can be. We humans tend to focus only on the seeming obvious; yet, the truth is, it is actually an accumulation of hundreds of small things. Young man, pay attention to life's subtleties because these make up the obvious."

I turned over and asked, "Master, how is it that only good things happen when we focus on our life, as this principle suggests? Is this Karma and its return activity?" His explanation came with a smile, "When we are focused on our life, we know all what we do each moment as it comes, and we do good things. Now because of this, Karma returns more of what we put forth, good things. When I suggest you focus on your life, this is not at all a selfish activity as one may first think. It is truly and more closely aligned to being totally self-less in every chosen action. We are all here to lift humankind, not to bring it down as most seemingly do by not focusing on their life. We are all here to knowingly be of service to humanity. This helps others, of course, and positive Karma returns to those in service. Unfortunately, we do not live in the highest manner we are capable of because, generally speaking, we have yet to do all things purely for honest reasons."

My teacher shared more with me, "Honest reasons do not come from our ego, the lower mindset. When we operate from ego, what we perceive as "honest" is actually not so at all because, in truth, it is created from a selfish mindset – the ego. If the act comes from ego, we make every attempt to impress others that we are performing a selfless act; however, the ulterior motive cannot be cloaked indefinitely, and we end up manipulating others to get what we want. The greatest acts are to do good things, to be of service, to act selflessly without anything expected in return. Any other way is not from an honest position; therefore, good things will not return, even if we

do get what we want. People are inherently good, Steven, but when they knowingly or unknowingly choose to operate from ego, they transform into something they were never intended to become. You have been taught here that the ego must be harnessed and trained to operate with our higher divine nature, instead of dominating and overshadowing it. When you return to your home in America, remember this idea. Allow your desires to become your teachers, as with everything else. Just as you focus on walking, learn to observe and accept all things as a teacher because each wants to show you an aspect of your self. Once these different aspects are known they are then changeable through the use of your objective self. Ego does not want to change and this you will come to realize with time."

"It is time to return for dinner and meditation," Master Lobsang reminded me aloud, just as I realized I was observing my thoughts about what my teacher had shared with me, rather than merely thinking about them as we all tend to do. As we strolled back to the monastery, he looked over at me, "Do you focus on what you do not have?" I replied without hesitation, "No, Master, I have everything I want right now." He then offered me more kernels of wisdom, "When we focus on what we do not have, we actually set a trap for ourselves in the material world because Karma, as you now know, will give us exactly that, more of what we do not have. Another point, if you focus on lack or ill health, lack or ill health are reinforced, hence their return, because they are what the Universe hears from you. In truth, *every single thought is a request for the Universe to give that thought to you.* Also, one cannot see lack and abundance at the exact same time. It can only be one or the other and this is what humans do as they move back and forth from one to the other while both are creating. The same holds true for your ideas of ill health and perfect health. When you focus on lack and ill health at any time, you do so, in truth, out of your pure desire for abundance and total health, meaning you do not already have them. Monks desire nothing because we already have all what we require in life. Now how is this? By focusing only on our own life and what we do each moment, nothing else. Remember, life itself is a precious gift and is the best reward each human can ever give to them self. Life is rewarding, but only when we are patient with it, and from patience, we ultimately live our dreams.

The eleventh Principle is termed the Law of Patience and Reward for this very reason."

After several steps, my teacher continued, "Desiring a thing implies you do not already have that thing, does it not? This is why people seek their desires without ever realizing the trap they had just set up for themselves. They now no longer understand or believe they already have all they truly need or require in life because this trap is a false guide, insatiably urging them to seek more and more things throughout their life. In truth, what does every human already have, without exception?" I am certain he paused for effect. "*We have who we are.* Merely becoming satisfied with who we are brings a sense of inner fulfillment which subsequently eliminates any desire; in other words, we shall never feel or believe we lack any one thing. From this position, our inner creative ability becomes more potent, thereby expanding outward more effectively into the material world from which all is given us automatically. The Christ Himself made this explicit point for our understanding, expressing this as our inner Kingdom. Young man, inner fulfillment is the most rewarding of all, for it returns abundant flow and optimum health into our life experience. It is perfectly fine to have all what you want, just as long as those things do not own or control how you see or feel about your self. Remember, you are not your things. You are you and things do not define this. Do not lose this perspective because, if you do, all the teachings will mean very little." Naturally, I did not realize the impact of his words until later.

Patience is the other part of this principle and it is a very gratifying experience, indeed, for it ultimately leads to total freedom from the so-called pressures of life. Do I wish to discuss its relation with the world and all its inhabitants? Not necessarily; after all, humans are going to be precisely who they need to be and are going to do precisely what they need to do. So allow them that. If we do not, then we are judging them based solely on our own experience. This judging is not for us to do, for judgment has the propensity to only downplay them and what they do. Also, it keeps them limited to only our perspective and not how they actually are in reality. If we limit others, then we become limited by the very same veil of illusion; besides, isn't this somewhat harsh? And sending a harsh vibration out into the world creates which Karmic return? I sense you know the answer.

Is there another side to patience? Most definitely! I now refer to the one pointing directly at our own self. The moment we lose our inner patience, we lose patience with the world, our personal circumstances, even with those most dear to us. Why would we do this, especially since we are literally condemning first ourselves and then the world? Two reasons: 1) our conditioning and seeming insatiable strive for perfection creates this in the first place, and 2) impatience truly ignites our ego to create a self-ingratiating attitude of "better than." As was pointed out in a previous chapter, "better than" is an untruth which will strictly lead to our downfall as Karma delivers the return lesson. Are you aware, that if you follow the path of self-condemnation, no way exists for you to ever realize your state of perfection, even though you constantly seek it?

Based on my teachings in the Far East, we are already perfect right now this instant because, "*We are perfection in a constant state of unfoldment,*" Master Lobsang once told me. The idea here is, why would someone look for what they already have? It is because we do not realize this, and through our inner condemnation – personal judgment through comparative thought – the path to higher perfection becomes blocked, though not permanently I assure you! By vigilantly maintaining patience with who you are, your external experience no longer clings to the path of resistance, a very major road block to your higher being. If you desire patience, take the road of least resistance known as the path of self-acceptance. Although not necessarily comfortable, smooth, or uncomplicated at first, this path is definitely well worth your journey.

From a commonsense approach, what other alternative do we have? Can we replace our skin? Can we switch minds? In truth, no other way exists, no matter what we believe or think because no other is supposed to exist. How may we change what naturally exists – our body? Besides, our skin and mind are not who we are internally since the physical outer appearance is more akin to our past life Karma. I would have to say we are internal first and external second; in fact,

one could say that what we are internally is what ultimately shows externally in our life. Or it could be stated that what we are internally, our life shows to us externally from the Law of the Mirrors reflecting back to us.

Patience is the very tool which brings to us our rewards in life. Sure, we are certainly capable of fighting and struggling for our every desire, something that is witnessed on a daily basis. However, you may be keenly aware of how this continuous life-long battle adversely impacts both our life and health. Please, it need not be this way! Where there is patience there is no struggle or fighting or judgment or anger or frustration. It appears we have simply been duped – conditioned – and have completely accepted this so-called tumultuous lifestyle. Case in point: do you remember the TV commercials airing throughout the 1950's? I laugh aloud because they move along so slowly compared with those broadcast today. Nowadays, the images constantly flash, blink, and pop in front of our faces nearly simultaneously, a mile a second, and in higher volume! No "hurry-up and buy-this-product" here! Additionally, and forgive me, I see many individuals wearing their wireless devices as though natural appendages to hips and ears, each alerting us to what we want to know right this very instant. This is not even close to the idea of patience; instead, it corresponds more closely to levels of selfishness, the "I must have it now!" syndrome. This is not stated in judgment; it is an observable truth. Such is our society today.

When you find yourself becoming impatient with the world, especially people, look within you to observe what the cause may truly be. Is it really them or is it you? Be objective in this to see truth. Switch the focus to your self. Look inside, for perhaps then you will calm down as your patience returns, while at the same time the external irritant gently disappears. Impatience is also nothing more than the teacher of patience in life; in fact, please allow my repetition because it bears repeating here. Always turn the coin to what you are feeling because only then will you discover the lesson. For example, expressing anger is the teacher of inner peace. Outward frustration is the teacher of inner harmony, and hating anything or anyone is the teacher of self love. When understood properly, each so-called

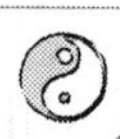

negative emotion is our ally, an internal teacher if you will. Always look within first before approaching the outer world because the outer is actually controlled by our inner nature, hence the reason why there are actually no coincidences or accidents or failures in our life. We are the ones who are in control, not life, and our life is totally our choosing. We are the ones who have complete and direct influence on all things through the idea of Karma. So learn to control you, if you choose; otherwise, the outer world has the control.

Allow me to share something once again with you by putting yourself in the following situation. During any activity in any space and time, see and feel yourself in a perfectly good mood. Feel wonderful? Great! Now suddenly, someone enters your space, saying or doing something which upsets you, instantly triggering your impatience. The question becomes: who is in control right now, you or the other person? They are. They are now controlling how you feel! This begs the next question: How did they physically trigger your impatience? Unless they strapped you to a chair under physical and emotional duress and pumped you with drugs, chances are you are the one who shifted how you felt at that moment, not them. Now think about this, can someone or something outside of you truly reach in your mind to flip your emotional switch? It is personally felt that the other individual did nothing more than to purely act as them self in that moment, not at all forcing you to change how you felt. The follow-up question is: why do you feel so drained after this incident? Here is a hint: who has the power during this experience? The answer is: you knowingly or unknowingly gave your power to an external cause by allowing the other person to shift your feelings and this creates the sense of being drained. This situation is not at all a coincidence since it reveals a different perspective about you and falls perfectly in line with the third mirror, Reflection of Loss, in the fifth Principle of Karma. Go back and read that section in chapter six for a refresher if you would like. It boils down to this: if you choose to accept your empowered being and a more rewarding life filled with rewarding experiences, do not give your power away to any one or any thing. Oh yes, one more thing. Gently release all blame. Well, how and where would blame exist when you only express your unconditional, loving, divine nature?

The soft voice of my teacher gently tugged my awareness out from my reflective mind and back to our walking as he offered more insight, "Young man, joy comes in life as a result of doing what we are meant to do, not doing according to what others or what we seemingly believe or think we should do." My face responded with yet another bewildered expression along with my silent question to which he knowingly smiled, "Life is not about what we have to or supposed to do. Yes, it is true there are things requiring our attention, but consider for a moment. All work in this monastery is entirely based on volunteers, is it not? When you painted, did you have to do that? Or when you plant and harvest, are you supposed to do this?" he asked. We all know my answer.

Master Lobsang continued, "When I use the words "supposed to" or "have to" or "must," these are different states of mind. That is all. But at the same time they seem to place internal pressure on the one who is thinking these things. When we think or believe we are to do an activity based on any one or more of these mindsets, our action can very easily develop into a heavy burden as Karma returns its like kind. In truth, there is nothing we are supposed to or have to or must do in life, other than to simply live life. When we think of our activity from any of these viewpoints, it becomes our teacher by giving us another view of our self." He paused a moment, "What happens internally if we do not want to do it? To the same degree we create internal pressure from our sense of having to do the thing, Karma returns to us an equal measure of resistance to the thing. There is no need for resistance because it strips our joy from the activity." Another nicely timed pause, "And now, does it not seem as though we are no longer in control of our life at this moment, instead feeling heavy and drained of energy? All of this merely because we feel or believe we must do a thing."

My teacher was on a roll, "It is not the idea that we are supposed to be in service, but the idea that we choose to be in service. Young man, by operating under this concept, you are honestly being of service to your fellow monks, both while you paint the monastery walls and while you plant or harvest in the fields, because you choose to do these things. Also, you are in service when you teach one another.

This honors all of life, each other, and our self at the same time, doing these things in joy. Viewed in any other fashion, we then see it as a "*supposed to*" or "*must*." Truly, our precious world can most dearly use many more people in honest service. Remember, being in service to others creates positive Karma and goes along with what Buddha once stated, "Success does not bring you joy, but joy can bring you success." If we place joy in everything we do, we are simply doing what we choose to do, ultimately living in joy only."

As we approached the monastery Master Lobsang did not stop talking, "Living in joy is the true natural state of the human. Joy creates humor and humor leads us to experience a more genuine lifestyle. Joy even helps make our decisions much easier, while at the same time, creates a much lighter life. Joy also creates a healthy body because we embody a healthier mind. Patience also becomes a natural state of our life when we live in a joyful manner, a life more rewarding for us in all ways." His pause sparked my question, "Master, what is the thing that pulls us from these natural states?" His answer smiled patiently at me, "Judgment. It is how we judge things to be, including the simplest and most benign judgment. Most humans see things as right or wrong, good or bad, and as many other forms. Seeing them in any of these ways moves us from our natural state. If we see something as bad and we have to do the task anyway, it makes the task much more difficult as we put forth more effort. This is yet another concept behind this principle. Anything in life may be simple or difficult, but is it not all in how we judge it to be? Imagine how easier or simpler all things become if we assign absolutely no judgment to them. If we think something as wrong or difficult, Karma will return a wrong or level of difficulty to us, thus the challenge in our situation." Okay, this actually made sense to me. So it all boils down to how we view the experience while we move through the experience, all the while constantly carrying the potential to create our own resistance to it. Allow me to offer a gentle reminder here. Each human is the creator of their life and every experience contained in it.

Would you like to remove all judgment from your life? Books, CD's, DVD's, workshops, retreats, religious affiliations, pilgrimages, even private counseling are really not required, unless of course, you

choose to pursue one or more of these experiences. This is perfectly fine. Even though each pursuit provides experiential information for you to understand who you are, do keep in mind however, that you may get a bit sidetracked from your path. The simple fact remains quite clear. You are going outside of yourself, looking for something inside yourself. Why not do the reverse and look inside instead of outside? How about the fast track, the absolutely certain, lightening-quick, gentle, and short-as-a-single-word path? Are you interested in knowing what that is? I offer you the path of patience. "Patience?! What does patience have anything to do with this?" I hear you asking. Yes, I know patience has been discussed earlier, but allow me to shed a different light by overturning another one of its stones.

In this part of the world we are conditioned to judge, pure and simple. We spend our whole life expressing it from our earliest childhood to our passing. The task of removing such a deep-seated, long-term mental habit certainly cannot be easy; yet, it can be accomplished. From genuine choice, mental discipline, perseverance, and constant observing, we can remove all forms and manner of judgment from our mind under the compassionate and peaceful name of patience. And here is the crux of the matter. Not until we accomplish viewing our self through objective eyes can we then see the world in the very same manner. The truth is revealed here, yet again; in other words, not until we first work with an inner aspect do we then see the appearance change in front of us, automatically for all time. Should you genuinely choose to make this journey, I offer another gentle reminder: there are absolutely no coincidences anywhere anytime with anyone or anything in our world. Live this rather than merely think it. Oh yes, the two are vastly different. Living this concept is to experience it which, by far, is the best and most efficient of all teachers, whereas thinking it is nothing more than storing it in our intellect.

Once you master and walk with this idea, your inner observation grows much more acute as judging no longer blinds your mind or colors your view. Personally speaking, only through patience and perseverance have I been able to develop such acute observation, and it now brings me so much closer to the actual experience in front of me. Life is now lived much more fully than ever before. Funny thing,

this supports my saying that life is an illusion, or put another way, as long as we continue to live from a conditioned mind layered with judgmental filters, our life remains an illusion simply because we do not "see" the actual life, only a filtered one. This is why we began this chapter with a quote which was realized by Zen Masters long ago. Would you like to permanently dissolve this filter and every colored lens of judgment from your eyesight? Then make the choice to be patient with yourself because, over time, you can completely dissolve this conditioned mindset, one which operates more from routine and judgment rather than spontaneity and joy. Would you like to step into your natural state of joyful living, to gain your unconditional nature with all people, places, things, with every individual experience? Simply form no opinion about anyone or anything. And allow all people and all things to be who and what they are, not who and what they are not, respectively.

Master your self by utilizing objective observation, then step into complete acceptance of all life, your truest form of unconditional love, your actual state of being. This in turn creates wonderful Karmic flow into your life. Initially, due to your conditioned mind and life, taking the steps toward self-empowerment may not come easily; however, the Law of Patience and Reward will work for you and with you, making the steps along the way quite effortless. Once freed from mental routines, the mind operates more spontaneously, relying just as much on feel as on your physical senses, thereby creating a more sensitive form of human. Believe me, this is well worth the journey, for it becomes inspiringly rewarding just as this principle suggests. Imagine a life completely free from the confines of conditioning! This is really living outside the box, is it not?

I now offer my final thought by presenting an ancient proverb. It is this: *Before you become enlightened, you must carry the water and till the soil.* What in the world does carrying water and tilling soil have to do with personal enlightenment? My wonderful and infinitely patient teacher, Master Lobsang, shared the following with me as we walked, "Young man, just as the Bible was never meant to be taken literally, the same holds true for the statement I just offered you." He repeated

the statement before continuing, "It makes no literal sense, does it? The true context of this proverb relates directly to the inner work we humans must do in order to reach higher consciousness. In this case, water symbolizes the internal weight on our mind which stems from all the yesterdays of life. Just as a bucket becomes heavier when more water is added, so also does the internal weight on our mind as we carry its constant accumulation over time, our shoulders feeling heavier as each day progresses."

"How do we release this weight? By tilling the soil. Of course, I do not mean a field of dirt. I mean tilling the field in our mind because this is where we plant the seeds each and every moment of our life, do we not? Only from cultivating our inner mind field can we then locate the old seeds and choking weeds we have been planting and accumulating from mental routines. Steven, do you recall when I asked you to remove both your shoes and to start over by putting on your left shoe first before the right one? Did this not reveal just how automatic you had actually become in your mind and life?" I chuckled over my memory of the event, for I quickly learned the degree of my imbalance when I stepped out of my shoe routine. Falling off the three-legged stool when I lifted my other leg first clearly demonstrated the degree and depth of my mental pattern, and revealed how my outer environment had been confined to this same pattern or routine. But hold on a second! Are we ever truly out of balance, or do we merely have the impression of imbalance simply because the experience is brand new and we feel so very different? Just as the farmer carefully watches his crops, every human can maintain a vigilant watch over their field of thoughts. Just as the farmer regularly cultivates and disks his fields to disturb unwanted weeds and aerate the soil, every human can till the soil of their mind with awareness and the gift of patience. We can disturb and shift our internal routines toward a new direction which instantly breaks up, aerates, and scatters the old patterns – *automatically*, including some of the judgments we have placed. Yes, even judgments are routine by their very nature! By tilling our soil, what do you suppose happens to our Karma? Will it not also shift and travel in the new direction with us?

From personal experience, I fully understand this process may not begin smoothly and effortlessly. I understand you have been saying and doing many things to many people in the same manner for many-many years. Unless you are willing and consciously choose to view these mental routines, they shall be most difficult to recognize as each inconspicuously arrives in your thought process in that perfect moment; however, I offer food for thought. Would you like to know precisely when a mental routine pops up? Easy. Each time you become impatient! Well, think about this. Any moment a personal routine becomes disrupted, do you not feel irritated or frustrated? These are simply two signs of impatience, or expressed honestly, impatience surfaces in that instant when we believe and feel things are not going our way. This is the exact perfect moment to stand back as the objective observer, to gently and patiently remind our self that life does not always go in the direction we think it should. Forgive me, but life solely goes in the direction it is meant to. Impatience, truth be told, reveals that we got in the way, not somebody or something else and certainly not life. We created the resistance. And do you know what Karma can only do in this instance? Resist right back, as it must.

This reminds me of a story once told to me by my very good friend, an Ayurvedic physician, Dr. Rajesh Kotecha. Though it has its own unique perspective, I feel it relates to this discussion. He shared, "One day there was this very intelligent crow. He was very intelligent and very thirsty. On this day he spied a vase that had water in it, but he could not reach the water as it was not full to the rim. You know, this day was very warm and he was so very thirsty. As he was walking around the vase he began to notice small pebbles on the ground. He looked at them and then at the vase, and he pondered for a moment. He then began to pick up some pebbles and began dropping them in the vase. As he was doing this, there were other not-so-intelligent crows in the trees watching him. He continued to drop the pebbles in the vase, one at a time, until the water reached the rim and he began to drink until his thirst was completely quenched. He then flew away. The other not-so-intelligent crows immediately flew down from the trees and flocked around the vase, mimicking him without any thought about what they were doing. They continued until there

was not one drop of water left in the vase because it had all overflowed onto the ground."

How does this story relate to what is being discussed in this Principle and Karma? Well, imagine our thoughts and actions, each as a pebble. Over the course of many years, our vase of life fills up with these pebbles because we repetitiously and continuously drop every pebble into it without ever thinking about what we are doing. Our vase soon becomes stuffed with pebbles and emptied of every drop of our spiritual water. Does life seem "dry" and "baseless" to you? What are you to do? I suggest you return to tilling your soil, to remove those pesky pebbles and all those root bound weeds so spirit can refill and water your life once again. This little story truly fits the first principle of Karma: *What you sow so shall you reap.*

Each and every moment, we fill our lives in a fashion similar to those crows watching from the trees. We are divine, unique creatures; yet, unlike the intelligent crow, do we not do what everyone else is doing by blindly following the status quo? Stop with your rationalizing. Just stop for a moment. In truth, are we not infinite beings with magnificent intellect? Then why have we not chosen to use it for personal understanding and expansion? Perhaps it is a wiser use of our time and personal effort to follow the intention behind my teacher's words, "*Before you become enlightened, you must carry the water and till the soil.*"

After a brief period of silent walking, Master Lobsang looked over at me with a pair of eyes telling me he was going to lift another stone and share its meaning with me. He offered, "Young man, there is another side to this proverb. Most people think that once they achieve enlightenment or consciousness they no longer need to carry the water and till the soil. Steven, this is pure illusion because the water and soil are always there. The only difference between the lower realm and enlightenment is higher understanding, the result of which makes the task of carrying the water and tilling the soil substantially easier. The truth is, the work of life is never over. I do not say this to discourage you, but to offer the reality of true life. As we climb towards higher consciousness, the more we realize how infinite in

scope these principles are, just as life. Every Master comes to know that our journey really begins after we rise above the pulls of Earthly flesh and physical materiality. Once the human attains this higher state, their work does continue, but at a more subtle level, for carrying the water and tilling the soil becomes simple. Even still, the water must be carried if one is to drink from the well of life; the soil must be constantly tilled if one is to promote sprouts of new growth, while at the same time uproot those choking weeds getting in the way of fresh new life. Would you not gladly do this if you realize the process becomes effortless?" An analogy comes to mind for me. When a young child, recognizing every word in order to read your favorite story all by yourself may have been an arduous task at first, but now, how much work does it take for your eyes to recognize the words on this page in front of you and for your mind to understand their meaning? I sense Master Lobsang intended for me to understand that carrying water and tilling soil with higher understanding would become as simple, smooth, and swift as speed reading.

What my teacher offered really made me think about the idea of enlightenment because I had always felt certain it would be all over after one achieves it! While listening again to his wisdom in my mind, a perpetual process actually made more sense. If the Creative Principle is infinite in nature, does this not imply a constant and continuous never-ending process? Since life falls within the Creator's infinite scope, does this not imply that life is also a constant and continuous, never-ending process? From the other side of the coin, if what my teacher had just shared with me is true, that learning is a perpetual process, then our life must also be perpetual and never-ending in its nature, correct? The two sides match perfectly! The second we choose to accept and enter higher learning, it stands to reason that the more we come to know, the more we come to realize we do not know as we travel from our initial set of finite circumstances to an infinite realm of possibilities. If the human opens their heart and mind to the Universe, they expand to accept all things and ideas, a perspective totally opposite to what is seen currently. The enlightened human views things totally free of all judgment and shackle-free from all anchors, an absolutely mind-bending experience as they slip out of their heavy coat of ego and struggle. By all means carry your water and till your soil. And choose to do these in joy and patience.

I am not at all discouraged to know that my water and soil needs constant attendance. We deeply hope you feel the same since carrying and tilling will seem as nothing to an enlightened mind, as Master Lobsang revealed. I think we all can handle no effort in patience, do you not feel the same? But then again, in truth, it all comes down to how we view what we say and do. So, is your life filled with effort? Is it filled with struggle? Frustration too, perhaps? Would you like a simpler life? A "Yes!" to any one or all of these questions points you to and reveals a choice to begin on the path being offered you, a very doable path leading to self-empowerment. To attain and maintain a simple life in this apparent complex world is not impossible because, with its infinite patience and unending guidance, Karma will create your life in whichever direction you choose. Remember, Karma makes no choices. It only says "Yes, my beloved!" to every one of your choices based solely on your interaction with life. Although life is ultimately a pure joy to experience, the human species spends so much time fighting and clawing at each other, while the truth remains, we do not have to. These actions are not found in the owner's manual. Trust this as I have already looked. I offer another pivotal point: if you fight life, life fights you back. This is Karma. Period. On the other hand, if you choose to practice a patient life, Karma returns it's like kind to you in full splendor, only to exponentially increase your joyful experience. What is it you would now choose? Is it the same course or a different one?

"One speaks at the right time, in accordance with facts, speaks what is useful, speaks of the Law and the discipline: one's speech is like a treasure, uttered at the right moment, this is called Right Speech."
Buddha

~ Chapter XIII ~
The Principle of Value and Upliftment

Although your experience in Monk 101 is nearly over, your learning and focusing in a sacred and honorable manner shall continue after the end of this class. This view and way of life should continue throughout the rest of your life – stay ever vigilant in this endeavor. The time is approaching to walk the path instead of merely scheduling and thinking about it only during moments of convenience, since Karma is a natural Law working perpetually. Indeed, you have traveled far towards the consciousness of true life and have taken into consideration your individual impact on all things. At the same time, you may recognize and accept all potential effects on your particular circumstance and every other human through the eyes of Karma. Perhaps you now realize how you have created Karma's return action, an unending and unbending activity by its very inherent nature. By discussing how each of us may apply Karma for positive returns, it is felt that our lives will become straighter, stronger, and more stable rather than haphazardly omni-directional, for we may now journey more tightly in a straight line in our growth and understanding.

As long as we honor our self, life will honor us. You see, it is our internal honor which automatically creates a life honoring us through

its Karmic return. And nothing else can honor our self to the degree and level of understanding than what is offered by the final sacred principle of Karma, the Principle of Value and Upliftment. Expressing the verb root "uplift" as a noun is purely intentional in honor of my teachers in the Far East. "Upliftment" shall be used precisely in this fashion and its meaning and great depth shall be revealed as this Law unfolds for you. Come travel with me now through the last of the twelve Principles of Karma.

One morning, long before the crescent rise of the brilliant sun, a band of thirty monks, my teachers, and I, arose to begin our journey to Dharmsala, home to his Holiness the Dalai Lama. Although the journey had not been planned specifically to meet him, I felt thrilled nonetheless, to merely be in the same proximity. Okay, I admit, there is always the chance he may be present; after all, he is the spiritual leader of the Tibetans and the Tibetan Buddhist path! Just like the other trips, I found this one just as fascinating and adventurous, for many lessons and teachings popped into my experience on a wide variety of subjects. Nothing was known about any other encounter or specific event along our way, only the knowledge of traveling from one monastery to the next. Is this not how life works? Do we ever really know how things are going to turn out? Even when we do have a plan, it is only the plan itself which we ever really know for certain. In my case, Dharmsala was my plan, for no other purpose existed in that present moment as we began our journey.

If you think about it, a plan does not detail the actual path; it merely affirms the results we desire – nothing more. A true plan would allow the path to show itself as we work within the plan. I offer a critical perspective here. It seems in this part of the world, once we formulate a plan, we believe it necessary to micro-manage every aspect of it, poking it from all angles. We keep kneading it with such intense manipulation, firmly believing we can actually sweep away every struggle from our path. Do you realize this degree of domination will, ironically, create the very struggle we do not wish to have? In our effort to achieve the very result we seek, such control will actually sway us – physically and emotionally – away from every teaching crucial to our profound and planned success. Read that sentence again if you so

choose. It is very understandable how we can enter times of struggle, even with our best of intentions and best laid plan. But is our struggle truly blocking us from success? From a Karmic perspective, is it even a struggle? Not at all on both counts! The so-called block is merely an illusion because, in reality, the plan continually remains obtainable so long as we remain aware of our ever-present Karma. What do we do? Simply allow each Karmic return to patiently steer us on a better course. Following the path of flexibility is the fast-track in any plan since it is filled with lessons for success; on the other hand, stumbling along the path of rigid adherence is the rocky road since it is filled with nothing but struggle. The truth is, our journey along either path is our teacher in life, and Karma remains our guide along both ways. It is best, though, to adapt and follow the path Karma outlines for us because the plan will still work but with less effort on our part. Simply follow where the path leads, for our goal shall greet us, presented by Karma.

The sun had blanketed the day with pleasing warmth by the time we left my monastery "home," my teachers sandwiching me as I hiked up front with them. On my right, Rinpoche Kiela turned to me, "Do you feel ready for the final principle of Karma?" With raised eyebrows I replied, "Yes, Master!" suddenly realizing I had been taught the Law of Patience and Reward several months ago. Upon reflection, I noticed how much more rewarding and vibrant my life had become since they introduced that principle to me. In fact, all turmoil had vanished from my life, for I had released my anger and frustration now that I understood the true purpose of life experience, and the reason things occur at the time and in the manner they do. I do not doubt there are many individuals who genuinely think they are aware of how life truly works, but I ask them, "Do you really?" With a yes answer, can they honestly proclaim, "I do not encounter any struggles or frustrations in my life!" If this is the truth for you, then you know and realize the wonders of pure joy in life.

You see, struggles approach us each time we feel our plan is not working according to the way we think it should, but the truth is it continues to work perfectly all the while in the background. Here is food for thought: 1) *everything* and *everyone* have purpose in our

life including the idea of struggle, 2) we need *only accept the teaching behind* every experience, and 3) we need not judge every single thing. Simplicity returns when we allow all people, places, and things to be exactly who and what they are without any need to transform them based on our internal memory tapes. Life has always been and always will be infinitely creative in nature; yet, the human must first realize their direct influence on life each and every moment by understanding, accepting, and utilizing the twelve self-empowering Principles of Karma.

As I continued my inner reflection, one aspect of these Laws suddenly came to mind. Each principle seemed more ethereal as I progressed, operating first from the obvious to the very subtle; in other words, my Master teachers introduced me to the principles of Karma in precise order, waiting patiently until I understood and internalized the current lesson before proceeding to the next. Is this not true for all things in life? As one extreme example, a student does not graduate from high school while in the first grade. One's journey starts at the beginning, not in the middle or end. And now, here I was, about to begin my journey into the twelfth and last Principle! Obviously, both my teachers keenly sensed my eagerness for the lesson because they purposely fell totally silent during our walk. Was this a lesson? I bet you know the answer.

On my left, Master Lobsang broke the silence with an intriguing question, "Steven, if you do something that makes no difference, what is the value of doing it?" Silence returned as this question was being pondered, fully aware of an underlying current, a dual meaning to it. He politely asked, "Do you understand the question being asked?" making me keenly aware of just how long my silence had lasted. I offered, "I am not sure, but I want to reflect on it some more..." Master Kiela cut in, "Young man, this is the very key to the twelfth Principle. A difference that makes no difference is no difference at all!" I added this kernel of information to the original question, mulling them both in my mind to see if I truly understood their meaning because I knew I would not get the rest of the information until I understood the seeming puzzle. Turning my head from one teacher to the other I simply blurted out, "Why would somebody do something that makes no difference if it makes no difference at all?"

"What a silly question," I thought to myself as my face flustered in embarrassment. Sure it sounds ridiculous, but curious enough, this actually occurs countless times each day in our part of the world. I asked myself, "Do I go through my routine motions, only to finally realize they are taking me absolutely nowhere simply because I am not making a difference or any change in my current circumstance?" This begged my next thoughtful question, "Do I make a difference in my life and in that of others?" Let us all really consider this question for a moment or two. Take your time. Forgive me, but it is observed how the majority of us will only do something because we want something in return, not because we simply had chosen to say or do it out of genuine, unattached kindness. Surprised? It is true, though, isn't it? Let us live to create a difference, not only in our field of endeavor, but also in *every thing* we say and do. Why? Because we can! Historically speaking, many individuals have made a significant difference, their words or actions affecting us deeply, even to the degree of changing our world forevermore. Why not you and I? When we do something for others without any regard for personal gain but purely out of choice, our presence, words, or actions will lift them and their esteem. Do we really lose anything by doing these things? Is public acknowledgement really required?

As if waiting for me to finish my thinking, Master Kiela responded to my question, "This is the impetus behind the twelfth Principle, termed as the Law of Value and Upliftment. Every thing we do should have some value to it, not for ourselves alone, but towards all things. If we do things to make a difference in our lives and those around us, a lifting effect returns to and takes place within all concerned based on Karma. The effect lifts others while it consequently moves us toward our higher divine mind, away from the lower realm of life. And, as we reach higher and higher toward our divine nature, the lower the impact on our life from Karmic return." After a pause he asked, "Do you remember the caterpillar?" I nodded. I remember being told, "…nothing in our world is insignificant," and my smile broadened. I shook my head in amazement. My teachers just tied together the significance and importance of all creatures in life to our every action.

He continued, "Steven, if we do a thing which makes no difference, we have done nothing for either humankind or ourselves. Acting selfish or self-centered, for example, makes no impact in life because these actions make no difference; in fact, they actually close us off from our true delight of life, a level of divine self where ego cannot reside." I remembered my own level of selfishness, self-centeredness, and confrontational nature before I traveled to India. Since my landing in Delhi, my teachers certainly opened my eyes and heart to my true nature! From conditioning, Western culture focuses more on the external concepts and ideas of life rather than the higher internal aspects of truly giving and making a difference. There is, of course, a wonderful and powerful exception. After a catastrophe or disaster, all personal and external concerns are stripped away as individuals from every socioeconomic level, station in life, or country of origin come together and unite. During this time, they all swiftly gather to form a human chain, truly linking up with helping hands and donations of every sort. For the most part, however, this chain erodes over a short period of time as each link rusts to oblivion while people return to their normal everyday routines. Must this be so? Yes, because deep down they are closed off to life! Sadly, this is true for the vast majority of humankind. Although we have the ability and are meant to become truly magnificent in all respects, it appears we prefer to restrain our self from this in all moments.

"Master," I asked, "is the twelfth Principle telling us that we must act in service to all people all the time?" Master Lobsang now responded, "That is one aspect. The complete idea behind this principle is about living life fully each and every moment. The "value" part has its basis in how much positive energy we actually put into all what we say and do. The "upliftment" part comes into our life through Karmic return and is equally proportional to the level of energy we had placed in those activities. If you choose to understand and accept it, Steven, the Law of Value and Upliftment will truly raise your awareness to the level where you can see that, as an individual, you actually do make a difference in everything you say, do, and offer to life."

When silence fell between us, I took this as my cue to move back in line with my fellow monks and to reflect on what my teachers shared with me. As you and I both know by now, many levels, sides and angles can appear in each lesson given by my teachers and other monks, not to mention the daily lessons I received merely by observing their actions. These gentle souls are truly wonderful examples of these principles, living in such humility, giving without fail or hesitation, without ever asking for a return. They remain fully engaged in life – each and every moment – wherever they may find themselves, no matter what they do at any given moment. Watching my teachers constantly lift others around them totally amazed my Western mind. Such high energy constantly remained within and all around them! And they expended such little effort! Not until now did I understand the reason. In my thirst to understand this principle in the fullest possible extent, I asked myself, "Am I truly open to giving to all people?", "What is the very best way to do this?", "Do I totally give myself up for others?", "I think I will ask my teachers for their input." So I returned to the front of the line, fell in step, and asked them these very questions without knowing what I had just walked into.

Master Lobsang replied first, "Steven, though most humans remain closed to it, life is actually all about being open, open to receive its true gifts. After all, if you are closed then how may you receive anything? It closes you off from receiving in most respects. When you arrived here you were very much closed; yet today, you are not. What created this change within you?" I answered, "I trust you, Rinpoche Kiela, and the other monks." His mouth curved upward ever so slightly before he offered, "Young man, if we are open only to those we trust, this implies we mistrust the rest of the world; therefore, we just stepped back into our small self as we remain closed, once more allowing judgment to overtake us. Being open to all of life will deepen your experience." After a pause he asked, "Are humans able to trust all things or some things?" I pondered this for few moments.

Indeed, if most of us do have very little trust, does this not imply that we literally pick the who's and what's to trust, even establishing the specific condition through which we will do it? Is this not now living in judgment? A-ha, I just realized something! Judgment, yet once again, can actually block us from being fully open and is the precise reason why we do not trust all things in our world. By living in

this manner, I reasoned that the Law of Value and Upliftment would be greatly diminished, for neither aspect could occur under judgment because they both require complete openness. I chuckled aloud and Master Lobsang glanced at me with a silent nod, acknowledging my new understanding. Allow me to offer food for thought here. How can a person receive if they are closed? They cannot, pure and simple. In this reality, they must take. But I ask, is taking not akin to stealing, like when taking something or someone who does not Karmically belong to you? And what is the Karmic return in this action? "Is this the underlying reason why people steal?" I found myself asking aloud. Both teachers responded in unison, "Yes!"

Rinpoche Kiela spoke this time, "Young man, we have shown you the value of this Law when it comes to the external world; yet, as with every principle, this Law also applies to our internal world as do all things in the end. Lobsang just spoke with you on the subject of being closed. Being closed to the outer world means we are first closed off internally." After a brief pause he continued, "We spoke with you about living in joy from the last principle. To accomplish this, to receive and live in the fullest extent, one may not be closed off from any part of life, both external and internal. This means we must first be open to life from the fullest part of our self. To have internal upliftment, one simply lives in joy and happiness at all times in every way. Steven, you recall the Great Law: *What you sow, so shall you reap*. This remains most significant and even applies directly to this, the last of the twelve Principles. If you plant the internal seeds of lifting yourself, then they grow automatically and extend into your outer world." A pause invited his question, "Are you happy being you?" I replied before breathing, "Yes, more than I ever have been! I feel very satisfied with me, especially after all what has been shown to me about my self and life. In fact, life is the only thing for us to realize." Both of my teachers smiled as we continued to walk on our journey.

It feels nice being in my body since I now realize and accept my past and where it has led me. Also, it feels good to know that my body never was, is, or ever will be broken! You see, I feel most humans truly believe they are broken in some form or fashion because of their seeming broken pasts, but this is a complete falsehood, an illusion

based entirely on one's perception of life all because of conditioning and being taught that they are stuck or in some way deserve their personal lot in life. Going out on another limb, I ask the following. If the Creator, your God, is truly a divinely infinite, an unconditionally loving and perfect force or Universal idea from every viewpoint, I put to you, how can such a loving, infinite, perfect concept create a so-called unloving, imperfect, broken human? How can It create anything other than what It is? How can It create something so totally opposite from Its own inherent nature – perfection – both in our world and the Universe? Loving, infinite, Perfection can only create in Its own image and likeness, an unconditional divine being. So how did we "fall?" Allow me to step way out there by asking, "Have we really ever "fallen," or does our conditioned perception judge it as the "fall?" If it is all God Stuff, then which aspect of the Universe or the world or our life or our self is other than? Do we believe we literally, physically exist outside of God? If so then this would represent the idea of the "fall." According to my teachers in the Far East, perhaps life exists solely for us to experience and grow, to evolve into remembering our true perception by seeing our true nature through the Principles and Mirrors of Karma. Perhaps it all comes down to how we personally choose to perceive life, the divine path within our Creator's reality of pure and total Perfection. This is just something for you to think about and consider as the truth of your reality.

Once more I was pulled from my lofty thoughts when Master Lobsang offered, "The value part of this principle comes from the level of energy – the quality of living – that we put into ourselves and life. Your Christ said to give all what we have, and we yet do not live in this manner. We still hold our self back from life and living. As you know, Karma will give back to us precisely what we put in – no more, no less; therefore, if you place very little in life, very little will come to you. Remember the second principle: *You attract to you what you are, not what you want*. This is all what Karma may give to you – all what you are, not what you want. If a person believes they deserve to hold very little self-value or importance, then no internal lifting or upliftment may take place. The true value of our life is based on the quality of energy we produce and put forth in all we say and do. If you choose to give this level of energy to another human in order to

lift them in their circumstance, you cannot lose it or be drained of it because more of the same is given to you through Karmic return. Do you understand this?" My response was yes while realizing another aspect of my past, for I was used to holding myself back and away from life.

My teacher continued, "Energy comes from many directions, Steven. It may come from your thoughts. It may come from your emotions. It may also come from your actions toward yourself, others, and life. Remember, a simple kind word may lift another human in their moment of distress. Holding the door for another or carrying their package may also lift them in that moment. Just your very presence with another in their difficult moment may uplift them, even without a word spoken or any action taken by you. The highest value, the highest energy you put into an action, comes to you only when you choose to perform the action freely and unconditionally, for this is an action based on true kindness and compassion, an action that shall make a difference. And you will have absolutely no desire for a physical, emotional, or monetary acknowledgment. The value of this activity creates its own upliftment for you."

Master Lobsang kept going with his instructions, "To make a difference in life, give to life all that you have; do so free of effort just as the Master Christ suggested to all of you in your so-called Bible. He said to give all you have, which applies to everything you may say and do. Even if a difficult moment occurs, by giving all you have, this Law will always lift you, for the quality of energy you had put forth will overcome the apparent struggle from others and by so doing you will also be lifted. If you give all your energy only to your self then this is nothing more than wasted energy because it is centered solely on you. This now creates the idea of self-centeredness which is far away from the intention of the twelfth principle. It is more about being self-less in what you do so that it, indeed, lifts others around you. It is the energy of peace and joy that you share while others are in your presence. In your journey, Steven, always attempt to help others feel better after you leave their space than before you entered it. This is the truth of your experiences with us here in India. This is what you have attained for your self while working with us. When

you look around at all the other monks this is what they do for and with each other every day."

He was not through with me just yet, for more wisdom was forthcoming. He knew and I then realized the degree to which my ears were pressed against his every word as I continued to listen intently, "Young man, whatever you contribute will uplift or decrease the whole of humankind. Every seed the human plants has its impact on the collective, known as mass consciousness, or in your part of the world referred to as super mind. Every human contributes to it, whether knowingly or unknowingly, and whatever we first place in it, our Karma returns to us its like kind. It was written long ago that a single human can lift or decrease the whole of consciousness. Consider our Lord Buddha. Consider also the Master, Jesus the Christ. Even Lao Tzu and many others lifted whomever they touched, each attempting to bring higher understanding to the whole of human consciousness. Make this your purest of intentions in all what you put forth."

"Then, of course, there are those in history who brought decrease to the whole through their oppression of humankind. [If I may add: not as a means to strike fear and resurrect the judgment termed "evil," but rather to serve as humankind's wakeup call, to act as its Karmic mirror by agitating and revealing to humankind its build-up of brown sludgy silt now bubbling from the bottom of global consciousness, ready to surface purely for its total release and complete healing through proper understanding and compassionate action.] Every human shares in this because every human is connected through consciousness by their very inherent nature. What we physically see in life is just the tip of the iceberg, for life runs much deeper as you may now realize. When placing the value of you in what you do, greater dynamics become created and extend outward to all of humanity, not only uplifting you, but also uplifting the whole as its consequence. Always be aware of what you place here, Steven. If possible, always place in your thought and deed only the higher good for humankind."

To think that each of us has this level of natural ability and responsibility is absolutely astounding to me! I remain baffled to witness that we still do not fully realize the depth of or the manner in

which we impact each other in all what we think, say, and do during each and every day, during each and every event. I am not at all surprised, nor do I wonder why there is so much turmoil in our world today. This is a perfect moment for you to again ask aloud, "What am I creating or placing in my crystal clear pool of consciousness?" Negative, reactionary, judgmental thoughts create the brown silt in our global consciousness, while our responses to life experience have churned that silt, now bubbling and rising to an already tumultuous surface, next spilling over its shoreline into our physical world. "Could this be a reason for the weather anomalies?" I just had to ask my teachers about this sudden impression of mine.

Master Lobsang responded first, "Young man, do you recall the story of the caterpillar?" I nodded. "Let us expand how seeming insignificant things connect, one to the other. In answer to your question, look into each principle of Karma which you have been taught since your arrival here. Do they each contain their own seed of return action?" I nodded. "Now, consider life and how, for the most part, the human does not give much credence to a simple, seeming insignificant thought. Remember, even these so-called trivial thoughts contain their own seed of creation and most certainly enter consciousness. Now, think of the idea of how all things are connected, including the caterpillar. If all of this is so, then would it not simply stand to reason that humans are also connected to the weather just as they are to all things? These things are merely created by and for the human in order to gain the higher realities of life, to learn the higher path. If we live in turmoil then would not the weather also reflect such turbulence back to us? How can we seek or expect something from a thing other than what we had originally placed in it? We simply cannot, for it is what we individually create. Knowingly or not is not the issue. Being present is the hardest of all lessons available to us because the path in this is realizing what we are creating in each moment which is why we use the "waking" stick in our teachings, to maintain presence, present with mind and thoughts."

He continued, "From our connection to all things, if we are capable of uplifting others when we only give from our unconditional peaceful nature, then do we not also uplift our surroundings in the same

fashion, including the weather? This is why all monks live in peace, Steven. Even during a severe storm, have you noticed how it seems so peaceful around the monastery?" The question joggled my memory and I reflected back, remembering the monsoon showers & winter storms in the Himalayas. My teacher was quite accurate, as my mind saw how each storm seemed to move right over the monastery, as if the building and immediate grounds were exempt from the torrential rains and thunderclaps. Even during the middle of winter in Nepal while at Gyuto Monastery, I witnessed only light snowfall; yet, a full-blown blizzard had encapsulated the landscape with ferocious winds just a few miles away. I chuckled aloud involuntarily as this memory returned. Only a handful of people back in the States would realize and understand this very real relationship, for the truth is, every human has always been and always will be connected to each other, to all things, and with any environment through the phenomenal reach of Karmic Law. This can be a truly mind-bending experience once it is realized and accepted! We do carry an impact on all things surrounding us in our world – including each other. This is the crux of what my teachers desired me to realize.

Master Kiela followed up with his wonderful counsel, "Young man, if every human throughout the world were to live in full individual peace with each other, the whole human race would witness its absolute level and depth of power in all what it does. Our minds and emotions are truly far-reaching; yet, we must keep our thoughts and our feelings on the idea of this last Principle. We must keep them focused on uplifting each other – even the weather – by remembering the second Principle: *You attract to you what you are, not what you want.* All things indeed overlap each other as does each Principle of Karma. If the majority of humankind is in upheaval then it would stand to reason that all things outside of us would represent what is going on inside of us. This would include the weather and geology." I was stunned at the full implications of this. Perhaps all what Rinpoche Kiela told me that day sounds too far-fetched for you – indeed for the Western mind. From personal experience and observation, however, his words ring very true for me. More inner turmoil occurs throughout the world in our current time than when I was a young child. The weather patterns today have become totally unpredictable

and ferocious. Our world is heating up. Geology is unsettling. Karma's alarm clock is clearly ringing for every human to wake-up, but the vast majority of us hit the snooze button, not yet willing to sit up and listen. Karmic return makes the external message self-evident, for its reflection constantly attempts to show us to our self. We simply have not put the pieces all together just yet. Both my teachers shared with me, "There will come a point when we will accomplish even this…" seeing our mirror and putting the puzzle together.

"Steven, I give you the key idea of life," my teacher offered. "All things outside of us – the external material world – merely represent what is predominantly going on inside the mind of humankind, a mind based on the collection of what each human puts forth. Then the mind reaps it. This means, with respect to the majority of humans, living with internal struggle may very well externalize as a struggling or turbulent weather pattern. Take a moment and look into specific areas of the world, regions where many individuals appear in struggle. Does the weather not reflect the same? There is only one way for certain this could be proved. Have humankind focus only on peace rather than hate, fear, frustration or personal struggle. If this is correct, what should reflect back to us in the form of weather, including geology? Yes, peace and calm."

Rinpoche Kiela does speak straightforward and his words may be a challenge to accept; however, has any one individual, family, community, or country ever taken the time and made the effort to perform this exercise? I sense it may very well be worth it! Master Kiela continued, "Karma is very far-reaching and it has been stated in many ways: Nothing is above the Law. Let us return to this principle and keep it in the realm of the individual because, after all, individuals make up the majority." After a slight pause he continued, "Young man, simply be who you are. Allow your example to shine for others. This method will uplift them and human consciousness to a higher state, and will override all else no matter what it may appear to be in the moment."

I noticed I had lowered and was slowly shaking my head as I absorbed all what my two teachers had just shared with me. I felt

overwhelmed! Interesting, this was the first time I felt like running away from such a high level of self-responsibility. But where do I hide from the Laws? I knew I could not because, after all: Wherever you go there you are. To realize we have such a profound effect, to realize the vast majority of humankind does not yet know or has never considered this connection, even as a remote possibility, is remarkable! What if this is correct? I mean, after all, we definitely affect each other directly, to that end there is no question. But the weather? Geology? I began to think of all the ways Karma could impact life, all of life. This was staggering in its scope and depth; in fact, it was infinite in its impact according to my teachers!

As our party of monks approached the crest of a hill I could see our destination in the far distance – Dharmsala! I distinctly felt my heart pound more strongly at the wonder of it all, such magnificent minds, easily and effortlessly lifting people. I continued to reflect on this principle until I heard a soft voice pulling me from my thought-filled mind. It was Master Lobsang this time, "Steven, if we all simply live and work in peace and joy, all of humanity will be lifted. This is the true purpose of the twelfth Principle, value and upliftment. It is not about the weather or anything else; it is simply about what you do to assist life. Maintain your focus right here and right now, no where else should it be. See each human and experience you encounter as the most important aspect of your life in that moment. Treat each of them as you would prefer to be treated and you will lift them because of your own personal dynamics. At all times be the divine nature that you are, nothing less, for this will lift others as you encounter them. The sage gives all they have and they are given yet more in return. Contribute the best in all moments and the best will come to you, through Karma of course."

He offered more advice, "Young man, if you are given information and you only understand it intellectually, it shall remain in your mind as such and be of little use to you. If, on the other hand, you experience that knowledge then you have great wisdom gifted you by its application in life, and it will change you and your experience. Intellect is simply a state of mind and thoughts, and truly contains nothing more than mental experience. To truly know these principles,

they must be lived and experienced by you until you become them, living them constantly. If this is not done, they will be of very little use to you in the long run. Do you understand this?" I could only answer, "Yes, Master."

My life transformed in a myriad of ways after my teachers introduced each Law to me. I knew my understanding was deepening and my awareness was growing, that a great depth was taking place within me because of these twelve simple Principles. Wouldn't it be nice if all people know them so they may transform their life as well? I also knew I had to bring them to this country, and at some point, share these Laws with my fellow Americans and everyone else so they, too, may choose to change their personal dynamics, to become a fully empowered and divine being throughout their life. My teachers and Karma revealed to me many lessons, one of which is this: in reality, the image we create of another is a simple projection of our self; subsequently, we only relate to this so-called self-projection with which we have cloaked the other person. We now can no longer relate to the truth of that individual; instead, we merely interpret their actions and words according to our own self-image, the self-projection placed upon them by us. We then enter the repetitious cycle of self-imposed judgment and all its limitations. And guess what? Karma will keep us in this never-ending loop until we decide to understand and see exactly what we are doing. Just how do we see? Become an objective observer through choice, discipline, and practice. Sooner, rather than later, you will easily see your self in each moment during each interaction.

Allow me to offer another perspective for you. Although your intention may be honorable, we suggest you not run out to help everyone around you just yet because this may be very draining to you. Perhaps you ought to first abide by the Great Law: *What you sow so shall you reap*. Yes, I repeat, Karma gives to us precisely what we give to life; therefore, it is always in our best interest to lift every individual along the way. How may you accomplish this? Go within your self first; go in your heart. Gently uproot and release the seeds of weeds that you had planted hours, days, weeks, even years earlier. And once you implement these tools, these Laws of life, your path will

automatically transform into one of peaceful ease as you live from your own internal level of unconditional love and compassion.

Living from unconditional nature, you cannot help but reach out to all humans, no matter their particular path or journey in life. You have a true and deep understanding of you, and are now able to focus on every fruitful seed you plant, to fully realize you now nurture them with wisdom, thus creating value and upliftment as you evolve into your true nature, your divine, powerful, creative being. Allow your true light to shine as though a city on a hill. Become an unconditional being filled with the urge to give all of you, your wisdom, your compassion, and your love to others throughout your magnificent world as a focused beacon of truth. You are now assisting in such ways that all people whom you encounter henceforth view their current path in a different light, possibly even changing their course towards higher understanding. Can it get better than this? Absolutely! Through Karmic return and your constant acceptance of divine nature, the cycle will empower your physical eyes to see only the truth: of your being, of your experience, of all others around you, and all of life. You are now no longer blind to the illusions while truth smiles back with deep blessings.

You can certainly ignore all of what has been shared about these simple ideas; however, your individual process of change may be challengingly slow and potentially arduous. Ultimately, though, you will change. From this no one may avoid! If, on the other hand, you genuinely accept and actively utilize these twelve Principles in each moment, your individual process shall surely shift at a pace dizzyingly faster than you could ever imagine. You see, we truly become fully empowered by having complete control over our mind which in turn will alter not only our life, but also every experience coming to us through Karmic return.

Once we begin to plant with perfect intention by utilizing these principles, then all what we do plant will surely come to full positive and divine fruition. We now operate with and toward divine fulfillment in all that we seek as all dreams become fully realized. Be constantly vigilant while keeping in mind we must bring these principles forth,

not purely from intellect but into our life as all things are given to us to have and to share. Would you like to have your circumstances altered for the better? Would you like to feel a deep, relaxing peace every moment, day and night? Would you like to attract your perfect mate? Allow me to clarify something here. You always have your perfect mate, Karmically speaking, because it is where you are right this very moment on your ladder of growth and understanding.

As you evolve with these principles, your circumstances and those around you may change naturally – automatically. When they do, simply release them without control. Would you accept greater abundance? A yes or no answer remains entirely up to you; therefore, choose genuinely with your heart and allow the guidance and wisdom of Karmic principles to work for you through every experience. I offer another clarification: Karma works for you no matter your answer; yet, being always conscious of it, you willhave – *again*, sooner rather than – all you may ever desire to have and live every dream of your intention. Regardless of what your circumstances may be mirroring for you, always feel yourself in abundance and learn from the experience so you may continually be fulfilled with the gifts of life. In truth, life is the gift for us to realize. It is simply missing the ribbon and the bow. Or is it?

We have begun and completed an amazing journey of higher being. My only sincere hope is that the messages contained within these pages have brought you the gift of being fully empowered within your own life. If not, then review them again to see what may have been overlooked or not fully internalized. My personal sense is, if we all fully understood the far-reaching ramifications of these ancient principles, then we would not have seen most of what we have already experienced in our life. Realize that a negative experience, in some fashion, is a misuse of these very same ideas, but once we use them in the appropriate manner, negativity is then removed from our life until such time we invite it back. Let us now move into the summation, a minor refresher course, if you will, to more fully understand all the principles. Use them with eternal wisdom and your life shall be filled with blessings.

"Free from desire, free from possessions,
free from attachment and appetite,
following the seven lights of awakening
and rejoicing greatly in his freedom in this world,
the wise person becomes themselves a light.
Pure, shining, free."
Buddha

~ Chapter XIV ~
Summation

Many, many years have passed since I first stepped off the plane in what is now New Delhi, India. Even to this day I vividly remember the majesty of the land and mind-boggling precepts of ancient wisdom. My firm American beliefs shattered like fine china falling onto a stone floor while I watched, listened to, and walked with my two Master teachers throughout northern India, Nepal, and Tibet. Without any hesitation or reservation, these incredibly giving souls shared with me such intricate knowledge of people, life, and energy dynamics of the Universe. Although this book is based solely on their teachings of Karma, they did not stop there. Oh-no! The monks also taught many different meditation techniques for my continual practice so I may live in the present moment, "…in a perpetual state of consciousness," my teachers termed it. Near the end of my sojourn, they fully integrated me as a monk and teacher to the neophytes – the new students – when they arrived at the front door to my northern India "home," Darjeeling monastery near Ladakh.

Literally hundreds of concepts and ideas were offered me, from the power of thought to meditation, from all of Buddha's sutras

to the twelve principles of Karma, in addition to retracing the path taken by Saint Issa, the one known as the Master Christ. So much to understand and remember! Perhaps so, but the truth is, these Universal Truths remain dormant in the mind of each and every human living today, no matter one's age, country of origin, chosen religion, gender, or even their tax bracket. This way of life was supremely more enjoyable to me than living either in the past or future; in fact, even today it feels like "no time," to offer a phrase for you. So, why in the world would I ever consider returning to my native country, my home in the Eastern Seaboard of the United States? I'll share my last heartfelt story with you now.

It was early fall and I had just finished my duties for the day. Before returning to the monastery, I decided to walk the short detour to my favorite meditation pond, to dive into its cool water for a relaxing swim, and to reflect on all the changes which had taken place within me and my subsequent outlook on all the events of my life. Entering the monastery late that afternoon, I felt the urge to grab a nice big pillow, then bound up the stairway leading to its rooftop, and enter my Akashic records for a short while before mealtime. This is a specific meditation technique used to help open our energy centers in order to view a past life or many of them. Yes, every human has them, tucked neatly away in what we term as our DNA, the Book of Life. Yes, these pages may be opened, read, and even experienced by anyone who seeks this level of knowledge about them self.

Buddha termed this exercise as "following the path of the seven lights." Do you suppose the seven lights correspond to our seven chakras? Continuing, I was pleased to find no one else on the roof, for it was always enjoyable to enter this meditation in seclusion and with a personal, expansive view of the Himalayan foothills. I settled on the pillow and became still before embarking on my inward journey. Certainly some time had passed, when suddenly, the projector of my mind exploded with flashes, as though warming up with a movie trailer, the light of my mind's eye flickering, awakening, and then illuminating lifetime after lifetime, so many cascading in my mind, one immediately after the other, each one depicted absolutely, perfectly and so clearly for me. Perhaps I had completely

transcended, for in this state of awareness, there was no sense of time or body. I did not know where I started or stopped as everything flowed together within me.

Returning to my physical self and slowly opening my eyes, I did not notice any discernable difference to either the temperature or ambient light. "Wow," I thought to myself, "this did not take very long at all!" You see, even though I entered my meditation during the setting sun, just before twilight actually, when my eyes adjusted to my surroundings after the exercise, it was apparently still twilight; in fact, I felt it was only a few moments later. I arose slowly, picked up the pillow, and gingerly walked across the roof, down the steps, back into the monastery. "Why is everyone looking and smiling at me?" I silently noticed as I placed the pillow on the floor before walking to the kitchen for my dinner meal. "What…?" my eyes widened when I finally recognized the food in everyone's bowl. "Breakfast?!… I meditated all night long?" I asked myself disbelievingly. Evidently so! Just then, Master Lobsang and Rinpoche Kiela both approached me, beaming with large smiles on their faces. They sat with me as we all ate together in silence, and I wondered, even my teachers were looking and smiling, beaming at me!

After we cleared our spaces, both teachers asked me to join them for a morning walk. And who decided to meet us outside the front gate? There sat my dear friend, Shanti Che! "Good to see you!" I expressed with my hard, vigorous hand-rubbing all over his lustrous coat. What a thunderous purr – still amazes me! As I looked over at my teachers, noticing how both were maintaining smiling faces, a thought just slipped into my consciousness, bringing to mind just how Master Lobsang and I had bonded into such a close relationship. I can effortlessly and openly admit he had become as a father to me. "And they are still smiling at me even while we walk in continued silence," I observed to myself, "and for some reason, everything looks so brighter and I feel so much lighter." While still smiling, Master Kiela broke the silence first, "Young man, tell me about your experiences last evening." I calmly gave a full report, "I went up on the roof to do my Akashic record meditation," and continued relating to both teachers my experience. He confirmed the depth of

my introspection by stating, "You had, indeed, been in meditation for nearly twelve hours." Then Master Lobsang chimed in with a twinkle in his eyes, "And, it is time for you to return home and share with your people what you have learned."

Life stopped in that moment. I was overwhelmingly stunned! Emotion waved over me, and with quivering lips I questioned and objected simultaneously, "No! Why?! This is my home! I never thought about returning!" My surroundings and the gentle faces of my teachers blurred as tears welled up over my eyes, "Why?!" I exploded, their smiles maintaining a constant vigil through all my stuttering and outcries. We stopped walking as Master Lobsang placed his warm, reassuring hand on my shoulder and softly stated, "The prophecy has been fulfilled, Steven. The Book of Knowledge is now known and shall pass from the East to the West. Young man, you have been gifted with a monks' greatest experience, and last night you unified with you and all of your vast experiences through many lifetimes, known as samadhi. This is something many monks aspire for but may never know, so it is indeed special. In fact, Buddha experienced samadhi while he sat under the banyan tree so many hundreds of years ago." Samadhi, I then realized, brings to our mind's eye not only all what we have done and where we have been in past lifetimes, but also reveals our so-called Karmic debt or circumstance for each lifetime, and how the debt of one lifetime interlaces with the debt of other lifetimes.

While viewing them, I observed how one debt led to the next and how my Karma was met and resolved, whether in one lifespan or another. I even realized there were times when I used several lives to work through just one issue because I had remained so stubbornly resistant to the solution, believing it as either too hard or extremely difficult in those previous times. So, allow me to offer a pivotal point here. Always take care of the issue the moment it enters your experience, and make every attempt to prevent it from festering, growing, or even carrying over to your next life. All Karmic debt can be resolved in a single lifetime provided you realize its presence. Do you have an addictive personality? Are you withdrawn? Are you selfish? These are keys to your Karmic debt. If you work to know

them, the rest would easily be shown to you, whether it takes seven lifetimes or a fraction of just one. You will know them – ultimately – just as I did that whole night on the monastery roof.

My teachers surely saw the degree of my shock and emotion in response to their pronouncement, and although I knew deep down in my heart they were perfectly correct, so many thoughts and feelings still swirled in my mind. Master Lobsang broke into my thoughts once more, "Steven, you have been here many years now and have made great strides in your lessons and with you. It is simply time for you to share with the Western minds what you have learned from us, to awaken your people to these ideas. It is time they awaken as you have. When you return to your homeland, we know this knowledge will lay dormant within you, but after about fourteen years it will all come flooding back, and when it does, you will begin to speak and even write seven books about all what you have learned, bringing Consciousness to many people." My head and eyes simultaneously rolled in total bewilderment in response as I testified to my mind, "I am not a speaker or writer! I never studied or envisioned these, and I have no desire for them!" Evidently, my testimony does not accurately represent what I now do today, does it? While watching my eyes roll, my closest teacher thoughtfully smiled and declared, "There you go, young man, resisting again." And he seemed to know my precise thoughts as he continued, "It is because you must learn to live this knowledge in your part of the world, away from the monastery. This will not come easy, for there will be many pulls from the material world." Oh-my, was he dead-on accurate! How little did I then realize the sheer magnitude and degree of all the external pulls of life I would need to confront, just so that my personal journey could evolve into one of truth and personal responsibility in all moments, no matter where I found myself!

Many more weeks had passed. Then one morning Master Lobsang approached me, "It is time to make the journey to Delhi for your trip home." The next day was a total blur. Not because of memory loss or time warp, mind you, but because of the tears that had welled up in my eyes once again as I approached the outer door of the monastery. You see, I followed a long train of fellow travelers, each shuffling through

a sea of monks who had come to see me off, every one my "brother," each bowing deeply as I passed by. While approaching the airport in Delhi several weeks later, Master Lobsang softly stated, "We shall depart now to return to the monastery." I faced my dearest friend, gave him my best bear hug then bowed deeply and thanked both him and my fellow monks for sharing all what they had. My heart sank as I watched them turn around, simply and quietly, without any gesture or turn of head. My feelings were not hurt, I would like to say, because this was their custom, to constantly and continually live in the present moment. Of course, this meant that I, too, must do the same when I turned to walk towards the ticket counter. When announced, I silently boarded the plane, and flew straight into the longest, most challenging journey of my life.

Taking in a sweeping retrospection, from the abusive beginnings of my childhood to my military deployment into Vietnam, from my incredible sojourn in the Far East – to this very moment in time, I fully realize my journey was set in motion at the very moment of my birth. This is absolutely remarkable! Who would have figured out that, from my early experiences with my father, I would come to honor and thank him for all what he had given me? Who would have known that I would meet my first teacher, a Zen Master living close to a war-torn village who would guide me to follow my intuitive senses? Who had pre-planned and planted the urge for me to fly to India of all places, so I could meet my Master teachers and walk the path of the Master Christ, all the while teaching me to interact with consciousness, to utilize meditation, and to fully understand Karma? Admit it now, if not Karma, did you arrange all this for me? Individual life is such a truly wondrous gift, such a perfect tool to use as our body of perfection moves forward and evolves throughout its journey!

It is now known for certain within my mind and heart that we live in Consciousness, the first key of life which we must come to realize and appreciate. And imagine – this is a world on which we all meet to understand it! In proportion to the human population, merely a handful realizes this concept, while by far the majority remains simply impervious to it. In truth, however, no human is excluded from the

so-called global pool of Consciousness because even the naïve and ignorant interact with it. Just as each drop of water interconnects to make up the oceans of the world, so too does each human mind interconnect to make up mass Consciousness. Hundreds of authors have written and spoken about this very subject to the Western mind; however, it still appears such crucial information falls on the deaf ear of the collective, for the majority has yet to accept and come to this level of understanding. I ask again, what generally occurs when you think about a particular family member or friend whom you have not seen in a long while? Do you not seem to run into or hear from them? Is this truly just pure coincidence or simple chance? I explain yet again, they heard your call in their mind through the free broadcast frequency of consciousness. And they answered. This follows the basic precept of Karma: like attracts like. This occurs at every level, from individual thought streams to entire countries because each of us emanates and projects who we are into the world, 24/7, and cannot be erased or avoided.

There are so many nuggets of wisdom my teachers shared with me, and it is my genuine desire to share them with those who choose empowerment and self-enlightenment, including those who are willing to at least listen. Karma is a significant lesson, a perfect guide to help us know our higher purpose in this world through developing a focused mind aimed directly at higher knowledge. It is also my desire for you to become actively aware of Consciousness because this is precisely the level from which Karma interacts with each and every one of us. Watching how monks co-operate with others and from my teachings, I now remember how quickly I came to realize that the ill-advised use of the blame game only creates a stubborn frame of mind which, in most cases, totally refuses any responsibility for one's life. This unconditionally contradicts self-empowerment, the awareness created by a divine frame of mind which, in all cases, totally accepts full responsibility for one's life. If it may be suggested, please read the previous two sentences as many times as you choose as they are important. If you are ever going to attain any modicum of empowerment, the blame game must rest, forever-locked in a dusty attic trunk. However, if you choose to unlock it, either knowingly or unknowingly, you have accepted the contract relinquishing all

your control to others and all outward circumstances. But wait, the contract can be cancelled at any time! Were we not told in the Bible that we have dominion – sovereign authority – over all things? This is all about our self and where our path must begin. The key is personal responsibility in your life, not the life of any other, for their life is for them to determine.

No one particular Law is any more important or significant than any other; however, if we trivialize or take any principle for granted that very one principle may just become the last stone left unturned on our path. If this occurs then you may potentially find your self tripping over it in the short run or creating a genuine difficulty in the long run. Remember, stones can pop up anywhere at any moment on our pathway simply because we stop paying attention to the subtleties always in front of us. Have you ever turned to your friend while walking, only to trip or stub your toe? Be aware! These principles will lead us to our higher purpose and divine greatness if we simply allow them to operate with the power of our knowing and proper us of them. Remember, you may use them or not, but they do not go away, for they are the power of life, the eternal equalizer in all things.

The twelve principles of Karma are universal, natural, simple, and compact. These Laws remain ever-present, entirely equitable, totally moral, and immutable. On the other hand, observe human laws. Generally speaking, they are lobbied and sponsored, then subcomittied and heavily revised – even favored – prior to a legislative vote conditioned on a majority rule. The resulting bill usually develops into a totally vague, insatiably verbose, inefficient, inequitable and costly law. One last question: based on the above, is the Internal Revenue Code a Universal or human law? You see, Karmic principles are strictly about our self, equally applicable to each of us as a unique individual, yet affecting all of humankind. Human laws attempt to control by herding every citizen in a box allowing specific behavior. Do human laws really work on the human? Look around you. Come to think of it, is the behavior of human governments really working? Look at world events. You see, Karmic Law simply guides each of us to see our self for who we truly are, which is ultimately and totally

unavoidable because no box exists in this context. Paying no mind or attention to our experiences simply increases the pressure of our Karmic return, much like stretching a rubber band. Trust me, there will come that ultimate moment in a life when you will clearly see no other choice but to snap back to attention, at which time you will truly open your mind to receive a deeper, greater understanding of your self and then infinite life.

It would be in our best interest to remain mindful of the truth that there exists no separation between anyone and anything, and it follows that no separation also exists between these twelve magnificent principles of life. Indeed, they are designed to constantly and continually point us toward Universal Truth; however, it all comes down to whether we actively choose to interact with them during every circumstance, consciously and knowingly. Sure I got poked and prodded from challenging circumstances, but as long as I objectively paid attention to the results of my actions, these principles kept me on the straight and narrow, each harmoniously working in concert. Forgive me for asking a personal question, but are you human? If so, you can, in fact, become an impersonal observer as you work with and learn every aspect of Karma. Life will unfold from this interaction as you gain complete control of it merely by using your direct influence on it. Doing so, you will attain complete fulfillment in each activity of choice. Up until this moment, I have introduced, picked apart, fully described, and lifted nearly every stone behind each principle. Yet, before my time with you comes to a close, I desire to place each principle in its natural sequence so you may realize the depth and degree to which they entwine. The fact is, they work in union by all what we do each moment in life, seamlessly moving into the next without any time or physical constraint whatsoever.

What you keep in mind, the seeds of thought you constantly sow, will grow and externalize precisely into what you shall reap, and their fruits are called life experience. This activates the first and Great Principle of Karma: *What you sow, so shall you reap*. These seeds sprout from every act, action, thought, emotion, and feeling you continually emit each and every moment. It can accurately be stated that they are all vibrant seeds in your garden of mind, ready and able

to sprout their like energy. They will sprout to become an obstructing water-sucking weed filled with hate, fear, anger, or a magnificent tree with hundreds of branches providing life-giving fruit of Divine understanding, each filled with joy, happiness, affluence, and love to name just a few. You have freedom of choice here; it is entirely up to you as to what you plant and what you shall also receive.

Do not feel overwhelmed or withdraw in despair because of current circumstances, for if you genuinely desire to plant the seeds of higher knowledge, you may do so in an easy and efficient way. Simply remain inflexibly focused on the fruitful seeds rather than the weeds, thereby potentially making your life a bit easier. No matter your current situation, no matter what you see, make every attempt to completely fill your every act, action, thought, emotion, and feeling with seeds of delightful joy, playful happiness, limitless affluence, and most of all, unconditional love. Having been there myself, your first step may not come with ease or grace. You may also feel utterly awkward or foolish, and entirely too aware of how others may think of you. Pay no mind to others; mind only your own business. In all you say and do, create in those moments all that you are able to send forth in front of you in the name of these more potent seeds. Sooner, rather than later, you shall witness the scope of their return activity unto you as these fruitful seeds sprout new experiences right in front of your eyes.

As you focus on planting only these new types of seeds in the garden of your mind, do they not automatically choke out the old weeds? The weeds subsequently wither away into oblivion, allowing space for yet more fruitful seeds. This new cycle now activates the second Principle of Karma: *You attract to you what you are, not what you want*, for you have suddenly created a new you with a mental routine focused only on joy, happiness, affluence, and love. Your mind, as the magnificent electro-magnetic field generator, now energizes the second Law, attracting to you these precise same attributes through people, places, and things, a life no different than what you yourself are right now because life is your exact mirror image by Karmic Law. And who knows? You may wake up one morning to find your life appearing totally opposite to what it was just days, weeks, or

years ago because your relationships, work expression, and personal well-being now matches what you are this moment. As improbable as it sounds, this actually now eliminates any semblance of struggle. The reason is simple. Even though you are still using what you have always had – a magnificent mind – the difference is now twofold: 1) you now know why, and 2) you now create with purpose.

What occurred for me may very well occur for you, too. As these first two principles soak into your very being, you may come to realize just how inspiring you are as a human and the true creative power all humans wield in life. Your eyes open, perhaps seeing for the very first time how awful – full of awe! – and humbling your experience has become, the perfect viewpoint to awaken the third Principle of Karma: *What you resist persists for you.* As you progress through each principle, higher energy naturally enters your mind in direct proportion to your acceptance of the higher knowledge offered by Karma. And, as the higher comes in, it is suggested that you release the lower without hesitation. Why? Karma is severing the chains to your anchored memories with its blade of truth, allowing the bubble of emotion from each memory to slowly and steadily rise to the surface of your awareness. Karma has just provided you with the perfect opportunity to do one of three things about each surfacing emotion: 1) Scream and run away from it, 2) resist and push the bubble of emotion back down which merely amplifies the emotion by reinforcing its anchor and memory, or 3) step back and observe; allow the bubble to burst while viewing and learning from the emotion through your objective mind. If I may offer, choosing the third option may guarantee you a very humbling and enlightening experience indeed!

Karma can release a bubble at any moment wherever you may be. Ever experienced an emotional outburst or two during your lifetime for no apparent rhyme or reason? Both my hands are raised! Such an incident effortlessly energizes the fourth principle of Karma, the Law of Growth: *Wherever you go there you are.* Yes, you can certainly run, but you cannot hide! Therefore, it is recommended that you accept this opportunity to constructively handle that emotion right where you are. Though you must ultimately face it, be reassured,

there is truly no thing and no one to fear! You see, based on your higher awareness from the first three principles and holding firm on who you have become, your understanding will grow, knowing fully in your heart there no longer exists any one thing, person, place, or even emotion you need to avoid about you. Realizing the memory's true purpose and then releasing its bond, you break free from the tethered emotion forevermore. This will now result in yet a higher sense of being because it is such a joy to more fully understand you, to be who you are, and to have the life that you do. Talk about positive feedback! In truth, you have no reason to avoid anything at all, for now you have the eyes to see only perfection all around you. What is so wonderful is that this becomes completely automatic! Does this not sound pleasurable to you? Would this not fill your life with more joy and blessings?

As the human, what is the biggest thing going on with us right now? I humbly repeat, it is how we feel about our self amid our every experience with each other and life, each and every day. And it can accumulate. Even the tiniest, subtle event is captured by the big mirror of life, only to return precisely how we feel about our self in that moment. Yes, the fifth Law of Karma now arises – the Principle of the Mirrors – and perfectly aligns to constantly reflect our understanding of not only what we judge, but also how we live within that judgment, so patiently guiding us to realize how we feel inside and tirelessly attempting to break our mental routine of mindless focus on every physical event out there. From the previous four principles, has not your mind and heart been filling with higher thoughts of joy, happiness, affluence, and unbounded love? What do you suppose life and experience would now reflect back to you? I am happy to report that each mirror has automatically realigned towards higher purpose, now only revealing the fullness and completeness within you…back to you! No longer must you rely and focus on the external physical world to create personal joy because you now understand you. The fruitful seeds of higher vibration have sprouted and are fully blooming within; therefore, all what you look upon can only reveal the beauty of your self and life, clearly demonstrating just how perfect reality truly is. It certainly appears that a whole new world has opened up for you to enjoy!

Perhaps you have the urge to jump up and dance or shout with joy right this very moment. By all means, go ahead, and allow the sixth Law of Karma, the Principle of Synchronicity, inspire you through each step! You have just entered that wonder-filled world of innocence which defies all your adult logic. You now appear in plain sight, aligning with and creating perfect symmetry between your physical form and divine nature by expressing perfect synchronicity within your self, with all others, and with all life. The truth is, you have humbled yourself as a small child, and allowed absolute pure innocence to return to your nature, the nature which finds only equality in every aspect of life, a life flowing freely and effortlessly as it has always been intended. At first, the lower weeds of forgetfulness, self-doubt and judgment may attempt to take root; however, turn away to focus on and continue to water only those higher seeds of joy, happiness, affluence, and love. Simply enjoy their flow in life as they flourish and surround you each moment. And the answer is? There is no answer, only your every activity playing out in perfect harmony. How could they not? What a brilliant, awe-inspiring gift to yourself!

As I have shared previously, in a world broiling in seeming discord, absolute harmony and a sense of completeness can completely take hold as you continue to plant and nurture the higher seeds in your personal garden, the result of which will totally free you from all inner division, a mental state from which you will constantly operate, single in focus and purpose. Now think for a moment. Without any division, how many paths will you attempt to walk on at the same time, let alone be interested in? Better yet, how many paths will you even see? Through the workings of the seventh Law, the Principle of Direction and Motives, a wonderful delight awaits as you walk the spiritual path, the only direction and motive by which to live, once and for all lifting the lifelong weight and illusion of dual nature. And without dual nature, you realize everyone lives and resides in sacred space each moment! Listening to spirit first, you will glide through each activity and circumstance, for spirit can alert you to something in error just as easily and quickly as to something in truth. And what does Karma do for you? It purely and solely returns to you more of what you ask for, all in accordance to your direction of focus and

motive. Does this path appeal to you more deeply than the one now tread upon by the vast majority?

The path to self-empowerment will awaken your true nature as you become willing to find out how things fit you, and at some point, demonstrate what you believe to be true. As mentioned earlier, in truth, you may only fit you once you discover who that is, and your higher personality will then be able to demonstrate this in your life. Having chosen to accept and utilize the guiding, ever-present principles of Karma, you realize that your own thoughts are the ones most valuable to you, no one else's. Living in this fashion, you get to know you, and by looking at your environment right now, you realize how powerful and life-changing your higher thoughts, your pure fruit-giving seeds, have been to help transform your circumstances. This moves you seamlessly into the eighth Law, the Principle of Willingness because, without any hesitation, you not only share what you have learned in life, but you also show it willingly. Sure you stumble by operating in error for a moment or two; however, you remember that error is neither good nor bad, that it is merely the steering mechanism guiding you back onto your true path of self and life. What a relief to realize you need not remain stuck in a past moment with a past thought! The Principle of Willingness is about the demonstration of truth which becomes easier to do since you are now true only to you. What do you suppose Karma reflects back? Possibly even a deeper understanding of truth?

As you progress through each principle, you will sense their harmonious interaction with both you and with each other. Also, they become much easier to realize, hence reducing the return impact upon your experience as they continue to gently nudge you towards a greater understanding of you and reveal your divine characteristics within. Having filled your garden with the newfound seeds of joy, happiness, affluence, and love, the ninth Law of Karma, the Principle of Be Here and Now, naturally approaches and guides you to mind each moment, to consciously live fully present, and to delight in spontaneous activity, all the while cheering your return to innocence, the home of your true self. As discussed before, you actually come home to the ultimate discovery of your peace with self, life, and all

its guiding experience, a life effortlessly moving on its own accord in the direction of your desires because you now have a clear mind, a mind which has nothing to do with the past but has everything to do with the present. In fact, you begin to trust Karma, allowing it to shift you into what you want. Talk about personal empowerment! From this empowerment and pure presence now developed within, you no longer find a valid reason to live either in the past or in the future because your present moment would only be filled with seeds of higher energy. Just guess where you go from here!

The pieces of the puzzle not only come to you effortlessly, but they also fit together quite nicely, do they not? Allow me to repeat what Master Lobsang had shared with me, italics mine, "Young man, all things in life have their time, place, and purpose. Every single experience that you have had in your life has its divine and perfect function on the path of knowledge, and it has been laid out just for you." It is no accident, therefore, that you created a broad diversity of experiences unique only to you, some even cyclic, and by utilizing the first nine principles, you have become the observer of your life, able to stand in pure presence and free of judgment, a forgiver of your past. The cycles now remaining in front of you energize the tenth Law of Karma, the Principle of Change, a guiding foundation helping you to easily recognize those repeating circumstances so that, once realized, you may open up to and accept their teachings for the necessary internal changes. As the cycles dissipate, your journey in life proceeds in a straight line, narrow and strong, and you would experience positive growth as things change through time while you move only forward. As you may realize by now, change is unavoidable in life, but your complete acceptance of it and total flexibility spurs your growth into higher dynamics, the currents of songha. Do you feel great joy and a sense of awe for being alive, to realize the entire Universe is behind you? For you? On your side? Eternally? What's that? You're not certain? A-h-h, you have a weed struggling for survival in your garden, that's all. Through compassion you accept its root based on the human perception that the Universe is against you, that life is hard. Utilizing the ten Principles of Karma and gently forgiving your self, you effortlessly release the weed once and for all.

Repeating from an earlier chapter, as you focus on your life by paying attention to all things both internal and external, you shall accomplish three things: 1) you totally understand what you do in any given moment, 2) you fully realize you are more closely aligned to acting self-less in every chosen action, and 3) you continually create a positive Karmic flow with which to operate. It is really no surprise to see good things happen to you. Oh, what joy! Living in joy, in fact, is our true natural state! I repeat, joy creates humor and humor leads you to experience a more genuine lifestyle. Joy even helps make your decisions much easier, while at the same time, creates a much lighter life. Joy also creates a healthy body because you embody a healthier mind. Truth be told, you like you! At this point the eleventh Law gladly steps in, the Principle of Patience and Reward, for when you walk the path of self-acceptance by living in a joyful manner, patience also emerges as a natural state of your life. Do you suppose life becomes more rewarding for you in every way? Absolutely! Because now you thoroughly enjoy who you are, and all stress easily washes away as you move through any change or look into any mirror. Life itself is a precious gift, most definitely the best reward you can ever give your self. Life is rewarding, in truth, but only when you are patient with it. And from patience, you ultimately live your dreams. Life simply becomes the one and only reward there is to have!

It is my desire to impress upon and remind every reader that there are no accidents, failures, rights, or wrongs in truth. Your body, personalities, and experiences are exactly as they ought to be and expressed at the perfect time. In truth, you are here in this world to only love, be loved, learn and grow, and to evolve into remembering your true perception by seeing your true nature through the principles and mirrors of Karma. Perhaps it all comes down to one thing: how you personally choose to perceive life. By utilizing and living with the first eleven Laws, your life and every aspect of the material world have been lifted to their highest point simply because you chose to plant only internal concepts of value and upliftment, the fruitful seeds of joy, happiness, affluence, and love. You are a fully conscious and aware human, living and working purely in joyful peace and unconditional acceptance with divine energy shining brightly both day and night, lifting global consciousness and all of humanity. This is the true purpose behind the twelfth Law of Karma, the Principle of Value and Upliftment.

As stated earlier, the "value" part depends on the quality of energy you put into every activity based on the value of you, while the upliftment part comes from its Karmic return. Expressing from true nature, all you can do is lift others around you, the return of which subsequently moves you towards higher divine mind. You automatically and effortlessly lose your white-knuckle clutch with the lower realm of looking only to the external – your physical nature – as you naturally and seamlessly reach for your divine realm of looking only to the internal – your spiritual nature. I repeat, through Karmic return and your constant acceptance of divine nature, the cycle will empower your physical eyes to see only the truth, be it your experience, all those around you, all of life, and even your own being. You have evolved and expanded into full consciousness, humbly aware of your sovereign dominion over all things, and capable of utilizing your full creative power backed by divine intention. You have gained self-empowerment – your Christhood – and you do not stand alone in this realm for you now are one with it all!

It is totally up to you to explore your greater dynamics. The same holds true for every human. I offer again, if you are given information and you only understand it intellectually, it shall remain in your mind as such and will be of very little use to you in the long run. On the other hand, to truly know these principles, they must be applied, lived, and experienced constantly and continually, after which time their great wisdom has been gifted, thereby changing you and your experience permanently. If you simply move through the material world in grace and harmony, you unfold into divine perfection as it moves into your realization, but certainly the choice is always yours to make.

It has been my only desire, therefore, to assist in creating purpose in your life, to reveal a better choice. If you use these simple and dynamic principles then your life fills with purpose and intention as you achieve all your dreams and desires. If you prefer such a fulfilling

life, absolutely free from every drama and struggle, then use these wonderful tools, for your life will shift into a whole new paradigm all on its own! Remember, in reality, you attract to you what you are, and what you are is your full, personal responsibility in life.

Make your journey one of grace, humility, love, openness, and of service, so you may receive all the rewards of your birthright. May you joyfully go forth as your perfection continually unfolds into your divine and unconditionally-loving nature in this wonderful world of ours! If I may, I will walk with you. Let us journey well and in light!

A Metaphysical Interpretation of the Bible

$39.95
ISBN: 0-9720080-5-5
808 pages
6.14" x 9.21"
Hardcover w/ Dust Jacket

What if what we are being taught by religion is incorrect?

How did the Churches gain so much power over the individual?

Are you aware that over ten million people were tortured and killed over the Bible?

Did you know that the word Satan is an ancient word that stands for ego?

Is Revelation really about the end times?

Is the antichrist a human or is it a state of being?

This book contains the answer to these and much more...

Reviews

"I strongly recommend this book for anyone wishing to gain a greater knowledge of the bible. It is the best book I have ever read!" - Denise T. Ticer (Santa Fe, NM)

"Well written and well presented book. It is a light that I am using to illuminate my path to awakening. I strongly recommend this book; you'll actually experience the movements in consciousness rising. Beautiful book Steven. I look forward to the next one." - Conrad Jones (Manchester, Jamaica)

"I was somewhat hesitant when I ordered this book, thinking just another literal rendition of the KJB. WOW! This is not only a great book, but a wonderful reference. You see, I am a metaphysical bookstore and spiritual center owner, and pastor. This is exactly what I was looking for to give Sunday lectures. (Don't like the word sermon.) Now I can use this book as a starting point for lecturing on taking back your own power and knowing that you DO create the world in which you live. Now Amazon will be sending me two of his other books. I look forward to adding them to my metaphysical reference library." - S. Burnett (Zephyrhills, FL)

"I challenge you to read this book and not be inspired. I challenge you to grasp the metaphysical concepts conveyed in this book. I challenge you to compare it to all other books, religious or otherwise. I challenge you to live by these lessons, parable by parable, until each moment brings you into 'the gaps between our thoughts' ... where silence hides ... and every soul finds peace waiting at the gates of __________. I challenge you to read this book ... and ever be the same." - Chad Lilly (Yakima, WA)

Other Books From Steven L. Hairfield

$24.95

0-9720080-0-4

Once Upon A Parable

This text is filled with valuable, researched information, principles and tested techniques, all aimed at spiritual growth. It has been written in the style of a Zen Kuan - or one very large parable - and it is designed for spiritual teachings, comprehension and attainment. It attempts to portray the Bible as a tool for such growth, by lessening its religious impact and introducing a new perspective through a metaphysical interpretation. It is merely giving a different light on the subject of the Bible, because of the Master's wish for our spiritual growth.

$19.95

0-9720080-2-0

Return To Innocence

This book reflects the philosophies found in the messages and teachings of the ancient Masters. They were researched in the Bible, the Nag Hammadi, the Dead Sea Scrolls and Tao Te Ching, amongst other great works. All these texts seem to show us how we may have divided ourselves into a false sense of duality and a dual world with great limitations. The messengers of old taught us about the ramifications of choice and what they may generate for us. If they create inner and outer disagreement, they may also create inner peace.

$14.95

0-9720080-3-9

Interview With An American Monk

Dr. Steven Hairfield, a Monk and Zen Priest, opens up to Chad Lilly and Rick LaFerla to give us a rare glimpse at the inner workings of Eastern thought. Trained by Monks hundreds of years old, witnessed miraculous metaphysical phenomena, and performed a few himself, Dr. Hairfield speaks frankly about the abilities of Monks and his experiences. If you have ever thought things like walking on water were possible, or if you gave that idea up long ago as fantasy, you will want to read this book. Not only are these things real, they are obtainable...by you. Read this book. And may you never be the same again."

$12.95

0-9720080-4-7

Interview With An American Monk:
Health and Healing

This is the second book of a series of interviews with an American Monk, Dr. Steven Hairfeld. His understanding of life, of energy and of the universe is unparalleled by most western minds. He has an extensive background in nontraditional education by our American standards. Each time that we have had a conversation with him, he has shifted our perspectives in a variety of directions and expanded our minds to other ways of looking into our selves and looking into and at life and our surroundings. He is open and very genuine in his perspectives on a variety of subjects.

Aware Talk Radio

Join Us - LIVE - 7 Nights A Week!!!
Or Listen To Past Archvies @:
www.innercirclepublishing.com

http://www.blogtalkradio.com/aware

Call In Number: *(646) 716-8138*

Aware Talk Radio incorporates all fields of science, from the normal to the paranormal, from the physical to the metaphysical. We seek to expand the awareness of humankind. Your Comments, Questions, and Guest Suggestions are welcome.

- Thank you for your support of Dr. Hairfield's work -
To receive a 15 Minute Free Spiritual Counseling with Steven call: (775) 826-5999 and give the Promo Code: KARMA09

LaVergne, TN USA
09 December 2009

166406LV00002B/16/P

9 780972 008068